STATISTICAL ANALYSIS
Quick Reference Guidebook

For E'Lynne and Beverly

STATISTICAL ANALYSIS
Quick Reference Guidebook
With SPSS Examples

Alan C. Elliott
University of Texas,
Southwestern Medical Center

Wayne A. Woodward
Southern Methodist University

SAGE Publications
Thousand Oaks ■ London ■ New Delhi

For information:

Sage Publications, Inc.
2455 Teller Road
Thousand Oaks, California 91320
E-mail: order@sagepub.com

Sage Publications Ltd.
1 Oliver's Yard
55 City Road
London EC1Y 1SP
United Kingdom

Sage Publications India Pvt. Ltd.
B-42, Panchsheel Enclave
Post Box 4109
New Delhi 110 017 India

Printed in the United States of America

Library of Congress Cataloging-in-Publication Data

Elliott, Alan C., 1952–
Statistical analysis quick reference guidebook: With SPSS examples / Alan C. Elliott, Wayne A. Woodward.
    p. cm.
Includes bibliographical references and index.
ISBN 978-1-4129-2560-0 (pbk.)
    1. Social sciences—Statistical methods. 2. Mathematical statistics. 3. Social sciences—Statistical methods—Computer programs. 4. SPSS/PC. I. Woodward, Wayne A. II. Title.
HA29.E4826 2007
300.285'555—dc22

                                                                2006005411

This book is printed on acid-free paper.

07   08   09   10   10   9   8   7   6   5   4   3   2

Acquisitions Editor:	Lisa Cuevas Shaw
Associate Editor:	Margo Beth Crouppen
Editorial Assistants:	Karen Gia Wong and Karen Greene
Production Editor:	Melanie Birdsall
Copy Editor:	Gillian Dickens
Typesetter:	C&M Digitals (P) Ltd.
Indexer:	Sheila Bodell
Cover Designer:	Edgar Abarca

Contents

List of Tables and Figures   xiii

Acknowledgments   xix

1. Introduction   1
    Getting the Most Out of This *Quick Reference Guidebook*   2
    A Brief Review of the Statistical Process   3
        Using Descriptive Statistics   4
        Using Comparative Statistics   5
        Using Correlational Statistics   5
    Understanding Hypothesis Testing, Power, and Sample Size   6
    Understanding the *p*-Value   9
    Planning a Successful Analysis   10
        Formulate a Testable Research Question (Hypothesis)   10
        Collect Data Appropriate to Testing Your Hypotheses   10
        Decide on the Type of Analysis Appropriate
            to Test Your Hypothesis   11
        Properly Interpret and Report Your Results   12
    Guidelines for Creating Data Sets   12
        1. Decide What Variables You Need
            and Document Them   12
        2. Design Your Data Set With One
            Subject (or Observation) Per Line   13
        3. Each Variable Must Have a Properly
            Designated Name   14
        4. Select Descriptive Labels for Each Variable   14
        5. Select a Type for Each Variable   15
        6. Additional Tips for Categorical
            (Character) Variables   15
        7. Define Missing Values Codes   16
        8. Consider the Need for a Grouping Variable   16

Preparing Excel Data for Import   16
Guidelines for Reporting Results   18
Guidelines for Creating and Using Graphs   19
Downloading Sample SPSS Data Files   20
Opening Data Files for Examples   20
Summary   20
References   21

2. Describing and Examining Data   23
    Example Data Files   24
    Describing Quantitative Data   24
        Observe the Distribution of Your Data   25
        Testing for Normality   25
        Tips and Caveats for Quantitative Data   26
        Quantitative Data Description Examples   27
        EXAMPLE 2.1: Quantitative Data With an
            Unusual Value   28
        EXAMPLE 2.2: Quantitative Data by Groups   34
        EXAMPLE 2.3: Quantitative Data With
            Unusual Values   36
    Describing Categorical Data   39
        Considerations for Examining Categorical Data   39
        Tips and Caveats   40
        Describing Categorical Data Examples   40
        EXAMPLE 2.4: Frequency Table for
            Categorical Data   40
        EXAMPLE 2.5: Crosstabulation of
            Categorical Variables   43
    Summary   45
    References   45

3. Comparing One or Two Means Using the *t*-Test   47
    One-Sample *t*-Test   48
        Appropriate Applications for a One-Sample *t*-Test   48
        Design Considerations for a One-Sample *t*-Test   48
        Hypotheses for a One-Sample *t*-Test   49
        EXAMPLE 3.1: One-Sample *t*-Test   50
    Two-Sample *t*-Test   54
        Appropriate Applications for a Two-Sample *t*-Test   54
        Design Considerations for a Two-Sample *t*-Test   55
        Hypotheses for a Two-Sample *t*-Test   56
        Tips and Caveats for a Two-Sample *t*-Test   57

Interpreting Graphs Associated With
the Two-Sample *t*-Test   58
Deciding Which Version of the *t*-Test
Statistic to Use   58
Two-Sample *t*-Test Examples   60
EXAMPLE 3.2: Two-Sample *t*-Test With
Equal Variances   60
EXAMPLE 3.3: Two-Sample *t*-Test With
Variance Issues   65
Paired *t*-Test   68
Associated Confidence Interval   69
Appropriate Applications for a Paired *t*-Test   69
Design Considerations for a Paired *t*-Test   70
Hypotheses for a Paired *t*-Test   70
EXAMPLE 3.4: Paired *t*-Test   71
Summary   75
References   75

4. Correlation and Regression   **77**
Correlation Analysis   78
Appropriate Applications for Correlation Analysis   79
Design Considerations for Correlation Analysis   79
Hypotheses for Correlation Analysis   80
Tips and Caveats for Correlation Analysis   80
EXAMPLE 4.1: Correlation Analysis   83
Simple Linear Regression   87
Appropriate Applications for Simple Linear
Regression   87
Design Considerations for Simple Linear Regression   88
Hypotheses for a Simple Linear Regression Analysis   89
Tips and Caveats for Simple Linear Regression   89
Interval Estimates   91
EXAMPLE 4.2: Simple Linear Regression   91
Multiple Linear Regression   95
Appropriate Applications of Multiple Linear
Regression   96
Design Considerations for Multiple Linear Regression   96
Hypotheses for Multiple Linear Regression   97
R-Square   98
Model Selection Procedures for Multiple Linear
Regression   99

	Tips and Caveats for Multiple Linear Regression	100
	Model Interpretation and Evaluation for Multiple Linear Regression	101
	EXAMPLE 4.3: Multiple Linear Regression Analysis	102
	Residual Analysis	105
	Bland-Altman Analysis	107
	Design Considerations for a Bland-Altman Analysis	108
	EXAMPLE 4.4: Bland-Altman Analysis	108
	Summary	111
	References	112
5.	**Analysis of Categorical Data**	**113**
	Contingency Table Analysis $(r \times c)$	114
	Appropriate Applications of Contingency Table Analysis	114
	Design Considerations for a Contingency Table Analysis	115
	Hypotheses for a Contingency Table Analysis	116
	Tips and Caveats for a Contingency Table Analysis	116
	Contingency Table Examples	117
	EXAMPLE 5.1: $r \times c$ Contingency Table Analysis	117
	EXAMPLE 5.2: 2×2 Contingency Table Analysis	123
	Analyzing Risk Ratios in a 2×2 Table	126
	Appropriate Applications for Retrospective (Case Control) Studies	128
	Appropriate Applications for Prospective (Cohort) Studies	128
	EXAMPLE 5.3: Analyzing Risk Ratios for the Exposure/Reaction Data	128
	McNemar's Test	131
	Appropriate Applications of McNemar's Test	132
	Hypotheses for McNemar's Test	132
	EXAMPLE 5.4: McNemar's Test	133
	Mantel-Haenszel Comparison	135
	Appropriate Applications of the Mantel-Haenszel Procedure	136
	Hypotheses Tests Used in Mantel-Haenszel Analysis	136
	Design Considerations for a Mantel-Haenszel Test	136
	EXAMPLE 5.5: Mantel-Haenszel Analysis	136
	Tips and Caveats for Mantel-Haenszel Analysis	139

Tests of Interrater Reliability 140
    Appropriate Applications of Interrater Reliability 140
    EXAMPLE 5.6: Interrater Reliability Analysis 140
Goodness-of-Fit Test 143
    Appropriate Applications of the Goodness-of-Fit Test 143
    Design Considerations for a Goodness-of-Fit Test 144
    Hypotheses for a Goodness-of-Fit Test 144
    Tips and Caveats for a Goodness-of-Fit Test 144
    EXAMPLE 5.7: Goodness-of-Fit Test 145
Other Measures of Association for Categorical Data 147
Summary 149
References 149

6. **Analysis of Variance and Covariance** 151
One-Way ANOVA 152
    Appropriate Applications for a One-Way ANOVA 152
    Design Considerations for a One-Way ANOVA 152
    Hypotheses for a One-Way ANOVA 154
    Tips and Caveats for a One-Way ANOVA 154
    EXAMPLE 6.1: One-Way ANOVA 154
    EXAMPLE 6.2: One-Way ANOVA With
        Trend Analysis 162
Two-Way Analysis of Variance 166
    Appropriate Applications for a Two-Way ANOVA 167
    Design Considerations for a Two-Way ANOVA 167
    Hypotheses for a Two-Way ANOVA 168
    Tips and Caveats for a Two-Way ANOVA 170
    EXAMPLE 6.3: Two-Way ANOVA 171
Repeated-Measures Analysis of Variance 175
    Appropriate Applications for a
        Repeated-Measures ANOVA 175
    Design Considerations for a
        Repeated-Measures ANOVA 176
    Hypotheses for a Repeated-Measures ANOVA 177
    Tips and Caveats for a Repeated-Measures ANOVA 177
    EXAMPLE 6.4: Repeated-Measures ANOVA 177
Analysis of Covariance 182
    Appropriate Applications for Analysis of Covariance 182
    Design Considerations for an Analysis of Covariance 182
    Hypotheses for an Analysis of Covariance 183
    EXAMPLE 6.5: Analysis of Covariance 184

	Summary	190
	References	190
7.	**Nonparametric Analysis Procedures**	**191**
	Spearman's Rho	192
	Appropriate Applications for Spearman's Rho	192
	Design Considerations for Spearman's Rho	193
	Hypotheses for Spearman's Rho	193
	Tips and Caveats for Spearman's Rho	193
	EXAMPLE 7.1: Spearman's Rho	194
	Mann-Whitney (Two Independent Groups Test)	195
	Hypotheses for a Mann-Whitney Test	196
	EXAMPLE 7.2: Mann-Whitney Test	196
	Kruskal-Wallis Test	198
	Hypotheses for a Kruskal-Wallis Test	198
	EXAMPLE 7.3: Kruskal-Wallis Test	198
	Sign Test and Wilcoxon Signed-Rank Test for Matched Pairs	201
	Hypotheses for a Sign Test or Wilcoxon Signed-Rank Test	202
	EXAMPLE 7.4: Wilcoxon Signed-Rank Test and Sign Test	202
	Friedman's Test	204
	Hypotheses for Friedman's Test	204
	EXAMPLE 7.5: Friedman's Test	204
	Summary	207
	References	207
8.	**Logistic Regression**	**209**
	Introduction to Logistic Regression	209
	Appropriate Applications for Logistic Regression	210
	Simple Logistic Regression	211
	Hypotheses for Simple Logistic Regression	211
	Tips and Caveats for Simple Logistic Regression	211
	EXAMPLE 8.1: Simple Logistic Regression	212
	Multiple Logistic Regression	215
	Tips and Caveats for Multiple Logistic Regression	216
	EXAMPLE 8.2: Multiple Logistic Regression	217
	Interpretation of the Multiple Logistic Regression Model	220
	Summary	223
	References	223

Appendix A: A Brief Tutorial for Using SPSS for Windows   **225**

   Working With Data in SPSS   227

      SPSS Step-by-Step. EXAMPLE A1:

         Entering Data Into the SPSS Data Sheet   229

      SPSS Step-by-Step. EXAMPLE A2:

         Importing a Data File From Microsoft Excel   231

      SPSS Step-by-Step. EXAMPLE A3:

         Performing an Analysis   233

   Transforming, Recoding, and Categorizing Your Data   234

      SPSS Step-by-Step. EXAMPLE A4: Creating

         a New Variable Using Computation   234

      SPSS Step-by-Step. EXAMPLE A5: Transforming Data

         to Make Data More Normally Distributed   235

      SPSS Step-by-Step. EXAMPLE A6: Removing

         Selected Data From Analysis Using Filtering   238

      SPSS Step-by-Step. EXAMPLE A7: Combining Groups

         and Creating Categories From Quantitative Data   239

      SPSS Step-by-Step. EXAMPLE A8: Transposing Data   241

Appendix B: Choosing the Right Procedure to Use   **243**

   How to Use the Tables   244

Index   **249**

About the Authors   **259**

List of Tables and Figures

Tables

Table 1.1	Hypothesis Test Decisions	8
Table 1.2	Sample Data Dictionary	13
Table 1.3	Table Showing the First Three Records in a Typical Data Set	14
Table 1.4	Sample Grouped Data	17
Table 2.1	Test for Normality on IRA Data	28
Table 2.2	Table Reporting Group Statistics: Baseline Characteristics of Patients in Study by Group	35
Table 2.3	Searching for Unusual Values	37
Table 2.4	Frequency Table for *How Arrived*	40
Table 2.5	Output for Crosstabulation Example	43
Table 3.1	Output for the Bolt Data	52
Table 3.2	Explore Output Showing the Confidence Interval for μ	52
Table 3.3	Fertilizer Data	60
Table 3.4	Two-Sample *t*-Test Output for Fertilizer Data	63
Table 3.5	Two-Sample *t*-Test Results for Job Placement Data	67
Table 3.6	Paired *t*-Test Output for EXAMPLE 3.4	71
Table 3.7	Paired *t*-Test Results Obtained Using a Calculated Difference Variable	74

Table 4.1	Matrix of Correlation Coefficients	85
Table 4.2	Results of Simple Linear Regression Analysis	93
Table 4.3	Output for Stepwise Model Selection	103
Table 5.1	Pearson's Crime Analysis Data	118
Table 5.2	Output for Crime Data	119
Table 5.3	Chi-Square Tests for Crime Data	120
Table 5.4	Exposure/Reaction Data	123
Table 5.5	Output for 2 × 2 Exposure/Reaction Data	124
Table 5.6	Statistical Output for 2 × 2 Exposure/Reaction Data	124
Table 5.7	Standard Risk Analysis Table	127
Table 5.8	Risk Analysis Results	129
Table 5.9	2 × 2 Table for Advertising Effectiveness Data	134
Table 5.10	McNemar's Test Results for Advertising Effectiveness Data	134
Table 5.11	Berkeley Graduate Admissions Data	137
Table 5.12	Mantel-Haenszel Results for Berkeley Graduate Admissions Data	138
Table 5.13	Berkeley Graduate Admissions Data Combined Across Departments	139
Table 5.14	Data for Interrater Reliability Analysis	141
Table 5.15	Results for Interrater Reliability Analysis	142
Table 5.16	Goodness-of-Fit Analysis for Mendel's Data	145
Table 6.1	Descriptive Statistics for a One-Way ANOVA	155
Table 6.2	ANOVA Table for COURSE.SAV Data	157
Table 6.3	Tukey Multiple Comparison Results	158
Table 6.4	Tukey Multiple Comparison Results as Reported by SPSS	158
Table 6.5	Dunnett's Test Results	160
Table 6.6	Contrasts for Course Data	161

Table 6.7   One-Way ANOVA Data for EXAMPLE 6.2   163

Table 6.8   Test for Trend   165

Table 6.9   Two-Way ANOVA Data   166

Table 6.10 Descriptive Statistics for Two-Way ANOVA   171

Table 6.11 Table for Two-Way ANOVA   172

Table 6.12 Tukey Comparisons for Sales by Display
Color in a Two-Way ANOVA   173

Table 6.13 Tukey Comparison Results in Graphical Form   174

Table 6.14 Example Table Showing Descriptive Statistics
for a Two-Way ANOVA   174

Table 6.15 ANOVA Results for Repeated-Measures Analysis   179

Table 6.16 Bonferroni Comparisons for
Repeated-Measures ANOVA   180

Table 6.17 Results of Bonferroni Comparison   181

Table 6.18 ANCOVA Analysis Containing
Test for Equal Slopes   186

Table 6.19 Analysis of Covariance Test for
Group Effects (on Method)   187

Table 6.20 Analysis of Covariance Pairwise Comparisons   187

Table 6.21 Adjusted Means for Analysis of Covariance   188

Table 7.1   Mann-Whitney Analysis   197

Table 7.2   Output for Kruskal-Wallis Analysis   200

Table 7.3   Output for Wilcoxon Signed-Rank Test   202

Table 7.4   Output for Friedman's Test   205

Table 7.5   Multiple Comparisons for Friedman's Test   205

Table 7.6   Graphical Representation of Friedman's Multiple
Comparisons   206

Table 8.1   Simple Logistic Regression Output   212

Table 8.2   Including All Predictor Variables in the
Logistic Regression Equation   217

Table 8.3   Results of Reduced Model   218

Table 8.4   Revised Model Using *Price100*   219

Table 8.5   Model Diagnostics   220

Table 8.6   Model Classification   222

Table A1   Sample Data   230

Table A2   Output From Descriptives Procedure   233

Table B1   Descriptive Statistics   245

Table B2   Comparison Tests   246

Table B3   Relational Analyses (Correlation and Regression)   247

Figures

Figure 1.1   Scatterplot of Schooling by Survey Score   6

Figure 2.1   Plots Used to Assess Normality
              Using *IRA Setup* Data   30–31

Figure 2.2   Revised Histogram to Assess Normality
              in the *IRA Setup* Data   32

Figure 2.3   Side-by-Side Boxplots Showing
              Outliers and Extreme Values by Group   38

Figure 2.4   Bar Chart for *How Arrived*   41

Figure 2.5   Pareto Chart for *How Arrived*   42

Figure 2.6   Clustered Bar Chart for SUV Data   44

Figure 3.1   The Bolt Data   50

Figure 3.2   Boxplot of the Bolt Data   51

Figure 3.3   SPSS Editor Showing Fertilizer Data   61

Figure 3.4   Boxplots for the Fertilizer Study   62

Figure 3.5   Side-by-Side Boxplots for Job Placement Data   66

Figure 3.6   SPSS Editor Showing Diet Data   72

Figure 3.7   Boxplot of the Differences for EXAMPLE 3.4   72

Figure 4.1   Pearson's Scatterplot of Heights of Fathers and Sons   78

Figure 4.2   Example Scatterplots Associated With $r = .72$ 82

Figure 4.3   Scatterplot of *Time1* by *Age*   84

Figure 4.4   Scatterplot Matrix   85

Figure 4.5   Scatterplot for Simple Linear Regression Example   92

Figure 4.6   Residual Plot for Simple Linear Regression Example   94

Figure 4.7   Matrix of Scatterplots for *Jobscore* Data   103

Figure 4.8   Residual Plot for JOBSCORE.SAV Data   105

Figure 4.9   Plot of Identity   108

Figure 4.10   Bland-Altman Plot   109

Figure 5.1   Bar Chart for Crime Versus Drinking Analysis   120

Figure 5.2   CRIME.SAV Count Form Data Set   122

Figure 5.3   First 14 Cases of EXPOSURE22.SAV   126

Figure 5.4   Interrater Reliability Data in SPSS   142

Figure 6.1   Boxplots for Course Data   156

Figure 6.2   Data Entered for a One-Way ANOVA   164

Figure 6.3   Mean Number of Flowers by Supplement Strength   165

Figure 6.4   Interaction Plots   168

Figure 6.5   Graph of Two-Way Interactions   172

Figure 6.6   Data for Repeated-Measures ANOVA   178

Figure 6.7   Plot of Means for Snoring Data   178

Figure 6.8   Analysis of Covariance Comparison Plot
With Reference Line for Pretest   185

Figure 7.1   Scatterplot of Grade Versus Attendance Data   194

Figure 7.2   Data for Kruskal-Wallis Example   199

Figure 8.1   Graph of Logistic Regression for Car Rebate Data   214

Figure A1   The SPSS Data Editor Grid   227

Figure A2   The SPSS Variable View Grid   229

Figure A3   The SPSS Variable Grid Showing Entered Definitions   230

Figure A4   Data in Excel for Import Into SPSS   231

Figure A5   Dialog Box for Excel Import   232

Figure A6   Data Imported From Excel   232

Figure A7   Dialog Box for Descriptives Analysis   233

Figure A8   Skewed Data   236

Figure A9   Transformed Data   237

Figure A10 Data Prior to Transposing   241

Figure A11 Data After Transposing   242

Acknowledgments

With the goal of writing a general statistics guidebook for students and researchers, it took much more than our own expertise to put together the material. Many discussions with colleagues over the years contributed to the selection of content for this book. Several colleagues helped by reading early versions and providing suggestions on various topics from their area of expertise. These include Paul Witt, PhD (Texas Christian University), Terry D. Bilhartz, PhD (Sam Houston State University), Doug Pollock (Tyco Electronics), and Linda Hynan, PhD (UT Southwestern Medical Center, Dallas).

We are also indebted to the fine editorial and production staff at Sage Publications and for the reviewers who provided valuable insights and suggestions. In particular, we'd like to thank Lisa Cuevas Shaw, Karen Gia Wong, Karen Greene, Melanie Birdsall, and Gillian Dickens. Thanks also to Laura Lewin and Katrina Bevan of Studio B for their efforts in finding a home for this book.

Above all, we wish to thank our wives, E'Lynne and Beverly, for their patience and support through the long process of writing and rewriting the book.

1

Introduction

Performing a statistical analysis may be as appealing to you as filling out a yearly stack of income tax forms. It's something you know you need to do, but you wish it weren't such a hassle. Although this book doesn't help with your taxes, it does attempt to make the data analysis part of your life a little easier. With over 50 combined years (egad!) of consulting and teaching experience behind us, we hope to bring a little sanity to the process that many researchers find unsettling.

This *Statistical Analysis Quick Reference Guidebook* is a practical handbook that "cuts to the chase" and explains the when, where, and how of statistical data analysis as it is used for real-world decision making in a wide variety of disciplines. It is designed to assist students and researchers who have general statistical knowledge in applying the proper statistical procedure to their data and reporting results in a professional manner consistent with commonly accepted practice. Each upcoming chapter discusses the following aspects of performing statistical analysis and interpreting your experimental data:

- How to make sure you are using an appropriate application of the statistical procedure
- What design considerations you should consider when using a particular statistical procedure
- An explanation of the hypotheses tested by the procedure
- A description of tips and caveats you should know about the procedure
- An example (or two) illustrating the use of the procedure on a data set

1

- How to report the analysis results using standard American Psychological Association (APA) and Modern Language Association (MLA) compatible formats (APA, 2001; Gibaldi, 2003)
- A description of the step-by-step directions for how to perform the computations using SPSS

Before moving on to chapters that discuss specific statistical procedures, the next few sections in this chapter contain general information that pertains to the data analysis process. We cover this information here in part, so it will not have to be repeated individually for later analyses. We encourage you to review the information in this chapter before moving on to the subsequent chapters.

Getting the Most Out of This *Quick Reference Guidebook*

The primary purpose of the *Quick Reference Guidebook* is to provide you with information about how to use and understand the statistical data analysis process. The analysis topics covered in the book are as follows:

- *Chapter 2: Describing and Examining Data.* Explains how to use descriptive statistics and graphs to understand and report information about your data.
- *Chapter 3: Comparing One or Two Means Using the t-Test.* Explains one-sample *t*-test, two-sample *t*-test, paired *t*-test, and appropriate confidence intervals.
- *Chapter 4: Correlation and Regression.* Explains correlation and simple linear regression with a brief discussion of multiple linear regression and the Bland-Altman analysis.
- *Chapter 5: Analysis of Categorical Data.* Explains methods that are applicable to count or categorical data, including contingency table analysis, measures of risk (including relative risk), and odds ratios and goodness of fit.
- *Chapter 6: Analysis of Variance and Covariance.* Explains several methods of comparing means, including one-way analysis of variance (ANOVA), two-way ANOVA, repeated-measures ANOVA, and analysis of covariance (ANCOVA).
- *Chapter 7: Nonparametric Analysis Procedures.* Explains nonparametric statistical procedures, including Spearman's correlation, sign test, the Mann-Whitney *U*, Kruskal-Wallis, and Friedman's test.
- *Chapter 8: Logistic Regression.* Explains logistic regression analyses, including the cases of single or multiple independent variables, variable selection, and evaluation of the model.

Along with each analysis in these chapters, we include a brief "step-by-step" section describing how to perform the calculations using SPSS. Additional information that may be helpful to you in analyzing the example data sets and selecting an appropriate analysis for your data is included in the following appendices:

- *Appendix A: A Brief Tutorial for Using SPSS for Windows*. This tutorial gets you started with the essential information needed to work through the examples in this book. We recommend that if your SPSS is rusty, if you have limited experience using SPSS, or if you are new to SPSS, you should go through the examples in this appendix before working the examples in the book.
- *Appendix B: Choosing the Right Procedure to Use*. This appendix includes a decision chart that can help you decide which statistical procedure is appropriate to address your research question.

The remainder of this chapter contains material that we believe is important for understanding the examples contained in this book. We know you are in a hurry, faced with a deadline, and anxious to get to your analysis. However, if you take only a few minutes to read the rest of the chapter, it may save you hours of frustration down the road. The remaining topics covered in this chapter are as follows:

- A Brief Review of the Statistical Process
- Understanding Hypothesis Testing, Power, and Sample Size
- Understanding the *p*-Value
- Planning a Successful Analysis
- Guidelines for Creating Data Sets
- Preparing Excel Data for Import
- Guidelines for Reporting Results
- Guidelines for Creating and Using Graphs
- Downloading Sample SPSS Data Files
- Opening Data Files for Examples

A Brief Review of the Statistical Process

Perhaps you are currently taking a statistics course or you struggled through a statistics course in the past and the concepts you once knew are a bit fuzzy. In this review, we remind you of the issues that typically motivate the use of statistical data analysis and illustrate the types of analyses that are most commonly used to describe data or make a decision based on observed data.

Although we expect that you have studied these concepts before, you might learn something new or gain some insights that hadn't occurred to you previously. In either case, we hope this review is helpful.

Most analyses can be categorized into one of these types:

- Description
- Comparison
- Association/correlation

Using Descriptive Statistics

Today's world is filled with information. By some estimation, there are more than two exabytes of new and unique information being created each year. Considering that an exabyte is a billion gigabytes, that's a lot of raw data! The computer enables us to gather and create more information than anyone can possibly remember and understand. Computer databases swell with information such as medical data, demographic information, environmental data, economic data—creating an almost enumerable list of numbers and figures. The challenge is to interpret this information in some logical and practical manner.

The best strategy is not to skim over the hundreds or thousands or tens of thousands of "raw numbers" that have been collected. What is needed is an intelligent summary of the information. You need to reduce the myriad of data values and facts to a few explanatory measures that will give you an idea of what's going on and what conclusions are warranted.

For example, suppose you have been funded by a government agency to evaluate the operation of two charity-sponsored counseling centers. As a part of the analysis, a satisfaction survey is given to 109 clients over a period of 1 month and measured on a scale of 1 to 100. In order to describe the results of the survey, you wouldn't want to present a list of raw results (109 scores). Instead, it would be more informative to report several summaries, such as the following:

Average satisfaction score: 80.3 (on a scale of 0 to 100)

Lowest score: 58.6

Highest score: 94.1

This descriptive information gives you (and your coinvestigators) an idea about the average level of satisfaction and something about the variability of scores.

Using Comparative Statistics

Since there are two counseling center locations, your research group might be interested in knowing if there is a difference in level of satisfaction among clients at the two locations. This could be important in deciding which center receives additional funding. You have the following summary data grouped by location:

Average score at the uptown location was 82.4 (based on 54 client scores)

Average score at the downtown location was 78.5 (based on 55 client scores)

Assuming that the clients are representative at each location, you have some evidence to make a decision about which center is more effective in terms of satisfaction score. Your data suggest that the uptown location may do a better job as far as the satisfaction score is concerned since the score for uptown is 3.9 points higher than the score for the downtown location. However, what if the average scores were only 1 point apart? Or 10 points apart? What level of difference would it take for you to conclude that the average score for one location was significantly higher than for the other? Could the difference in scores be due to some random fluctuation? If you did the survey again during some other time period, is there a reasonable chance that the downtown location would produce a better score? These questions are addressed with a properly designed and executed statistical analysis.

Using Correlational Statistics

To learn more about your survey results, you could examine your data in another way. Ignoring for a moment the location of the center, you may want to compare the relationship between educational level of clients and satisfaction scores. The variables *survey scores* and *years of schooling* are plotted on a scatterplot in Figure 1.1, and a measure of how they are related is summarized in a number called the correlation coefficient, which is found to be $r = 0.37$. From this measure of association, you have evidence that suggests there is a mild relationship between years of schooling and satisfaction score. There is a tendency for clients with a higher education to have a higher satisfaction score. (Correlation is discussed in more detail in Chapter 4: Correlation and Regression.)

In each of these example analyses, the raw data are summarized into summary statistics or a graph that allows you to discover important information about the data and to provide the basis for making informed decisions. This

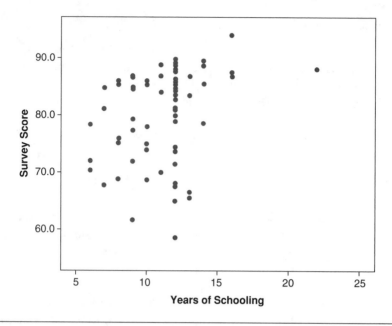

Figure 1.1   Scatterplot of Schooling by Survey Score

Quick Reference Guidebook provides you with the information needed to use these and other types of statistical procedures and to interpret the results.

Understanding Hypothesis Testing, Power, and Sample Size

To properly interpret a statistical analysis, you must understand the concept of hypothesis testing. Otherwise, the entire process is so much gibberish. This brief discussion is designed to refresh your memory about these concepts.

Many people have likened hypothesis testing to a jury trial. You assume the defendant is not guilty. Evidence is then presented to show guilt. If there is a preponderance of evidence of the defendant's guilt, you should conclude that the defendant is indeed guilty (you reject innocence). In the same way, a statistical analysis is based on a "null" hypothesis (labeled H_0) that there is "no effect" (e.g., no treatment differences). In research terms, the null hypothesis will typically be a statement such as the following: There is no difference in group means, no linear association between two variables, no difference in distributions, and so on.

An experiment is designed to determine whether evidence refutes the null hypothesis. If your evidence (research result) indicates that what you observed was extreme enough, then you would conclude that you have "significant" evidence to reject the null hypothesis. However, if you do not gather sufficient evidence to reject H_0, this does not prove that the null hypothesis is true, only that we did not have enough evidence to "prove the case."

In general, null and alternative hypothesis are of the following form:

- A "null hypothesis" (H_0) is the hypotheses of "no effect" or "no differences" (i.e., the observed differences are only due to chance variation).
- An alternative hypothesis (H_a) states that the null hypothesis is false and that the observed differences are real.

In the following chapters, the null and alternative hypotheses related to each statistical test will be presented. They appear in the following form:

H_0: $\mu_1 = \mu_2$ (the population means of the two groups are the same).

H_a: $\mu_1 \neq \mu_2$ (the population means of the two groups are different).

These particular hypotheses are for a two-sample t-test as described in Chapter 3: Comparing One or Two Means Using the t-Test. In most cases, we will present the hypotheses in both a mathematical form (such as $\mu_1 = \mu_2$) and in words.

The alternative hypothesis is usually what the investigator wants to show or suspects is true. The alternative in the example above is called a two-tailed alternative (also called a two-sided alternative.) That is, reject H_0 if there is sufficient evidence that the null is not true. For a one-tailed alternative (e.g., H_a: $\mu_1 > \mu_2$), we would reject H_0 only if the evidence against H_0 tends to support H_a. Further discussion of one- and two-tailed alternatives will be given when appropriate for the discussion of various tests in future chapters.

In hypothesis testing, two types of errors can occur, as illustrated in Table 1.1. The top classification is the "truth" that you do not know. The left categories are your decisions. For example, if you reject H_0 when it is false, you've made a correct decision. However, if you reject H_0 when it is true, you've made a "Type I error." Notice that of the four possible outcomes summarized in the table, two are errors.

The Type I error is controlled by your choice of a decision-making criterion, called alpha (α) or the level of significance. It is usually set small, at 0.05. Thus, you are willing to make a Type I error 5% of the time, or 1 in 20 times.

Table 1.1   Hypothesis Test Decisions

	Truth	
Our decision	H_0 true	H_0 false
Reject H_0	Type I error (α)	Correct decision ($1 - \beta$ or power)
Do not reject H_0	Correct decision ($1 - \alpha$)	Type II error (β)

If H_0 is false and you do not reject H_0, you commit a Type II error. The probability of committing a Type II error is called beta (β). The power of the test is defined to be one minus β. When a test has low power, it means that you are likely to make a Type II error (i.e., fail to reject H_0 when it is actually false). Looking at it the other way, the higher the "power," the better your chance of rejecting H_0 when it is false—the better your chance of finding a difference when it in fact exists.

An important point is that there are many ways in which a null hypothesis can be "not true." For example, if the null hypothesis is that there is no difference in two population means (measured in inches), then, for example, this hypothesis is "not true" if the actual difference between the two means is 1″, 5″, or 50″. It may be very difficult to develop a test for which we are able to detect a difference in population means of 1 inch. In fact, such a difference may be of no practical importance. On the other hand, it will likely be the case that a true difference of 50″ may be very easy to detect. That is, if the true difference is 50″, the power of the test will be large.

Another important point is that for any given level of significance (α), power can be increased by increasing the sample size. Thus, sample size should be a consideration when embarking on an experiment. Many negative (nonsignificant) studies reported in the literature are the result of inadequate sample size (resulting in poor power) (Friedman, Chalmers, Smith, & Kuebler, 1978). Therefore, the process of selecting a sample size for your analysis should begin early in your study. To follow with this example, the experimenter should determine the level of difference it is desirable to detect and then select a sample size that will detect this difference with an acceptable power (say, at least 0.80). Often, a pilot study will be undertaken to help determine the necessary sample size. SPSS offers a separate program called SamplePower that allows you to calculate a sample size for a given power or range of powers you select. Other commercial programs (PASS, nQuery, and SAS) are also available for these purposes. Or, consult your friendly local statistician for help. For more concerning hypothesis testing, see a standard statistical text such as Moore and McCabe (2006). For a good discussion of power and sample size, see Keppel and Wickens (2004).

Understanding the p-Value

The "evidence" used to reject a null hypotheses is summarized in a probability called a p-value. The p-value is the probability of obtaining results as extreme or more extreme than the ones observed given that the null hypothesis is true. Thus, the smaller the p-value, the more evidence you have to reject the null hypothesis.

When your rejection criterion, α, is set at 0.05, then if your p-value for that test is 0.05 or less, you reject H_0. All of the examples illustrating statistical tests in this *Quick Reference Guidebook* use the criterion that a p-value less than 0.05 indicates that the null hypothesis should be rejected.

However, don't base your entire decision-making criterion on the p-value. For example, suppose two sample means for systolic blood pressure (SBP) differ by one point and are found to be statistically significantly different (i.e., $p < 0.05$). This could occur if the sample sizes are large, but such a finding may have no practical or therapeutic significance, even though the results are statistically significant. On the other hand, an observed difference in mean SBP of 20 based on small sample sizes may not be statistically significant (i.e., $p > 0.05$). However, such a finding may be of sufficient practical importance that this (nonsignificant) result may indicate the need for further investigation with larger sample sizes to increase the power to the extent that you would have a good chance of detecting a difference of 20 if it really exists. The point here is that the p-value is a valuable decision-making tool, but it should not be the only criterion you use to judge the results of your research.

A word of warning: If you perform multiple statistical tests within the same analysis, you should adjust your α level for individual tests to protect your overall Type I error rate. For example, if 10 independent statistical tests are reported for the same analysis (such as in a table comparing baseline values between two groups), each conducted at the 0.05 significance level, there is a 40% chance that one or more significant differences would be found even if there are no actual differences. That should be unacceptable to you—and is usually unacceptable to journal reviewers. The proper response to this is to adjust p-values in multiple tests using a standard technique such as the Bonferroni correction. To perform this simple adjustment, divide your rejection criterion value (α) by the number of tests performed. For example, if you are testing at the $\alpha = 0.05$ level and 10 tests are performed, then your rejection criterion for each test should be 0.05/10 = 0.005 in order to maintain your 0.05 overall Type I error rate (Miller, 1981). To report these results in your paper, use wording such as "$p < 0.005$ was considered statistically significant for baseline comparisons according to a Bonferroni correction. . . ."

> All of the examples illustrating statistical tests in this *Quick Reference Guidebook* use the criterion that a *p*-value less than 0.05 indicates that the null hypothesis should be rejected.

Planning a Successful Analysis

Statistical data analysis begins with planning. Entire university courses are devoted to properly designing experiments. An improperly designed experiment can make data analysis a nightmare. Therefore, it is to the researcher's advantage to spend some up-front time considering how an experiment will be analyzed before collecting the data. Although this book cannot cover all the aspects of good experimental planning, a few important considerations are the following:

Formulate a Testable Research Question (Hypothesis)

Formulate a testable research question (hypothesis) before you collect your data and formulate your research question in a way that is statistically testable. For example, you might test the null hypothesis that there is no difference in satisfaction scores from the two counseling centers in the previous example. You "test" this assumption by gathering data and determining if there is enough information to cast sufficient doubt on your null hypothesis. If there is such evidence, then you may reject the null hypothesis in favor of the alternative (one location has a better satisfaction score than the other).

Collect Data Appropriate to Testing Your Hypotheses

Consider the types of variables you will need to answer your research question:

An Outcome Variable. (Sometimes also called the dependent or response variable.) This outcome variable measures the characteristic that you want to test or describe in some way. It could be some outcome such as death, sales amounts, growth rate, test score, time to recovery, and so on.

Predictor Variable(s). (Sometimes called independent or explanatory variables, or factors.) The predictor variables are often manipulated by the experimenter (e.g., level or dosage, color of package, type of treatment), although they may also be observed (such as cigarette smoking, blood pressure, gender, amount of rainfall).

For Correlational Studies. If you are performing a correlational study (examining the association between variables), you will not have a specific outcome variable. Keep in mind, however, that a correlational study by itself cannot be used to conclude cause and effect.

Scales of Measurement. The method you use to measure an observation affects the type of analysis that may be performed. As you design your study, keep in mind these general ways of measuring data:

- Categorical scales include nominal and ordinal measures.
- Continuous scales include interval and ratio measures.

As various statistical analyses are discussed in this text, reference will be made to the measurement types appropriate for the analysis. (More about how SPSS classifies variables can be found in Appendix A: A Brief Tutorial for Using SPSS for Windows.)

Decide on the Type of Analysis Appropriate to Test Your Hypothesis

Do you need a descriptive, comparative, or association/correlation analysis? See Appendix B: Choosing the Right Procedure to Use for help in deciding which type of data analysis to use for testing your hypotheses. In general, select the simplest statistical procedure that adequately answers your research question. Wilkinson and the Task Force on Statistical Inference (1999) state,

> The enormous variety of modern quantitative methods leaves researchers with the nontrivial task of matching analysis and design to the research question. Although complex designs and state-of-the art methods are sometimes necessary to address research questions effectively, simpler classical approaches often can provide elegant and sufficient answers to important questions. Do not choose an analytic method to impress your readers or to deflect criticism. If the assumptions and strength of a simpler method are reasonable for your data and research problem, use it. (p. 598)

Properly Interpret and Report Your Results

As a part of the discussion of each analysis method in this *Quick Reference Guidebook,* suggestions for interpreting your results and reporting them in a professional manner are presented.

While the above items are important considerations for your data analyses, they are not comprehensive and cannot substitute for the expertise of a professional statistician. If you do not understand the relevance of these issues to your own analysis, we recommend that you consult a professional statistician.

Guidelines for Creating Data Sets

A savvy information guru once remarked that data are no more information than 50 tons of cement is a skyscraper. Like a builder that transforms raw materials into a functional skyscraper, statistical data analysis transforms raw data into meaningful and useful information. However, before you can begin to perform your data analysis, you must get that raw data into the software program.

Before entering data for analysis, there are several data issues you should address. This discussion describes how to prepare a data set for use in any statistical software program. For specific requirements in SPSS, see Appendix A: A Brief Tutorial for Using SPSS for Windows. Also, for a more complete general discussion of this topic, see Elliott, Hynan, Reisch, and Smith (in press).

1. Decide What Variables You Need and Document Them

Your research question determines which variables are needed for your analysis. Researchers should document their variables in a "data dictionary" that contains the important information defining the variables. (Some texts refer to this as a data codebook.) For an example of a data dictionary, see Table 1.2.

This table is a document you create during your planning stage. It can be created using a spreadsheet or a word processor. Creating this simple "dictionary" before you collect your data not only forces you to consider which variables you will need in your data set, their types, and how they will be named, but it also provides documentation that can be a valuable tool in performing and interpreting your analyses later on.

Variables may contain values that are either string (such as M and F or A, B, and C) or numbers (such as 0 and 1) whose meaning may not be

Table 1.2   Sample Data Dictionary

Variable Name	Label	Type (Width)	Value Codes	Missing Code
ID	Identification number	String (4)	None to be missing	Not allowed
Age	Age on January 1, 2005	Numeric (3.0)	None	−99
Sex	Gender	Numeric (1.0)	1 = Female 2 = Male	9
Tdate	Test date	Date (10) (mm/dd/yyyy)	None	Blank, "." Or 11/11/1111
Score	Initial test score	Numeric (6.2)	None	−99

completely clear. For example, if you coded a *gender* variable as 1 and 2 and *race* as AA, C, H, O, and X, you will want to define those codes in your data dictionary, as illustrated for the *sex* variable in Table 1.2.

Note that when you create a categorical variable, you should include an "other" designation when the list does not include an exhaustive collection of possibilities. For example, if you have a variable for "What magazine do you enjoy the most?" and you include a list of 10 magazines, you should also include an "Other" category since the answer for the person filling out the questionnaire may not be in your list. You might also include "None" as an answer for those people who don't read magazines at all.

2. Design Your Data Set With One Subject (or Observation) Per Line

The vast majority of data analyses require your data set to contain one subject (or entity) per row. A properly designed data set should look something like Table 1.3.

Notice how this data set is designed. Each row contains data from a single subject. Each column contains the data from a single variable. You may be tempted to have multiple rows per subject or to design your data set with subjects as columns, but if you enter your data in that manner, you are only asking for problems later on in most cases. If your data are already in a data set where the subjects are in columns and your variables are in rows, see the transpose example in Appendix A: A Brief Tutorial for Using SPSS for Windows for a way to realign your data file.

Table 1.3   Table Showing the First Three Records in a Typical Data Set

ID	Age	Sex	Tdate	Score
1001	45	M	07/10/2006	60
1002	34	F	06/12/2006	55
1003	65	M	12/02/2006	62

3. Each Variable Must Have a Properly Designated Name

Variable names are often short designations such as ID for subject identification number, SSBP (supine systolic blood pressure), and so on. Each statistical package has a set of restrictions for naming variables. The guidelines given here will help you design your data dictionary with variable names that are acceptable to most statistical programs:

- Variable names should begin with a letter but may also include numbers.
- Keep variable names short. Some programs require variable names of 8 or fewer characters, although many allow names up to 64 characters in length.
- Do not use blanks or special characters (e.g., !, ?, ', and *).
- Variable names must be unique; no duplicate names are allowed.
- Case usually does not matter. Use any mixture of uppercase and lowercase characters when naming or referring to your variables.

4. Select Descriptive Labels for Each Variable

Creating a variable label allows you to associate a descriptive label with each variable name. Variable labels are important because they help you more clearly understand and interpret statistical output, particularly if the variable names are ambiguous, similar, or difficult to decipher. Typical names and labels might be the following:

Age: Age on January 1, 2005

SBP: Systolic blood pressure

S1 to S50: Answers to a satisfaction survey

Gender: Male or female

SWQ1: Sales for the southwest region during the first quarter

5. Select a Type for Each Variable

Each variable designates a particular type of information. The most commonly used variable types are numeric (a quantitative value) and character (also called string or text and often used for categorical-type data). A good rule of thumb is to designate as numeric only those variables that could be used in a calculation or that are factor or grouping codes for categorical variables. For example, a Social Security number, an ID number, and a telephone number are not really "numbers" that are used in calculations, and they can be designated as character values. This prevents the program from accidentally using that number in a calculation. However, it is common to designate dichotomous or grouping variables using numeric codes such as 0 and 1 or 1, 2, and 3, but care must be taken if you use these numbers in calculations. Also, never use codes such as "NA," "Missing," "> 100," or "10 to 20" as entries in numeric fields (which may occur if you first enter your data into a spreadsheet such as Excel and then import the data into your statistics program). For a list of specific data types in SPSS, see the section in Appendix A titled "Working With Data in SPSS."

6. Additional Tips for Categorical (Character) Variables

Keep Case Consistent. For coded variables that are of the character (string or text) type, it is always good advice to maintain consistent case in data values. For example, use all uppercase ("M" and "F") or all lowercase ("m" and "f") for a character-type gender variable. Even when case does not matter for variable names, it does matter for the data contents of the variables. The computer recognizes uppercase *M* as a different character than lowercase *m*. Therefore, if you haphazardly use *M, m, F,* and *f* as data entries, your program may recognize the data as having four categories instead of two.

Avoid Long Data Codes. Avoid long (and easy to misspell) string variables such as Influenza or Timer Clock Malfunction. Use shortened codes such as FLU and TCM instead. The Label field (see item number 4) can be used for a more complete description of the variable if needed.

Consider Binary Coding. If your data are binary (having only two levels such as male and female), creating a numeric variable that uses the values 0 and 1 may save time later since some analyses (such as regression) require numeric data.

7. Define Missing Values Codes

Sometimes data are lost or never collected. For example, a test tube is broken, a subject refuses to answer, or a patient fails to show up for an appointment. This type of data should be coded using a missing value code. Always select a missing value code that is an "impossible value" for the particular variable. For example, a –99 (negative 99) is an appropriate missing value code for *age, weight,* or *height* since that value would never be observed for those variables. Specifically, avoid using a blank or a 0 as a missing value code since that may cause confusion as to whether the data value was ever recorded and may cause an incorrect number to be used in a calculation. For a date variable, you can use a "highly unlikely" date such as 11/11/1111 as a missing value code (assuming your data do not include observations from the 12th century!). Once you specify a missing value code in your statistics program, the program will take that missing value into account when performing an analysis.

8. Consider the Need for a Grouping Variable

A grouping variable is a code that tells the statistical program how to separate records into groups—such as control group and experimental group. Therefore, if your data set contains information on two or more groups, you should include a variable that specifies the group membership of each observation. A grouping specification could be a single character (A, B, C), numeric (1, 2, 3), or names (CONTROL, TRT1, TRT2). For example, suppose you will be comparing the mean heights of 24-month-old males who were fed regularly with breast milk and those who were fed on formula. You could choose numeric grouping codes to be 1 and 0, where 1 means breast-fed and 0 means formula-fed. Or you could use string grouping codes such as B and F or BREAST and FORMULA or any other designation that makes sense to you. For example, Table 1.4 contains a grouping variable (named *group*) as well as two other variables, *subject* and *height*.

From this example, you can see how the program can tell that the height 30.4 belongs to Subject 1001 in Group B, the height 35.9 belongs to a subject in Group F, and so on.

Preparing Excel Data for Import

A number of researchers choose to first enter data using the Microsoft Excel program and then subsequently import that data set into a statistical program. This section describes how you should prepare your data in Excel

Table 1.4   Sample Grouped Data

Subject	Group	Height
1001	B	30.4
1002	F	35.9
1003	B	30.2
1004	B	38.0
1005	F	34.3
etc.		

(or any other spreadsheet or database program) for importation into a statistics program. Using the guidelines in the previous section, here are several additional items you should keep in mind. (The procedure for importing an Excel spreadsheet into SPSS is illustrated in Appendix A: A Brief Tutorial for Using SPSS for Windows.)

1. Row 1 of your Excel spreadsheet should contain only variable names. Do not extend names to row 2.

2. Each subsequent row (line) in the Excel spreadsheet should contain data for a single subject or observed entity (in almost all cases).

3. Avoid blank rows—it will complicate your import and analysis.

4. If you have missing data in your data set, define a missing value code and place that code in any cell that contains missing data.

5. Always use date variables with four-digit year formats in Excel. That is, enter the date in Excel using the format 01/01/2005 and not 01/01/05. Otherwise, the old Y2K gotcha can still be a problem for date calculations, where the date 1/1/05 could either represent the year 1905 or 2005.

6. Use your data dictionary (previously discussed), making sure to include all of the variables you will need. Use the specifications in the data dictionary such as codes, formats, and data ranges to determine how you will enter your data into Excel.

7. If you have the time or resources, enter your data twice (preferably using two different data entry people) and compare the two files. See Elliott et al. (in press) for an example of how to do a simple double-entry comparison in Excel.

8. Avoid putting any extraneous text into your spreadsheet. Instead, put explanatory information in other sheets in the same spreadsheet file. Extraneous data in your primary spreadsheet can make importing the data more difficult.

Guidelines for Reporting Results

All the statistics in the world will not get your point across unless you properly report your results. Most journals and publications have guidelines that you must follow when submitting your results. Along with each example in this *Quick Reference Guidebook,* we illustrate how you might report your findings using statements that are compatible with generally accepted formats. Since a number of guidelines are commonly adopted when reporting statistics results, we present these general rules:

- Computer programs tend to report statistics to more digits than are necessary or meaningful. A generally accepted practice is to report statistics to one decimal place more than the resolution of the original measurements. For example, if age is measured as integer, report the average age using one decimal place. Occasionally, if precision is important, you may report more decimals. APA guidelines state that two or three significant digits (e.g., digits that convey information and are not merely placeholders) are usually sufficient for reporting any statistic. (However, you should use all decimal places reported in the computer output when using these results in further calculations.)

- For very large numbers, you may want to limit the number of significant digits depending on the nature of the measure. For example, if you are reporting the average salary of corporate presidents, you might report a mean of $723,000 and a standard deviation of $59,000 rather than $723,471.20 and $59,356.10.

- Whenever a number is less than 0, place a zero before the decimal. For example, use 0.003 instead of .003.

- When reporting percentages, include the counts as well. For example, "There were 19% males (12 of 64) represented in the sample." Note also that the percentage was rounded. In general, give percentages as whole numbers if the sample size is less than 100 and to one decimal place if the sample size is larger than 100 (Lang & Secic, 1997, p. 41).

- When using the APA format for reporting statistics, use the appropriate abbreviations for common statistical measures. Examples are the following:

Mean: $M = 1.34$

Standard deviation: $SD = 3.21$

Sample size: $N = 203$

p-value: $p = 0.03$ or $p < 0.001$

t-statistic with degrees of freedom: $t(13) = 2.12$

Chi-square results: $\chi^2(2, N = 97) = 7.6$, $p = 0.02$

F-test: $F(2, 21) = 3.33$, $p = 0.04$

Guidelines for Creating and Using Graphs

The old adage about a picture being worth a thousand words may be altered slightly when dealing with data. Our revised adage states, "A graph is worth a thousand numbers."

Graphs can be useful for identifying problems or interesting data points in your data set. When reporting your results, graphs are useful for clarifying findings. In general, graphs should be used as an alternative to tables when the table would contain too many entries to be easily understood or when the graph more clearly illustrates your results. Any number of textbooks and journal specifications contain guidelines relating to the use of graphs (see Tufte, 1983). Here are a few general guidelines for using and reporting graphs:

1. Use simple graphs when possible. Avoid three-dimensional graphs since they often distort your message and contain spurious and distracting information.

2. Label all plots and axes clearly.

3. When creating two or more graphs that will be compared in some way, the range of values for each axis on every graph should be the same. Axes should generally begin with zero if that is the natural minimum. Otherwise, use the minimum value of the measurement as the minimum value for the axis.

4. Axis intervals on plots should be equal.

5. Use bar charts instead of pie charts. (In *The Visual Display of Quantitative Data*, Edward Tufte [1983] wrote, "The only worse design than a pie chart is several of them" [p. 176]).

6. Stick with standard charts when possible. Avoid custom complex charts that attempt to display several messages at once.

Downloading Sample SPSS Data Files

This *Quick Reference Guidebook* references a number of data files that are used to illustrate the procedures described in this book. These data files are available for you to download from the Internet. To download these files onto your local hard drive, point your browser to the following site (enter in all lowercase):

http://www.alanelliott.com/spssdata

Follow the instructions on this Web page to download and install the files onto your computer. Examples in the subsequent chapters assume that the data files have been downloaded and stored in a directory (folder) on your computer and that you know the name of the directory where the files are stored.

> Examples in the subsequent chapters assume that the data files have been downloaded and stored in a directory (folder) on your computer and that you know the name of the directory where the files are stored.

Opening Data Files for Examples

Once you have downloaded the sample data onto your hard drive, you can open these data files in the SPSS program using the following steps:

1. Begin SPSS. From the main menu select **File/Open/Data. . . .**

2. In the "Look In" option on the Open dialog box, drill down to the C:\SPSS-DATA folder on your computer (or wherever you stored your data).

3. Select the file to open (such as EXAMPLE.SAV) and click OK. (Or simply double-click on the file name.) The data will be opened into the SPSS data grid.

4. You are now ready to use that data in an analysis.

In the examples referenced in subsequent chapters, you should use the above steps to open designated data files to perform the analyses under discussion.

Summary

This chapter includes a description of the goals of this book, a brief review of statistical concepts, guidelines for creating a data set, entering data into

Excel, presenting results, and instructions on how to download example data. The next chapter plunges you into the analysis process, beginning with a look at how to describe your data.

References

American Psychological Association (APA). (2001). *Publication manual of the American Psychological Association* (5th ed.). Washington, DC: Author.

Elliott, A. C., Hynan, L. S., Reisch, J. S., & Smith, J. P. (in press). Preparing data for analysis using Microsoft Excel. *Journal of Investigative Medicine.*

Friedman, J. A., Chalmers, T. C., Smith, H., & Kuebler, R. R. (1978). The importance of beta, the Type II error and sample size in the design and interpretation of the randomized control trial. *NEJM, 299,* 690–696.

Gibaldi, J. (2003). *MLA handbook for writers of research papers* (6th ed.). New York: Modern Language Association of America.

Keppel, G., & Wickens, T. D. (2004). *Design and analysis: A researcher's handbook* (4th ed.). Mahwah, NJ: Pearson Prentice Hall.

Lang, T. A., & Secic, M. (1997). *How to report statistics in medicine.* Philadelphia: American College of Physicians.

Miller, R. G. (1981). *Simultaneous statistical inference* (2nd ed.). New York: Springer Verlag.

Moore, D., & McCabe, G. (2006). *Introduction to the practice of statistics* (4th ed.). New York: Freeman.

Tufte, E. (1983). *The visual display of quantitative information.* Cheshire, CT: Graphics Press.

Wilkinson, L., & the Task Force on Statistical Inference, APA Board of Scientific Affairs. (1999). Statistical methods in psychology journals: Guidelines and explanations. *American Psychologist, 54*(8), 594–604.

2

Describing and Examining Data

Information is the currency of research. However, unlike real money, there is often too much information. In most cases, data must be summarized to be useful.

The most common method of summarizing data is with descriptive statistics and graphs. Even if you're planning to analyze your data using a statistical technique such as a *t*-test, analysis of variance, or logistic regression, you should always begin by examining your data. This preliminary step helps you determine which statistical analysis techniques should be used to answer your research questions.

In fact, this process of examining your data often reveals information that will surprise or inform you. You may discover unusually high or low values in your data. Perhaps these "outliers" are caused by incorrectly coded data, or they may reveal information about your data (or subjects) that you have not anticipated. You might observe that your data are not normally distributed. You might notice that a histogram of your data shows two distinct peaks, causing you to realize that your data show a difference between genders. Insights such as these often result from the proper use of descriptive techniques.

The following sections of this chapter discuss the most commonly used tactics for understanding your data for reporting information or preparing your data for further analysis. The two major topics discussed in this chapter are as follows:

- Describing quantitative data using statistics and graphs
- Describing categorical data using statistics and graphs

Each section includes, where appropriate, methods for reporting your data in a standard manner for a report or journal article.

> Recall that the purpose of this *Quick Reference Guidebook* is to "cut to the chase" and discuss only material that is typically important in performing a well-planned and -analyzed experiment. Therefore, some statistics, tests, and graphs that are presented in standard computer output are not discussed.

Example Data Files

Before continuing, there is one bit of housekeeping we need to cover; we assume that you've installed the sample data sets on your computer, as described in Chapter 1 in the section "Downloading Sample SPSS Data Files." What? You haven't installed the sample data? Go back. Do not pass Go. Do not collect $200.

Welcome back. Now that you have the sample data stored on your computer, you are ready to proceed.

Describing Quantitative Data

Quantitative data are data on which computations such as addition and subtraction make sense. (SPSS calls this "scale" data.) This type of data is also referred to as numeric data. Quantitative data are sometimes categorized as continuous (possible values fall along a continuum) and discrete (there are a countable number of possible outcomes). Examples of continuous quantitative data are height and weight, while examples of discrete data are number of children in your family, number of years of schooling, and so on. Other classifications of quantitative data include ratio (has a natural zero) and interval (no natural zero) scaled data. We'll use the general term *quantitative data* to include all these types. Quantitative data are usually observed as measurements or counts as in the example above. Examples of the types of data that would fall into the quantitative category include the following:

- Rainfall (measured)
- Systolic blood pressure (measured)
- Number of peaches harvested from each tree (count)
- Years of smoking (count)

It makes sense to talk about the average value of each of these variables (even if there is no such thing as a part of a peach growing on a tree).

> The determination of whether arithmetic computation for the data makes sense is a key component in the decision regarding whether your data are quantitative.

Observe the Distribution of Your Data

Since many common statistical procedures assume normally distributed data, you may want to examine your data to determine whether they fit this criterion. There are a number of ways to check the normality of your data. For example, you can observe the shape of the data's distribution using graphs such as a histogram (which for normal data should produce a graph that approximates a bell-shaped curve). Other plots that are helpful include boxplots and normal probability plots. You must have a sufficient sample size for these graphical methods to give you interpretable results. Several graphical techniques can be used to assess the normality of your data. These include the histogram, boxplot, Q-Q plot, and stem-and-leaf plot. These will all be described in an upcoming example. These graphical methods are not only valuable for assessing the normality of your data; they are also useful in detecting unusual values that need further examination.

Testing for Normality

To supplement the graphical assessment of normality, you can formally test for normality. For example, the Kolmogorov-Smirnov and Shapiro-Wilk test reported in the SPSS Explore procedure can be used to test the hypothesis that the distribution is normal. (SPSS recommends these tests only when your sample size is less than 50.) The hypotheses used in testing data normality are as follows:

H_0: The distribution of the data is normal.

H_a: The distribution of the data is not normal.

If a test does not reject normality, this suggests that a parametric procedure that assumes normality (e.g., a t-test) can be safely used. However, we emphasize again that it is always a good idea to examine data graphically in addition to the formal tests for normality.

The term *normal distribution* used here and in the remainder of the book indicates that histograms of data sampled from this distribution will approximate a bell-shaped curve. The normal distribution is also referred to as a Gaussian distribution (after the mathematician Karl Friedrich Gauss). We will refer to data from a normal distribution as "normal data." Figure 2.2, shown in a later example in the chapter, shows a bell-shaped curve fitted to data.

Tips and Caveats for Quantitative Data

How to Use the Information About Normality

Given the fact that there is emphasis on normality in statistical procedures, you'd think it was a "make-or-break" criterion for your analysis. This is not necessarily the case. In fact, true normality is usually a myth. What is important is to ascertain whether your data show a serious departure from normality. Data showing a moderate departure from normality can usually be used in parametric procedures without loss of integrity. Also, if you are comparing means and your sample size (for each group) is "large" (say, greater than 40), you can invoke the central limit theorem (CLT) to justify using parametric procedures even when the data are not normally distributed. Briefly, the CLT states that sample means are approximately normal for sufficiently large sample sizes even when the original populations are nonnormal. In the criterion above, we define "large" to be 40 or more. However, if your sample size is not large or you are not comparing means and are concerned that your data are not normally distributed, you might consider one of the following options.

- Perhaps there is some functional transformation of your data (e.g., logarithm or square root) that produces approximate normality.
- Consider recoding your data into categories to create a categorical variable. (See Appendix A: A Brief Tutorial for Using SPSS for Windows for information on transforming, recoding, and categorizing your data.)
- Nonparametric tests may be available for your particular need (see Chapter 7: Nonparametric Analysis Procedures).

If Data Are Not Normally Distributed, Don't Report the Mean

Describe distinctly nonnormal data with the median and range or interquartile range (Lang & Secic, 1997). Another way to report this type of data is by using a five-number summary consisting of the minimum,

25th percentile, 50th percentile, 75th percentile, and maximum. This five-number summary is the basis for the boxplot.

When in Doubt, Report the SD Rather Than the SEM

When reporting descriptive statistics, there is sometimes a dilemma regarding whether to report the standard deviation (*SD*) or standard error of the mean (*SEM*), which is the *SD* divided by the square root of the sample size. You should report the *SD* if you are describing the variability of the data and the *SEM* if you are reporting the variability of the mean. Some texts and journals recommend that you always report the *SD* since the *SEM* can be calculated easily from the *SD* and sample size, and the *SEM* may give an uninformed reader a false impression about the variability of the data. If you are unsure, the safe bet is to report the *SD*.

Use Tables and Figures to Report Many Descriptive Statistics

If you are reporting two or three descriptive measurements in a report or article, we recommend that you include the statistics in the text. However, if you have more than two or three measurements, consider using a table or graph.

When You Have Large Sample Sizes

As mentioned earlier, if your sample size (for each group) is "large" (say, greater than 40), you can invoke the central limit theorem to justify using parametric procedures based on means, even when the data are not normally distributed.

Break Down Descriptive Statistics by Group

Descriptive statistics should be broken down by group (i.e., calculated separately for each group) for populations composed of distinct groups rather than looking at aggregate data. For example, a mixture of normal subpopulations will usually not have a normal appearance.

Quantitative Data Description Examples

The following examples illustrate techniques for describing quantitative data using statistics and graphs.

EXAMPLE 2.1: Quantitative Data With an Unusual Value

Describing the Problem

Hypothetical data from several branch banks in Southern California contain information on how many IRAs (individual retirement accounts) were set up in 19 locations during a 3-month period. The variable is called *IRA Setup*. These data are counts and are appropriately classified as quantitative data since, for example, it makes sense to calculate a mean number of accounts per bank. Before calculating and reporting the mean or other parametric measures of these values, you may want to assess the normality of the data. One way to do that is to perform a statistical test. Table 2.1 shows the results of two statistical tests used to assess normality of the *IRA Setup* variable.

Table 2.1   Test for Normality on IRA Data

Tests of Normality

	Kolmogorov-Smirnov[a]			Shapiro-Wilk		
	Statistic	df	Sig.	Statistic	df	Sig.
IRA Setup	.173	19	.136	.878	19	.019

a. Lilliefors Significance Correction

The "Sig." values in the "Tests of Normality" table are the p-values based on testing the null hypothesis that the data are normally distributed. Both tests are designed to determine whether the observed data closely fit the shape of a normal curve. The Shaprio-Wilk test result is significant ($p = 0.019$), which suggests that the data are not normal, while the Kolmogorov-Smirnov test result is nonsignificant ($p = 0.136$). This leaves you without a convincing argument one way or another.

To further examine these data (and perhaps understand the reasons for the discrepancy), you can visualize the distribution of the data using graphical displays such as a histogram, boxplot, stem-and-leaf diagram, and normal Q-Q plot (see Figure 2.1).

Here is a brief explanation of how to interpret each of these plots in the context of normality:

- *Histogram*. When a histogram's shape approximates a bell curve, it suggests that the data may have come from a normal population.
- *Boxplot*. A boxplot that is symmetric with the median line in approximately the center of the box and with symmetric whiskers somewhat longer than the

subsections of the center box suggests that the data may have come from a normal distribution.

- *Q-Q Plot.* A quantile-quantile (q-q) plot is a graph used to display the degree to which the quantiles of a reference (known) distribution (in this case, the normal distribution) differ from the sample quantiles of the data. When the data fit the reference distribution, then the points will lie in a tight random scatter around the reference line. For the IRA data, the curvature of the points in the plot indicates a possible departure from normality, and the point lying outside the overall pattern of points indicates an outlier.
- *Stem-and-Leaf Plot.* A stem-and-leaf plot is a method of displaying data that shows the data in a histogram-like pattern but retains information about actual data values. Each observation is broken down into a stem and a leaf where, typically, the stem of the number includes all but the last digit and the leaf is the last digit.

All four of these plots for *IRA Setup* indicate something unusual. There is one small value (Case 15, as indicated by the boxplot) that is a potential outlier (an unusually large or small value). Suppose that after carefully examining the source documentation for these data, you discover that the branch location for Case 15 was closed for 21 days because of localized wildfires. After this type of discovery, you might be justified in excluding this branch location from your analysis.

When this data value is excluded from the data set and the data are reanalyzed, the Shapiro-Wilk test yields a *p*-value of 0.73, and the Kolmogorov-Smimov *p*-value is greater than 0.2, indicating that there is no reason to be concerned about the normality assumption. Furthermore, after the removal of the extreme data value, the revised histogram looks considerably more normal (as does the boxplot). The histogram for the revised data is shown in Figure 2.2. The superimposed normal curve helps you assess the normality assumption. Although not a perfect fit, the histogram suggests that it is reasonable to assume that the data are from a normal population. The boxplot, not shown here, is relatively symmetric and typical of normally distributed data containing no outliers or extreme values. The other plots also suggest normality. The point of this example is to show that it is important to not only look at statistics and tests but also to look at graphical displays based on your data.

Once you are satisfied that a normality assumption makes sense for your data, you can use statistics such as means, standard deviations, and so on to describe your data. In the example here, note that we were justified in removing the extreme value. In addition to reporting the sample mean of the data, you may also want to report a confidence interval. For example, a 95% CI (confidence interval) on the mean is based on the standard error of the

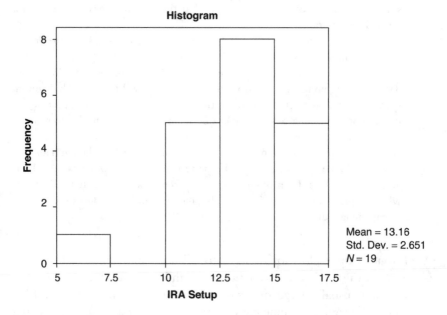

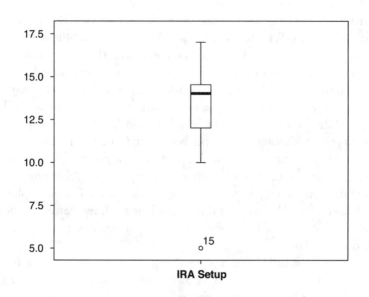

```
IRA Setup Stem-and-Leaf Plot
Frequency                 Stem  &  Leaf

   1.00 Extremes              (=<5.0)
   1.00                  10  .  0
   1.00                  11  .  0
   3.00                  12  .  000
   3.00                  13  .  000
   5.00                  14  .  00000
   2.00                  15  .  00
   2.00                  16  .  00
   1.00                  17  .  0


Stem width:     1
Each leaf:          1 case(s)
```

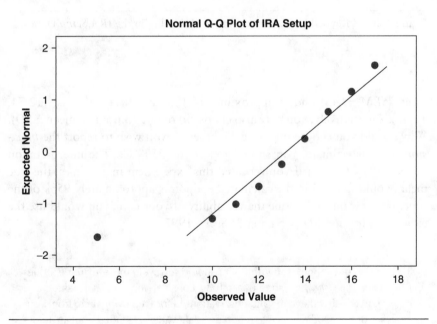

Figure 2.1   Plots Used to Assess Normality Using *IRA Setup* Data

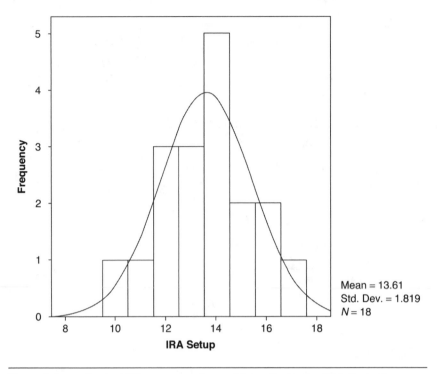

Figure 2.2   Revised Histogram to Assess Normality in the *IRA Setup* Data

mean (*SEM* = .43) and is approximately 13.6 ± 2 × .43, that is, (12.74, 14.46). Alternatively, you may also choose to report 13.6 ± 1.8 (mean ± *SD*). Why should you choose one over the other? If you wish to report the *precision* of your estimate, you should report the 95% CI. The interpretation of the 95% CI is that if you repeated this experiment many times, the true mean would fall within the calculated endpoints approximately 95% of the time. If you want to describe the variability of your data, you would use the expression mean ± *SD* (see Lang & Secic, 1997).

This example does not imply that you should always remove extreme values from your data set. You should carefully consider any unusual values and determine whether they are valid observations before removing them from your analysis. (It is a good practice to report any data values excluded from an analysis in your write-up and to justify your actions.)

Reporting Results for EXAMPLE *2.1: Quantitative Data With an Unusual Value*

The results for the analyses on the IRA data could be reported in the following ways:

Narrative for the Methods Section

"One value in the data for IRA setups was eliminated because the bank was closed for 21 days during the evaluation period. Descriptive statistics were calculated on the remaining 18 values."

Narrative for the Results Section

"IRA setups averaged 13.6 per branch ($SD = 1.8$, $N = 18$)."

or

"The mean ($\pm SD$) IRA setups was 13.6 (± 1.8)."

If you are reporting the precision of your estimate, you could state the following:

"The mean was 13.6 (95% CI = 12.71 to 14.52) IRA setups per branch."

If you decide that you want to analyze the data *without* removing the extreme value and therefore not make a normality assumption, you could report your findings using the median and interquartile range. For example:

"The number of IRA setups per branch ranged from 5 to 17 setups with a median (interquartile range) of 14 (3)."

Another way to describe nonnormal data is with a five-number summary that consists of the minimum, 25th percentile, median, 75th percentile, and maximum values of a data set. For example:

"A five-number summary of the IRA setups is (5, 12, 14, 15, 17)."

SPSS Step-by-Step. EXAMPLE *2.1: Quantitative Data With an Unusual Value*

Use the following steps to obtain the output for the IRA data analysis:

1. Open the data set IRA.SAV and select **Analyze/Descriptive Statistics/Explore.**

2. Select the *IRASetup* variable for the dependent list.

3. Click on the Plots button and select the "Normality plots with tests" check-box and "Histogram." Click Continue and OK. Table 2.1 is displayed (along with other output).

4. To eliminate the outlying value (*IRASetup* = 5), return to the data editor and select **Data/Select Cases . . .** and select the option "If condition is satisfied. . . ." Click on the "If . . ." button. In the formula text box, enter the expression "*IRASetup* > 5" (without quotes). Click Continue and OK. A slash appears in the IRA data file next to record 15, indicating that the record will not be included in subsequent analyses. (For more information about filtering cases, see "Transforming, Recoding, and Categorizing Your Data" in Appendix A.)

5. To display the revised histogram, select Graphs/Histogram and select *IRASetup* as the analysis variable. Select the "Display normal curve" check-box and click OK. The graph shown in Figure 2.2 is displayed.

6. To calculate the 95% confidence interval, select **Analyze/Descriptive Statistics/ Explore**. Select *IRASetup* as the variable and click OK.

7. To remove the "Select cases" criterion and calculate the interquartile range and five-number summary using all of the data, return to the data editor and select **Data/Select Cases . . .** and select the option "All cases" and OK. Select **Analyze/Descriptive Statistics/Explore**. Select *IRASetup* as the variable. Click the Statistics button and select the Percentiles option. Click Continue and OK. The interquartile range appears in the Descriptives table output.

EXAMPLE 2.2: Quantitative Data by Groups

Describing the Problem

A survey was administered to 79 clinic patients to measure their satisfaction with clinic services. Two versions of the survey were randomly assigned to the participants. The following demographic information (by group) is shown in Table 2.2.

The purpose of this table is to compare the respondents to the two types of surveys on several important demographic variables. The *p*-values refer to a test of the null hypothesis that the means are equal (see the two-sample *t*-test examples in Chapter 3: Comparing One or Two Means Using the *t*-Test). In this table, it appears that the number of years of schooling was significantly higher for those who took the old survey.

Researchers disagree over whether to include the "*p*-Value" column in tables of this type. The controversy arises in part over the known problem of performing multiple tests within the same experiment. For a discussion of *p*-values, see Chapter 1.

Table 2.2   Table Reporting Group Statistics: Baseline Characteristics of
Patients in Study by Group

| | Mean (SD) | | |
| | Old Survey | New Survey | |
Characteristic	N = 34	N = 45	p-Value
Age	34.3 (11.6)	30.2 (9.21)	0.08
Schooling	12.2 (2.43)	10.5 (2.33)	0.003
Temperature	99.1 (1.24)	99.5 (1.51)	0.27
Minutes	532 (337)	429 (309)	0.16

As described in Chapter 1, when multiple p-values are used in an analysis, it is good practice to use Bonferroni-adjusted significance criteria. In this case, the adjustment would entail using the p-value $0.05/4 = 0.0125$ as the rejection criterion for these tests. Thus, the only significant result in this table would be for the schooling variable (where the reported p-value is 0.003).

Reporting the Results for EXAMPLE 2.2: Quantitative Data by Groups

Narrative for the Methods Section

"The two versions of the survey were randomly assigned to patients as they registered at the clinic."

Narrative for Results Section

When there are several means to report, it is often clearer to the reader if you report the results in a table such as the one shown in Table 2.2. If you use a Bonferroni-adjusted p-value for your rejection criterion, you should include a statement such as the following:

"To maintain the $\alpha = .05$ significance level for the table comparisons using a Bonferroni adjustment, a p-value must be less than $p = 0.0125$ (i.e., $0.05 \div 4$) to be considered statistically significant."

In either case, the *schooling* difference remains the only significant comparison. We assume that the observed difference of 1.7 years of schooling is a meaningful difference.

When creating a table for publication, you should check the specifications for the particular publication to which you will be submitting your article.

SPSS Step-by-Step. EXAMPLE 2.2: Quantitative Data by Groups

To calculate descriptive statistics for the survey data, follow these steps in SPSS.

1. Open the data set SURVEY.SAV and select **Analyze/Descriptive Statistics/Explore.** . . .

2. Select *Age, Years of Schooling (Edu), Arrival Temperature (Temp)*, and *Minutes in Clinic (Stayminutes)* for the dependent variables and *Survey Version* for the factor list. Click OK to produce output that includes the means and standard deviations listed in Table 2.2.

3. To calculate the *p*-values, select **Analyze/Compare Means/Independent samples *t*-test** and select *Age, Years of Schooling (Edu), Arrival Temperature (Temp)*, and *Minutes in Clinic (Stayminutes)* as the "test variables" and *Survey Version* as the "grouping variable." Click on the "Define groups" button and enter 1 and 2 for the group values. Click Continue and OK. In the resulting "Independent Samples" table, the *p*-values for each comparison are listed in the "Equal variances assumed" row in the "Sig. 2-tailed" column. More about the *t*-test and this table is discussed in Chapter 3: Comparing One or Two Means Using the *t*-Test.

EXAMPLE 2.3: Quantitative Data With Unusual Values

Describing the Problem

Suppose you are interested in exploring the variables in a data set from the U.S. Department of Energy (2005) containing fuel economy information on 2005 model year automobiles. Your first strategy might be to look for unusually large or small data values by finding the minimum and maximum for each quantitative variable of interest. The results are shown in Table 2.3 for four of the variables.

In this output, the minimum value for the *cylinders* variable is –1. This seems impossible, but by examining the data, it can be seen that there are two Mazda RX-8 models that have rotary engines without conventional cylinders. The data are correct, but the –1 code indicates that the data for rotary engines indicates a "missing" value rather than an actual number of cylinders. Before analyzing the data, you should define this missing value for

Table 2.3   Searching for Unusual Values

Descriptive Statistics

	N	Minimum	Maximum	Mean	Std. Deviation
Engine Size	1081	1.3	8.3	3.307	1.1748
Cylinders	1081	-1	12	5.78	1.587
CityMPG	1081	10	60	19.29	4.605
HwyMPG	1081	13	51	25.67	5.323
Valid N (listwise)	1081				

that variable. On the other side of the scale, notice the very high miles per gallon (mpg) ratings of 51 (city) and 60 (highway). These are legitimate mpg ratings for the hybrid Honda Civic and Toyota Prius models. If your study deals only with cars having conventional engines, you may want to exclude both the rotary engine cars and hybrids from your analysis. (Assigning missing values and selecting cases in SPSS is discussed in Appendix A: A Brief Tutorial for Using SPSS for Windows.)

> Checks for extreme values will not find a slight miscoding of a data value. For example, if an mpg were entered as 32 instead of 23, this procedure would not catch the error.

Continuing with the automobile data, suppose you want to examine *city mpg* between SUVs and non-SUVS in the 2005 automobile data set and you want to investigate whether the normality assumption makes sense for each group. The following graph in Figure 2.3 shows the boxplots for that assessment.

Notice in these side-by-side boxplots that some observations (on the high end of mpg) are indicated as outliers (marked as an "o") and some as extreme values (marked as an "*"). An outlier is defined (in SPSS) as a value from 1.5 to 3 interquartile ranges (IQRs) beyond the 75th (or below the 25th) percentile, and an extreme value is greater than 3 IQRs beyond the 75th (or below the 25th) percentile. Figure 2.3 shows that there are a number of outliers for non-SUV automobiles, but the data for SUVs are less variable, with only two extreme values (both hybrid models).

SPSS Step-by-Step. EXAMPLE *2.3:*
Quantitative Data With Unusual Values

To create the output in Table 2.3 and Figure 2.3, follow these steps in SPSS:

1. Open the data set CARS2005.SAV and select **Analyze/Descriptive Statistics/Descriptives. . . .**

2. Select the variables *EngineSize, Cylinders, CityMPG*, and *HwyMPG*.

3. Click OK, and the table in Table 2.3 is displayed.

4. To set the *Cylinders* missing value at –1, click on the Variable View tab in the SPSS editor and click on the cell for *Cylinders* in the Missing column. Click on the ellipses (. . .) and enter –1 as a discrete missing value.

5. To create the side-by-side boxplots in Figure 2.3, again using the CARS2005.SAV data set, select **Graphs/Boxplot. . . .**

6. Select the "Simple" option and choose the radio button for "Summaries for groups of cases." Click the Define button.

7. Select *CityMPG* as the "Variable," *SUV* as the "Category Axis," and *Model* for "Label Cases by."

8. Click OK to produce Figure 2.3.

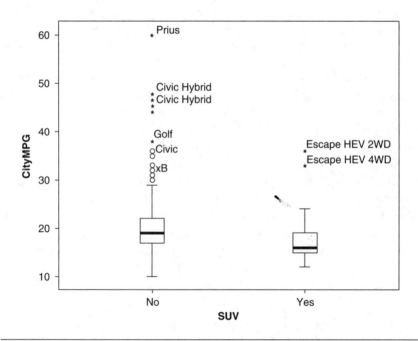

Figure 2.3   Side-by-Side Boxplots Showing Outliers and Extreme Values by Group

Describing Categorical Data

Categorical data record a characteristic such as race, gender, presence of a disease, or the color of a car model. Think of the word *categories* when you're analyzing categorical data. This data type is sometimes called *qualitative* and is further divided by the terms *nominal* (order not important) and *ordinal* (having order). We will assume categorical data to be nominal unless specified. In this section, two types of descriptive analyses are illustrated for categorical data. They are as follows:

- Frequency tables
- Crosstabulations

Examples illustrate methods for examining categorical data and reporting your results. Categorical variables include the following:

- Presence of a disease (1 = yes, 0 = no)
- Method of delivery (1 = USPS, 2 = UPS, 3 = FedEx, 4 = other)
- Marital status (1 = married, 2 = single never married, 3 = single divorced, 4 = single widowed)
- Stage of a disease (1, 2, 3, or 4)

Each of these variables is an observation that places the subject or entity into two or more categories. When we observe summaries of these variables, they are typically given as counts (the number of subjects placed into each category) and/or the corresponding percents.

Considerations for Examining Categorical Data

Notice in the examples above that some categories have order and some do not. For example, in the marital status variable above, there are four unordered categories, and although these categories are recorded in the data set as numbers (1 to 4), these numbers are simply codes and are not meaningful numerically. They should not be interpreted as implying an ordering of the categories, nor should they be used in arithmetic calculations (e.g., mean, etc.). For the purposes of analysis, these categorical data are reported as counts, frequencies, or percentages of subjects falling into various categories. In the marital status example, the categories have no order and are thus nominal variables. On the other hand, stage of cancer (from 1 to 4), rank in the military, and finish order in a race (first place, second place, etc.) are ordinal categorical variables since categories have a logical order.

Tips and Caveats

When Categorical Variables Can Be Treated as Quantitative Data

Sometimes, ordinal data such as responses using a Likert scale (1 = strongly disagree, 2 = disagree, 3 = neutral, 4 = agree, 5 = strongly agree) are treated as quantitative data. As a general guideline, in order for the mean and other arithmetically obtained quantities (e.g., standard deviation) to make sense, it must be reasonable to assume that the differences between any two categories are equal. For example, if the categories are 1, 2, 3, 4, 5, then it must be reasonable to consider the difference between categories 2 and 3 to be the same as the difference between 4 and 5, and so on.

Describing Categorical Data Examples

The following examples illustrate techniques for assessing and describing categorical data using statistics and graphs.

EXAMPLE 2.4: Frequency Table for Categorical Data

Describing the Problem

In a survey of 79 patients at a clinic, information was collected on how they arrived (car, bus, or walked). You may want to examine the data using a frequency table to report the number and percentage of patients who arrived using each travel method along with a bar chart showing a visualization of these percentages. Table 2.4 displays a frequency table for this data set, and Figure 2.4 shows the associated bar chart. Note that the bar chart information is displayed in percents rather than counts. We could optionally have produced a similar chart using frequencies (counts).

Table 2.4   Frequency Table for *How Arrived*

How Arrived

		Frequency	Percent	Valid Percent	Cumulative Percent
Valid	BUS	11	13.9	13.9	13.9
	CAR	66	83.5	83.5	97.5
	WALK	2	2.5	2.5	100.0
	Total	79	100.0	100.0	

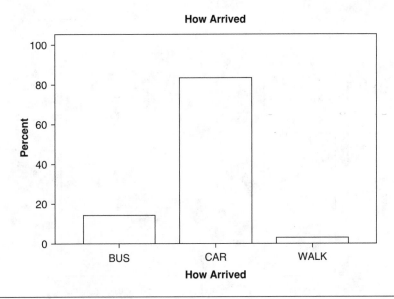

Figure 2.4   Bar Chart for *How Arrived*

In Table 2.4, the frequency is the number of patients who arrived using each method of transportation. The percent (and valid percent, which is the percent after removing missing values) tells you the percentage of patients arriving by each method. It is clear both from the frequency table and the bar chart that most patients arrived by car.

Some researchers prefer to display the bars in a bar chart for nominal data in descending order of bar heights. This makes it easier to find the categories with the most and fewest occurrences as well as view the categories in order of frequency of occurrence. This type of bar chart is called a Pareto chart. Figure 2.5 shows a Pareto chart for these data.

Reporting Results for Frequency Data

Narrative for Methods Section

"Arrival methods were examined by finding the number of subjects arriving at the clinic using a car, bus, or by walking."

Narrative for Results Section

"Subjects arrived by car 83.5% of the time (66 of 79), 13.9% by bus (11 of 79), and 2.5% by walking (2 of 79). (Round-off error makes the total slightly under 100%.)"

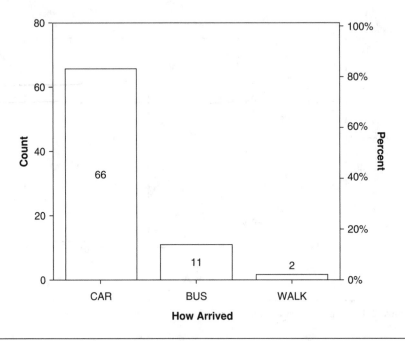

Figure 2.5   Pareto Chart for *How Arrived*

SPSS Step-by Step. EXAMPLE *2.4:* *Frequency Table for Categorical Data*

To create the output in Table 2.4 and Figure 2.4, follow these steps in SPSS:

1. Open the data set SURVEY.SAV and select **Analyze/Descriptive Statistics/ Frequencies.**

2. Select *How Arrived* as the analysis variable.

3. Click on the Charts button and select Bar Chart, Percentages, Continue, and OK.

To display the Pareto chart in Figure 2.5, follow these additional instructions:

4. Using the SURVEY.SAV data set, select **Graphs/Pareto.**

5. Choose Simple type chart, select the radio button for "Counts or sums for groups or cases," and click on the Define button.

6. Select *How Arrived* as the Category Axis and deselect the Display Cumulative Line button and press OK to display the chart displayed in Figure 2.5.

EXAMPLE 2.5: Crosstabulation of Categorical Variables

Describing the Problem

Using the 2005 automobile data, suppose you want to crosstabulate two variables. Table 2.5 contains a crosstabulation of the variables *SUV* (sport utility vehicle) and *AWD* (all-wheel drive).

Table 2.5   Output for Crosstabulation Example

SUV * AWD Crosstabulation

			AWD No	AWD Yes	Total
SUV	No	Count	752	50	802
		% within SUV	93.8%	6.2%	100.0%
		% within AWD	76.5%	51.0%	74.2%
		% of total	69.6%	4.6%	74.2%
	Yes	Count	231	48	279
		% within SUV	82.8%	17.2%	100.0%
		% within AWD	23.5%	49.0%	25.8%
		% of total	21.4%	4.4%	25.8%
Total		Count	983	98	1081
		% within SUV	90.9%	9.1%	100.0%
		% within AWD	100.0%	100.0%	100.0%
		% of total	90.9%	9.1%	100.0%

Specific statistical tests to analyze this type of table are discussed in Chapter 5: Analysis of Categorical Data. In this example, we are only interested in the descriptive information contained in the table. For example, observe that 17.2% (48 of 279) of the SUVs in this data set have all-wheel drive. Also note that 49% (48 of 98) of all-wheel-drive vehicles are SUVs and that 9.1% (98 of 1,081) of all vehicles are SUVs with all-wheel drive. A bar chart for these data is shown in Figure 2.6.

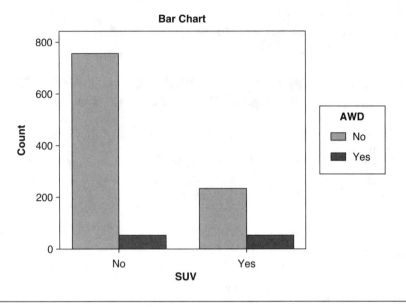

Figure 2.6   Clustered Bar Chart for SUV Data

This bar chart allows you to visualize the relationship between SUVs and whether they have all-wheel drive. In this chart, it is visually clear that most non-SUVs do not have all-wheel drive, while a larger percentage (although about the same number) of the vehicles classified as SUVs have all-wheel drive. You can also see that there are many more non-SUVs than there are SUVs in this data set.

Reporting Crosstabulation Results

To describe the information in a frequency table or crosstabulation in your report or article, you should always include counts along with percentages (Lang & Secic, 1997). For example, your description (from the information in the crosstabulation above) might be as follows:

Narrative for Methods Section

"The relationship between model type and all-wheel drive was examined using crosstabulation."

Narrative for Results Section

"This table shows that 17.2% (48 of 279) of SUV models and 6.2% (50 of 802) of non-SUV models have all-wheel drive."

SPSS Step-by Step. EXAMPLE 2.5:
Crosstabulation of Categorical Variables

Follow these steps to create the crosstabulation output from the CARS2005 data set:

1. Open the data set CARS2005.SAV and select **Analyze/Descriptive Statistics/Crosstabs. . . .**

2. From the dialog box, select the variable named *SUV* as the row variable and *AWD* as the column variable.

3. Click on the Cells button and select Row, Column, and Total Percentages. Click Continue.

4. To display the bar chart, select the "Display clustered bar charts" checkbox.

5. Click OK to display the results as shown in Table 2.5.

Summary

Understanding your data is the first step in any data analysis. This chapter explains how to use descriptive statistics and graphs to understand and report information about your data. Once you are satisfied that your data are clean and that you understand the types of variables you are using, then you are ready to move on to the following chapters that enter the realm of inferential statistics.

References

Lang, T. A., & Secic, M. (1997). *How to report statistics in medicine*. Philadelphia: American College of Physicians.

U.S. Department of Energy. (2005). *Model 2005 model year fuel economy data*. Retrieved from http://www.fueleconomy.gov/feg/FEG2005_GasolineVehicles.pdf

3

Comparing One or Two Means Using the *t*-Test

The bread and butter of statistical data analysis is the Student's *t*-test. It was named after a statistician who called himself Student but whose real name was William Gossett. As an employee of Guinness Brewery in Dublin, Ireland, he tackled a number of practical statistical problems related to the operation of the brewery. Since he was discouraged from publishing under his own name, he adopted the Student moniker.

Because of Gossett's work, today's researchers have in their toolbox what is probably the most commonly performed statistical procedure, the *t*-test. The most typical use of this test is to compare means, which is the focus of the discussion in this chapter. Unfortunately, because this test is easy to use, it is also easily misused.

In this chapter, you will learn when, why, and how to appropriately perform a *t*-test and how to present your results. There are three types of *t*-tests that will be discussed in this chapter. These are the

1. One-sample *t*-test, which is used to compare a single mean to a fixed number or "gold standard"

2. Two-sample *t*-test, which is used to compare two population means based on independent samples from the two populations or groups

3. Paired *t*-test, which is used to compare two means based on samples that are paired in some way

These three types of *t*-tests are discussed along with advice concerning the conditions under which each of these types is appropriate. Examples are given that illustrate how to perform these three types of *t*-tests using SPSS software. The first type of *t*-test considered is the simplest.

One-Sample *t*-Test

The one-sample *t*-test is used for comparing sample results with a known value. Specifically, in this type of test, a single sample is collected, and the resulting sample mean is compared with a value of interest, sometimes a "gold standard," that is not based on the current sample. For example, this specified value might be

- The weight indicated on a can of vegetables
- The advertised breaking strength of a type of steel pipe
- Government specification on the percentage of fruit juice that must be in a drink before it can be advertised as "fruit juice"

The purpose of the one-sample *t*-test is to determine whether there is sufficient evidence to conclude that the mean of the population from which the sample is taken is different from the specified value.

Related to the one-sample *t*-test is a confidence interval on the mean. The confidence interval is usually applied when you are not testing against a specified value of the population mean but instead want to know a range of plausible values of the unknown mean of the population from which the sample was selected.

Appropriate Applications for a One-Sample *t*-Test

The following are examples of situations in which a one-sample *t*-test would be appropriate:

- Does the average volume of liquid in filled soft drink bottles match the 12 ounces advertised on the label?
- Is the mean weight loss for men ages 50 to 60 years, who are given a brochure and training describing a low-carbohydrate diet, more than 5 pounds after 3 months?
- Based on a random sample of 200 students, can we conclude that the average SAT score this year is lower than the national average from 3 years ago?

Design Considerations for a One-Sample *t*-Test

The key assumption underlying the one-sample *t*-test is that the population from which the sample is selected is normal. However, this assumption is rarely if ever precisely true in practice, so it is important to know how concerned you should be about apparent nonnormality in your data. The following are rules of thumb (Moore & McCabe, 2006):

- If the sample size is small (less than 15), then you should not use the one-sample *t*-test if the data are clearly skewed or if outliers are present.
- If the sample size is moderate (at least 15), then the one-sample *t*-test can be safely used except when there are severe outliers.
- If the sample size is large (at least 40), then the one-sample *t*-test can be safely used without regard to skewness or outliers.

You will see variations of these rules throughout the literature. The last two rules above are based on the central limit theorem, which says that when sample size is moderately large, the sample mean is approximately normally distributed even when the original population is nonnormal.

Hypotheses for a One-Sample *t*-Test

When performing a one-sample *t*-test, you may or may not have a preconceived assumption about the direction of your findings. Depending on the design of your study, you may decide to perform a one- or two-tailed test.

Two-Tailed *t*-Tests

The basic hypotheses for the one-sample *t*-test are as follows, where μ denotes the mean of the population from which the sample was selected, and μ_0 denotes the hypothesized value of this mean. It should be reiterated that μ_0 is a value that does not depend on the current sample.

H_0: $\mu = \mu_0$ (in words: the population mean is equal to the hypothesized value μ_0).

H_a: $\mu \neq \mu_0$ (the population mean is not equal to μ_0).

One-Tailed *t*-Tests

If you are only interested in rejecting the null hypothesis if the population mean differs from the hypothesized value in a direction of interest, you may want to use a one-tailed (sometimes called a one-sided) test. If, for example, you want to reject the null hypothesis only if there is sufficient evidence that the mean is larger than the value hypothesized under the null (i.e., μ_0), the hypotheses become the following:

H_0: $\mu = \mu_0$ (the population mean is equal to the hypothesized value μ_0).

H_a: $\mu > \mu_0$ (the population mean is greater than μ_0).

Analogous hypotheses could be specified for the case in which you want to reject H_0 only if there is sufficient evidence that the population mean is less than μ_0.

SPSS always reports a two-tailed p-value, so you should modify the reported p-value to fit a one-tailed test by dividing it by 2 if your results are consistent with the direction specified in the alternative hypothesis. For more discussion of the issues of one- and two-sample tests, see the section "Hypotheses for a Two-Sample t-Test" in this chapter.

EXAMPLE 3.1: One-Sample t-Test

Describing the Problem

A certain bolt is designed to be 4 inches in length. The lengths of a random sample of 15 bolts are shown in Figure 3.1.

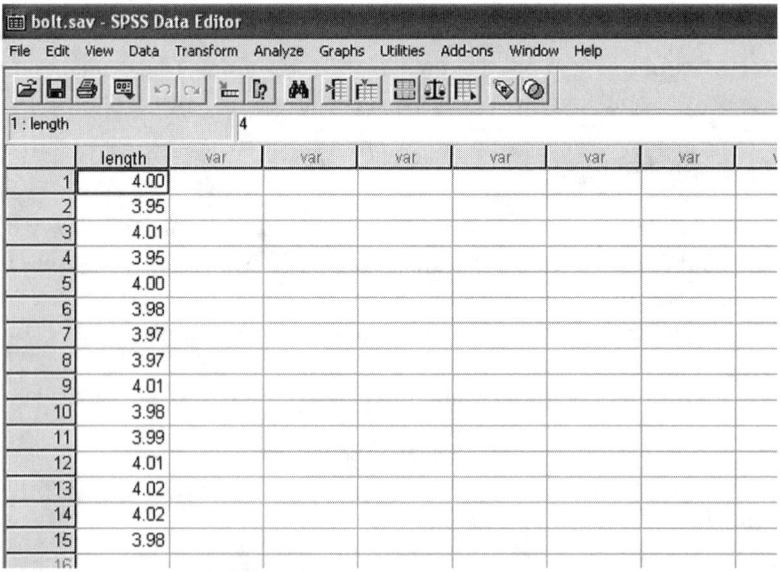

bolt.sav - SPSS Data Editor							
File Edit View Data Transform Analyze Graphs Utilities Add-ons Window Help							
1 : length		4					
	length	var	var	var	var	var	var
1	4.00						
2	3.95						
3	4.01						
4	3.95						
5	4.00						
6	3.98						
7	3.97						
8	3.97						
9	4.01						
10	3.98						
11	3.99						
12	4.01						
13	4.02						
14	4.02						
15	3.98						
16							

Figure 3.1   The Bolt Data

Since the sample size is small ($N = 15$), we need to examine the normality of the data before proceeding to the t-test. In Figure 3.2, we show the boxplot of the length data from which it can be seen that the data are reasonably symmetric, and thus the t-test should be an appropriate test.

See the section "Observe the Distribution of Your Data" in Chapter 2 for a discussion of tests for normality.

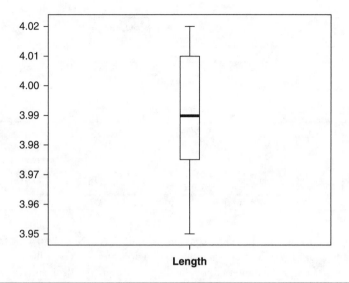

Figure 3.2   Boxplot of the Bolt Data

Since the bolts will be out of design whether they are too short or too long, we test the following hypotheses:

Null hypothesis (H_0): $\mu = 4$ (the population mean is equal to 4 inches).

Alternative hypothesis (H_a): $\mu \neq 4$ (the population mean is not equal to 4 inches).

The output needed to perform this test is shown in Table 3.1.

In the "One-Sample Statistics" box, it can be seen that the sample mean of the lengths is 3.9893 inches, with a standard deviation of 0.02314. (You should report these values to fewer digits, as discussed in Chapter 1.) In the "One-Sample Test" output, we see that $t = -1.78$ with a *p*-value of 0.096. Thus, at the $\alpha = .05$ level of significance, we do not reject the null, and we do not conclude that there is a problem with the lengths.

We make the following comments concerning the output:

- The "mean difference" value of -0.01067 given in the table is $\bar{X} - \mu_0$ (i.e., $3.9893 - 4$).
- The confidence interval above is given as $(-0.0235, 0.0021)$. It should be noted that this is a 95% confidence interval on the difference $\mu - \mu_0$ instead of an interval for μ. Thus, the fact that this interval contains zero indicates that

Table 3.1   Output for the Bolt Data

One-Sample Statistics

	N	Mean	Std. Deviation	Std. Error Mean
length	15	3.9893	.02314	.00597

One-Sample Test

	Test Value = 4					
				Mean Difference	95% Confidence Interval of the Difference	
	t	df	Sig. (2-tailed)		Lower	Upper
length	-1.786	14	.096	-.01067	-.0235	.0021

the test would not be rejected at the $\alpha = .05$ level. Note also that this is a nonstandard way of presenting the confidence interval. You will usually want to find a confidence interval for the mean μ, not a confidence interval for the difference $\mu - \mu_0$.

To obtain a confidence interval for the mean μ, you can modify the interval above by adding 4 to the lower and upper endpoints, or you can use the SPSS Explore procedure to produce the table shown in Table 3.2. The 95% confidence interval for the mean is (3.9765, 4.0021), and this is the interval you would usually report.

Table 3.2   Explore Output Showing the Confidence Interval for μ

Descriptives

			Statistic	Std. Error
length	Mean		3.9893	.00597
	95% Confidence Interval for Mean	Lower Bound	3.9765	
		Upper Bound	4.0021	
	5% Trimmed Mean		3.9898	
	Median		3.9900	
	Variance		.001	
	Std. Deviation		.02314	
	Minimum		3.95	
	Maximum		4.02	
	Range		.07	
	Interquartile Range		.04	
	Skewness		-.346	.580
	Kurtosis		-.919	1.121

Reporting the Results

The following examples illustrate how you might report this *t*-test in a publication format.

Narrative for the Methods Section

"A one-sample Student's *t*-test was performed to test the hypothesis that the mean bolt length is 4 inches."

Narrative for the Results Section

"The bolt lengths were not significantly different from 4 inches, $t(14) = -1.79$, $p = 0.10$."

Or, to be more complete,

"The mean bolt length (mean = 3.989, *SD* = 0.023, *N* = 15) was not significantly different from the hypothesized value of 4 inches, $t(14) = -1.79$, $p = 0.10$."

A description of the confidence interval would read as follows:

"A 95% confidence interval on the mean bolt length using a Student's *t* distribution with 11 degrees of freedom is (3.977, 4.002). Since this interval contains 4 inches, there is not significant evidence that the mean bolt length is different from 4."

SPSS Step-by-Step. EXAMPLE 3.1: One-Sample t-Test

To run the one-sample *t*-test on the bolt data, follow these steps:

1. Open the data set BOLT.SAV and select **Analyze/Compare Means/One-Sample T Test. . . .**

2. Select *Length* as the test variable and specify 4 as the test value.

3. Click OK, and Table 3.1 is displayed.

4. To display the boxplot in Figure 3.2, select **Analyze/Descriptive Statistics/Explore,** add *Length* to the Dependent List, click on the Plots radio button at the bottom left of the screen, and click Continue and then OK.

To obtain the confidence interval using the SPSS Explore procedure, follow these steps:

1. Open the data set BOLT.SAV and select **Analyze/Descriptive Statistics/Explore. . . .**

2. Add *Length* to the Dependent List.

3. Click OK, and the output includes the information in Table 3.2.

Two-Sample *t*-Test

The two-sample (independent groups) *t*-test is used to determine whether the unknown means of two populations are different from each other based on independent samples from each population. If the two-sample means are sufficiently different from each other, then the population means are declared to be different. A related test, the paired *t*-test, to be discussed in the next section, is used to compare two population means using samples that are paired in some way.

The samples for a two-sample *t*-test can be obtained from a single population that has been randomly divided into two subgroups, with each subgroup subjected to one of two treatments (e.g., two medications) or from two separate populations (e.g., male and female). In either case, for the two-sample *t*-test to be valid, it is necessary that the two samples are independent (i.e., unrelated to each other).

Appropriate Applications for a Two-Sample *t*-Test

In each of the following examples, the two-sample (independent group) *t*-test is used to determine whether the population means of the two groups are different.

- *How Can My Flour Make More Dough?* Distributors often pay extra to have products placed in prime locations in grocery stores. The manufacturer of a new brand of whole-grain flour wants to determine if placing the product on the top shelf or on the eye-level shelf produces better sales. From 40 grocery stores, he randomly chooses 20 for top-shelf placement and 20 for eye-level placement. After a period of 30 days, he compares average sales from the two placements.
- *What's the Smart Way to Teach Economics?* A university is offering two sections of a microeconomics course during the fall semester: (1) meeting once a week with taped lessons provided on a CD and (2) having three sessions a week using standard lectures by the same professor. Students are randomly placed into one of the two sections at the time of registration. Using results from a standardized final exam, the researcher compares mean differences between the learning obtained in the two types of classes.

- *Are Males and Females Different?* It is known that males and females often differ in their reactions to certain drugs. As a part of the development of a new antiseizure medication, a standard dose is given to 20 males and 20 females. Periodic measurements are made to determine the time it takes until a desired level of drug is present in the blood for each subject. The researcher wants to determine whether there is a gender difference in the average speed at which the drug is assimilated into the blood system.

Design Considerations for a Two-Sample *t*-Test

The characteristics of the *t*-tests in the above examples are the following:

A Two-Sample t-Test Compares Means

In an experiment designed to use the two-sample *t*-test, you want to compare means from a quantitative variable such as height, weight, amount spent, or grade. In other words, it should make sense to calculate the mean of the observations. This measurement is called your "response" or "outcome" variable. Also, the outcome measure *should not* be a categorical (nominal/discrete) variable such as hair color, gender, or occupational level, even if the data have been numerically coded.

You Are Comparing Independent Samples

The two groups contain subjects (or objects) that are not paired or matched in any way. These subjects typically are obtained in one of two ways:

- Subjects (or items) are selected for an experiment in which all come from the same population and are *randomly* split into two groups (e.g., placebo vs. drug or two different marketing campaigns). Each group is exposed to identical conditions except for a "treatment," which may be a medical treatment, a marketing design factor, exposure to a stimulus, and so on.
- Subjects are randomly selected from two separate populations (e.g., male vs. female) as in the medical example above.

The t-Test Assumes Normality

A standard assumption for the *t*-test to be valid when you have small sample sizes is that the outcome variable measurements are normally distributed. That is, when graphed as a histogram, the shape approximates a bell curve.

Are the Variances Equal?

Another consideration that should be addressed before using the *t*-test is whether the population variances can be considered to be equal.

The two-sample t-test is robust against moderate departures from the normality and variance assumption, but independence of samples must not be violated. For specifics, see the section below titled "Deciding Which Version of the t-Test Statistic to Use."

Hypotheses for a Two-Sample t-Test

As with any version of the t-test, when performing a two-sample t-test, you may or may not have a preconceived assumption about the direction of your findings. Depending on the design of your study, you may decide to perform a one- or two-tailed test.

Two-Tailed Tests

In this setting, there are two populations, and we are interested in testing whether the population means (i.e., μ_1 and μ_2) are equal. The hypotheses for the comparison of the means in a two-sample t-test are as follows:

H_0: $\mu_1 = \mu_2$ (the population means of the two groups are the same).

H_a: $\mu_1 \neq \mu_2$ (the population means of the two groups are different).

One-Tailed Tests

If your experiment is designed so that you are only interested in detecting whether one mean is larger than the other, you may choose to perform a one-tailed (sometimes called one-sided) t-test. For example, when you are only interested in detecting whether the population mean of the second group is larger than the population mean of the first group, the hypotheses become the following:

H_0: $\mu_1 = \mu_2$ (the population means of the two groups are the same).

H_a: $\mu_2 > \mu_1$ (the population mean of the second group is larger than the population mean of the first group).

Since SPSS always reports a two-tailed p-value, you must modify the reported p-value to fit a one-tailed test by dividing it by 2. Thus, if the p-value reported for a two-tailed t-test is 0.06, then the p-value for this one-sided test would be 0.03 if the results are supportive of the alternative hypothesis (i.e., if $\overline{X}_2 > \overline{X}_1$). If the one-sided hypotheses above are tested and $\overline{X}_2 < \overline{X}_1$, then the p-value would actually be greater than 0.50, and the null hypothesis should not be rejected.

If you intend to use a one-sided test, you should decide this before collecting the data, and the decision should never be based on the fact that you could obtain a more significant result by changing your hypotheses to be one-tailed. Generally, in the case of the two-sample *t*-test, if there is any possibility that there would be interest in detecting a difference in either direction, the two-tailed test is more appropriate. In fact, you will find that some statisticians (and some reviewers) believe that it is almost always inappropriate to use a one-sided *t*-test.

Tips and Caveats for a Two-Sample *t*-Test

Don't Misuse the *t*-Test

Be careful! Don't be among those who misuse the two-sample *t*-test. Experimental situations that are sometimes inappropriately analyzed as two-sample *t*-tests are the following:

- *Comparing Paired Subjects.* A group of subjects receives one treatment, and then the same subjects later receive another treatment. This is a paired design (not independent samples). Other examples of paired observations would be fruit from upper and lower branches of the same tree, subjects matched on several demographic items, or twins. This type of experiment is appropriately analyzed as a paired test and not as a two-sample test. See the "Paired *t*-Test" section later in this chapter.
- *Comparing to a Known Value.* Subjects receive a treatment, and the results are compared to a known value (often a "gold standard"). This is a one-sample *t*-test. See the "One-Sample *t*-Test" section.

Preplan One-Tailed *t*-Tests

As previously mentioned, most statistics programs provide *p*-values for two-tailed tests. If your experiment is designed so that you are performing a one-tailed test, the *p*-values should be modified as mentioned above.

Small Sample Sizes Make Normality Difficult to Assess

Although the *t*-test is robust against moderate departures from normality, outliers (very large or small numbers) can cause problems with the validity of the *t*-test. As your sample sizes increase, the normality assumption for the two-sample *t*-test becomes less of an issue because of the central limit theorem (i.e., sample means are approximately normal for moderately large sample sizes even when the original populations are nonnormal). Refer back to the guidelines regarding normality and sample size given in the section

"Design Considerations for a One-Sample *t*-Test." Studies have shown that the two-sample *t*-test is more robust to nonnormality than the one-sample methods. The two sample methods perform well for a wide range of distributions as long as both populations have the same shape and sample sizes are equal. Selection of sample sizes that are equal or nearly so is advisable whenever feasible (see Posten, 1978). In fact, if your sample sizes are nearly equal, then the one-sample *t*-test guidelines about sample size requirements regarding normality can be thought of as applying to the sum of the two sample sizes in a two-sample *t*-test (see Moore & McCabe, 2006). A more conservative approach is to base your decision on the smaller of the two sample sizes, especially when sample sizes are very different. If your sample sizes are small and you have a concern that your data are not normally distributed, an alternative to the two-sample *t*-test is a nonparametric test called the Mann-Whitney test (see Chapter 7: Nonparametric Analysis Procedures).

Performing Multiple t-Tests Causes Loss of Control of the Experiment-Wise Significance Level

If an experiment involves the strategy of comparing three or more means, the investigator may consider using the familiar *t*-test to perform all pairwise comparisons. However, this strategy leads to the loss of control over the experiment-wise significance level (i.e., the probability of incorrectly finding at least one significant difference in all possible pairwise comparisons when all means are equal). A more appropriate procedure for comparing more than two means is an analysis of variance (see Chapter 6: Analysis of Variance and Covariance for more information).

Interpreting Graphs Associated With the Two-Sample *t*-Test

Graphs are useful tools in understanding an analysis. A graph produced by many software programs in association with the *t*-test is the side-by-side boxplot. This plot aids in the visual assessment of the *normality (symmetry)* of the data as well as the *equal variance assumption*. In addition, the boxplots allow you to visually assess the degree to which the two data sets are separated. The histogram and normal probability plots are also helpful. For additional information on the use of graphs, see Chapter 2: Describing and Examining Data.

Deciding Which Version of the *t*-Test Statistic to Use

Most statistics packages compute two versions of the *t*-statistic, denoted here as t_{EQ} and t_{UNEQ}. The statistic t_{EQ} is based on the assumption that the two population variances are equal, and a pooled estimate of the (equal) population variances is used. Since the population variances are assumed to be equal in this case, the pooled estimate of the common variance is a weighted average of the two sample variances. The statistic t_{UNEQ} does not assume equal variances.

There are two common methods for determining which of the two versions of the t-test to use for an analysis. Both methods make the same assumptions about normality.

1. A simple conservative approach used by a number of recent statistics texts (see, e.g., Moore & McCabe, 2006; Watkins, Scheaffer, & Cobb, 2004) is to *always* use the t-test that does not assume equal variances unless you have evidence that the two variances are equal. This is a conservative approach and is based on studies that have shown that tests to determine equality of variances are often unreliable.

2. The classical approach to deciding which version of the t-test to use is to formally test the equal variance assumption using an F-test. The results of these tests are typically provided in the output from statistical packages. (SPSS uses Levene's version of the F-test.) Typically, the decision criteria for deciding on equality of variances are as follows: If the p-value for the F-test is less than 0.05, you conclude that the variances are unequal and use the t-test based on unequal variance. If the p-value for the F-test is greater than 0.05, you use the t-test based on a pooled estimate of the variances.

If you don't know which of these two approaches to use, we recommend that you use the conservative criterion. That is, always use the "unequal" version of the t-test unless there is evidence that the variances are equal. In most cases, both versions of the t-test will lead to the same conclusion. Here are several items to consider when deciding which version of the t-test to use:

1. Although test statistic t_{UNEQ} does not actually follow a t-distribution even when the populations are normal, the p-value given in the statistics packages provides a close approximation. The degrees of freedom may not necessarily be an integer.

2. There are a number of journal reviewers and professors who follow the classical decision-making procedure that a test for equality of variances (and maybe also for normality) be performed to determine which version of the t-test to use.

3. If one or more of the sample sizes are small and the data contain significant departures from normality, you should perform a nonparametric test in lieu of the t-test. See the section "Tips and Caveats for a Two-Sample t-Test" above.

Two-Sample *t*-Test Examples

The following two examples illustrate how to perform a two-sample *t*-test, create appropriate graphs, and interpret the results.

EXAMPLE 3.2: Two-Sample *t*-Test With Equal Variances

Describing the Problem

A researcher wants to know whether one fertilizer (Brand 1) causes plants to grow faster than another brand of fertilizer (Brand 2). Starting with seeds, he grows plants in identical conditions and randomly assigns fertilizer "Brand 1" to seven plants and fertilizer "Brand 2" to six plants. The data for this experiment are as follows, where the outcome measurement is the height of the plant after 3 weeks of growth. The data are shown in Table 3.3.

Table 3.3   Fertilizer Data

Fertilizer 1	Fertilizer 2
51.0 cm	54.0 cm
53.3	56.1
55.6	52.1
51.0	56.4
55.5	54.0
53.0	52.9
52.1	

Since either fertilizer could be superior, a two-sided *t*-test is appropriate. The hypotheses for this test are H_0: $\mu_1 = \mu_2$ versus H_a: $\mu_1 \neq \mu_2$ or, in words, the following:

Null hypothesis (H_0): The mean growth heights of the plants using the two different fertilizers are the same.

Alternative hypothesis (H_a): The mean growth heights of the plants using the two fertilizers are different.

Arranging the Data for Analysis

Setting up data for this type of analysis is not intuitive and requires some special formatting. To perform the analysis for the fertilizer data using most statistical software programs (including SPSS), you must set up the data using two variables: a classification or group code and an observed (outcome/response) variable. Thus, the way the data are listed in Table 3.3 (although it may make sense in your workbook or spreadsheet) is *not* how a statistical software program requires the data to be set up to perform a two-sample *t*-test. Instead, the data should be set up using the following format:

- *Select a Grouping Code to Represent the Two Fertilizer Types.* This code could be numeric (i.e., 1, 2) or text (i.e., A, B or BRAND1, BRAND2). For this example, use the grouping code named *Type*, where 1 represents Brand1 and 2 represents Brand2.
- *Name the Outcome Variable.* The outcome (response) variable is the observed height and is designated with the variable named *Height*.
- *The Grouping Codes Specify Which Observation Belongs to Which Type of Fertilizer.* Thus, to set up the data for most statistics programs, place one observation per line, with each data line containing two variables: a fertilizer code (*Type*) and the corresponding response variable (*Height*).

Figure 3.3 illustrates how the data should be set up for most statistics programs, where it should be noted that there is one item (plant) per row.

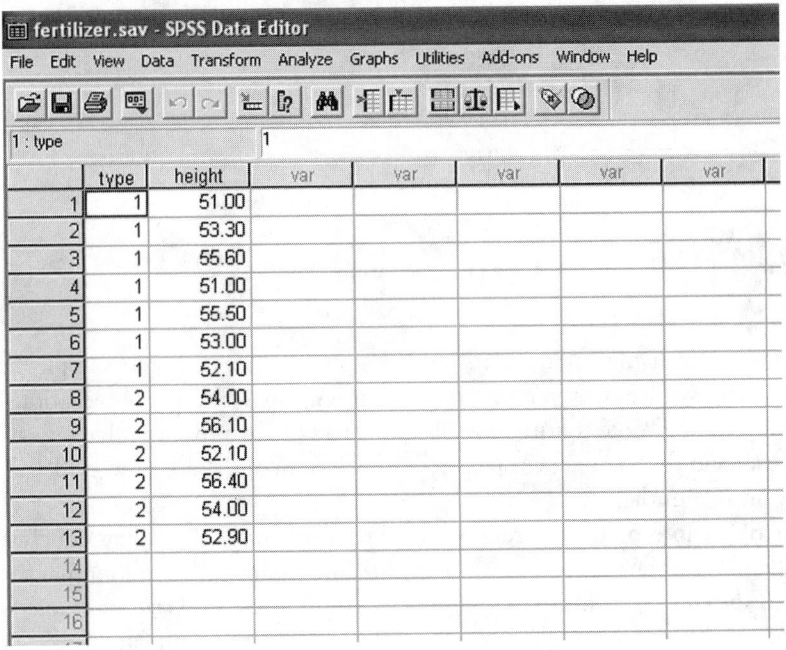

Figure 3.3   SPSS Editor Showing Fertilizer Data

The values 1 and 2 in the "type" column represent the two brands of fertilizer and the "height" variable is the outcome height measurement on the plants. (The codes 1 and 2 in this data set were arbitrarily selected. You could have used 0 and 1 or any other set of binary codes.)

Before performing the t-test, you should check to see whether your data meet the assumptions of normality and equality of variances. A visual way to check those assumptions is with a boxplot. The boxplot for these data is shown in Figure 3.4.

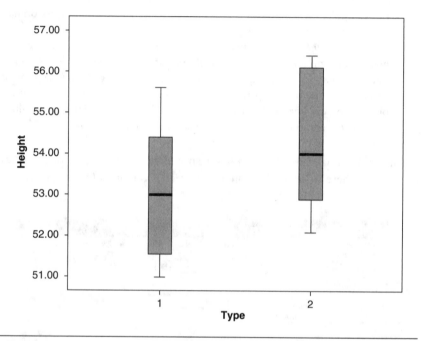

Figure 3.4   Boxplots for the Fertilizer Study

From the listing of the data and boxplot, notice that the sample sizes are small, with only seven observations in Group 1 and six observations in Group 2. Also note that the distributions of both groups are relatively symmetric, and the variances appear to be fairly similar. There is no evidence of any sizable outliers.

Do not interpret the large overlap in the boxes as providing conclusive evidence that the means are not different. Although it will turn out that there is no difference in this example, when sample sizes are large, you may see considerable overlap in the boxes even when there is a significant p-value for the t-test. (This would indicate that there is evidence that means are different even though there is sizable overlap between the populations.)

With this information in hand, you can proceed to perform a *t*-test. The resulting output is shown in Table 3.4. The "Group Statistics" table shows that the standard deviations (variances) for the two groups are similar, as was visually seen in the boxplot. (Remember that the variance is the square of the standard deviation.)

From the "Independent Samples Test" in Table 3.4, first notice the results of the *F*-test (Levene's test) for evaluating the equality of variance. There it

Table 3.4   Two-Sample *t*-Test Output for Fertilizer Data

Group Statistics

	type	N	Mean	Std. Deviation	Std. Error Mean
height	1	7	53.0714	1.90938	.72168
	2	6	54.2500	1.70968	.69797

Independent Samples Test

		Levene's Test for Equality of Variances		t-test for Equality of Means						
									95% Confidence Interval of the Difference	
		F	Sig.	t	df	Sig. (2-tailed)	Mean Difference	Std. Error Difference	Lower	Upper
height	Equal variances assumed	.075	.790	-1.163	11	.269	-1.17857	1.01329	-3.40881	1.05166
	Equal variances not assumed			-1.174	10.963	.265	-1.17857	1.00398	-3.38922	1.03208

can be seen that the *p*-value is 0.79, which indicates that the variances are not significantly different. You now have two pieces of information that indicate the variances are similar (the boxplot and Levene's test).

Therefore, if you are comfortable with this information, the appropriate *t*-test is the one that assumes equal variances. However, if you choose to go with the conservative approach, you will use the "equal variances not assumed" *t*-test. In this case, your final decision for the significance of the *t*-test would not be different.

The following information discusses methods of interpreting the output from the "Independent Samples Test" table.

- *Making a Decision Based on the p-Value.* The *p*-value for the equal variances *t*-test is $p = 0.269$. Since this *p*-value is greater than 0.05, the decision would be that there is no significant difference between the two groups. (Do not reject the null hypothesis.) Thus, there is not enough evidence to conclude that the mean heights are different. If you use the approach in which equal variances are not assumed, the p-value is $p = 0.265$, which is almost identical to the "equal variance" p-value. Thus, your decision would be the same.

- *Making a Decision Based on the Confidence Interval.* The 95% confidence intervals for the *difference in means* are given in the last two columns of Table 3.4. The interval associated with the assumption of equal variances is (−3.41 to 1.05), while the confidence interval when equal variances are not assumed is (−3.39 to 1.03). Since these intervals include 0 (zero), we again conclude that there is no significant difference between the means using either assumption regarding the variances. Thus, you would make the same decisions discussed in the p-value section above. The confidence interval gives more information than a simple p-value. Each interval above indicates that plausible values of the mean difference lie between about −3.4 and 1.0. Depending on the nature of your experiment, the information about the range of the possible mean differences may be useful in your decision-making process.

Reporting the Results of a (Nonsignificant) Two-Sample t-Test

The following sample write-ups illustrate how you might report this two-sample t-test in publication format. For purposes of illustration, we use the "equal variance" t-test for the remainder of this example:

Narrative for the Methods Section

"A two-sample Student's t-test assuming equal variances using a pooled estimate of the variance was performed to test the hypothesis that the resulting mean heights of the plants for the two types of fertilizer were equal."

Narrative for the Results Section

"The mean heights of plants using the two brands of fertilizer were not significantly different, $t(11) = −1.17, p = 0.27$."

Or, to be more complete,

"The mean height of plants using fertilizer Brand 1 ($M = 53.07, SD = 1.91, N = 7$) was not significantly different from that using fertilizer Brand 2 ($M = 54.25, SD = 1.71, N = 6$), $t(11) = −1.17, p = 0.27$."

A description of the confidence interval would read as follows:

"A 95% confidence interval on the difference between the two population means using a Student's t distribution with 11 degrees of freedom is (−3.41, 1.05), which indicates that there is not significant evidence that the fertilizers produce different mean growth heights."

SPSS Step-by-Step. EXAMPLE 3.2:
Two-Sample t-Test With Equal Variances

To run the two-sample *t*-test on the FERTILIZER.SAV data, follow these steps:

1. Open the data set FERTILIZER.SAV and select **Analyze/Compare Means/Independent Samples T Test. . . .**

2. Select *Height* as the test variable and *Type* as the grouping variable.

3. Click on the Define Groups button and define the group values as 1 and 2.

4. Click Continue and OK, and the tables shown in Table 3.4 are displayed.

5. To display the boxplot in Figure 3.4, select **Graphs/Boxplot** and choose Simple Boxplot and then Define. Select *Height* as the variable and *Type* as the category axis. Click OK.

EXAMPLE 3.3: Two-Sample *t*-Test With Variance Issues

Describing the Problem

Seventy-six subjects were given an untimed test measuring the dexterity required for a particular job skill as a part of a research project at a job placement center for inner-city youth. The sample consisted of 17 males and 59 females. Time to complete the test was recorded (in minutes). The researcher wants to know whether the test is gender neutral. As a part of that analysis, she wonders if the average time to complete the test will be the same for both male and female participants.

Since the researcher is simply interested in determining whether there is a difference in the average times for males and females, a two-sided *t*-test is appropriate. The hypotheses for this test could be written (in words) as follows:

Null hypothesis (H_0): The mean times to finish the skills test are the same for both genders.

Alternative hypothesis (H_a): The mean times to finish the skills test differ for the two genders.

The data for this analysis are entered into a data set in a format similar to the previous example, using one line per subject, with a group variable (*gender*) containing two values (M and F) and a variable containing the response variable (*time*). As in EXAMPLE 3.2, it is a good practice to look at a plot of the data. For this example, boxplots are shown in Figure 3.5.

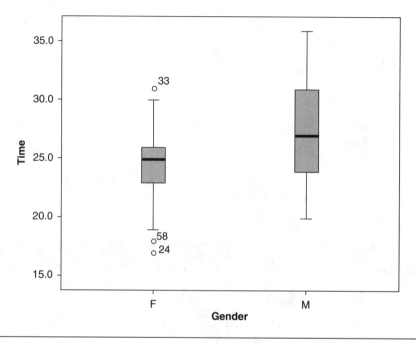

Figure 3.5   Side-by-Side Boxplots for Job Placement Data

The side-by-side boxplots show that the data are fairly symmetric and thus consistent with approximate normality. The dots labeled "33," "58," and "24" show that there are several "outliers," although none appear extreme. The difference in sizes of the boxes illustrates that the equality of variances may be questionable.

Table 3.5 shows the results of performing the two-sample *t*-test. From the "Group Statistics" table, note that there are 59 females and 17 males in the sample. Also note that the standard deviation for males is almost twice as large as that of the females.

In the "Independent Samples Test" table, the test for equality of variances, labeled "Levene's Test," yields a significant *p*-value (Sig.) of $p = 0.013$. This indicates that, according to this criterion, the variances cannot be considered to be equal. This result indicates that you should use the "equal variances not assumed" *t*-test. Using the conservative approach mentioned earlier, you would also choose to use the unequal variances *t*-test.

Table 3.5   Two-Sample *t*-Test Results for Job Placement Data

Group Statistics

	Gender	N	Mean	Std. Deviation	Std. Error Mean
Time	M	17	27.529	4.7318	1.1476
	F	59	24.627	2.8881	.3760

Independent Samples Test

		Levene's Test for Equality of Variances		t-test for Equality of Means						95% Confidence Interval of the Difference	
		F	Sig.	t	df	Sig. (2-tailed)	Mean Difference	Std. Error Difference		Lower	Upper
Time	Equal variances assumed	6.450	.013	3.126	74	.003	2.9023	.9285		1.0521	4.7525
	Equal variances not assumed			2.403	19.557	.026	2.9023	1.2077		.3795	5.4251

- *Making a Decision Based on the p-Value.* Because equal variances are not assumed, you should use the set of statistics labeled "equal variances not assumed" in the "*t*-test for equality of means" section of the "Independent Samples Test." The *p*-value for this version of the *t*-test is $p = 0.026$. Since this *p*-value is less than 0.05, the decision would be that there is a significant difference between the two group means. (Reject the null hypothesis.) Thus, there is evidence to conclude that the mean times to complete the test differ by gender. (Regardless of the statistical results, the researcher should evaluate whether an average difference of 2.9 minutes [27.529 minus 24.627] is important in terms of the goals of the research.)
- *Making a Decision Based on the Confidence Interval.* To analyze these data using confidence intervals, refer to the section of Table 3.5 labeled "95% confidence interval of the difference" on the second line of statistics labeled "equal variance not assumed." The interval for the difference in means (male minus female) is (0.3795, 5.4251). Since the interval does not include 0 (zero), the conclusion is that (at the 0.05 level of significance) you should reject the null hypothesis and conclude that there is a statistically significant difference in the population means. Also, since the confidence interval contains only positive values for the (male minus female) difference in the means, there is evidence that males take longer on average to perform the task.

Reporting Results for EXAMPLE *3.3:*
Two-Sample t-Tests With Variance Issues

The following sample write-ups illustrate how you might report this *t*-test in publication format:

Narrative for the Methods Section

"Since a preliminary Levene's test for equality of variances indicated that the variances of the two groups were significantly different, a two-sample t-test was performed that does not assume equal variances."

Narrative for the Results Section

"There is evidence within the setting observed that males take a significantly longer time on average to complete the untimed skills test than do females, $t(19.6) = 2.40$, $p = 0.03$."

Or, more completely,

"The mean time required for females to complete the untimed aptitude test ($M = 24.6$ minutes, $SD = 2.89$, $N = 59$) was significantly shorter than that required for males ($M = 27.53$ minutes, $SD = 4.73$, $N = 17$), $t(20) = 2.40$, $p = 0.03$."

SPSS Step-by-Step. EXAMPLE 3.3: Two-Sample t-Tests With Variance Issues

To create the side-by-side boxplots, use the following steps:

1. Open the data set JOB.SAV and select **Graph/Boxplot/Simple . . .** and click Define.

2. Select *Time* as the variable and *Gender* for the category axis.

3. Click OK, and the plot shown in Figure 3.5 will be displayed.

To create the t-test output in SPSS for this example, follow these steps:

1. Using the data set JOB.SAV, select **Analyze/Compare Means/Independent Samples T Test. . . .**

2. Select *Time* as the test variable and *Gender* as the grouping variable.

3. Click on the Define Groups button and define the group values as M and F.

4. Click Continue and then OK, and the output shown in Table 3.5 appears.

Paired t-Test

The paired t-test is appropriate for data in which the two samples are paired in some way. This type of analysis is appropriate for three separate data collection scenarios:

- Pairs consist of before and after measurements on a single group of subjects or patients.
- Two measurements on the same subject or entity (right and left eye, for example) are paired.
- Subjects in one group (e.g., those receiving a treatment) are paired or matched on a one-to-one basis with subjects in a second group (e.g., control subjects).

In all cases, the data to be analyzed are the differences within pairs (e.g., the right eye measurement minus the left eye measurement). The difference scores are then analyzed as a one-sample *t*-test.

Associated Confidence Interval

The confidence interval associated with a paired *t*-test is the same as the confidence interval for a one-sample *t*-test using the difference scores. The resulting confidence interval is usually examined to determine whether it includes zero.

Appropriate Applications for a Paired *t*-Test

The following are examples of paired data that would properly be analyzed using a paired *t*-test.

- *Does the Diet Work?* A developer of a new diet is interested in showing that it is effective. He randomly chooses 15 subjects to go on the diet for 1 month. He weighs each patient before and after the 1-month period to see whether there is evidence of a weight loss at the end of the month.
- *Is a New Teaching Method Better Than Standard Methods?* An educator wants to test a new method for improving reading comprehension. Twenty students are assigned to a section that will use the new method. Each of these 20 students is matched with a student with similar reading ability who will spend the semester in a class using the standard teaching methods. At the end of the semester, the students in both sections will be given a common reading comprehension exam, and the average reading comprehension of the two groups is compared.
- *Does a New Type of Eye Drops Work Better Than Standard Drops?* A pharmaceutical company wants to test a new formulation of eye drops with its standard drops for reducing redness. Fifty subjects who have similar problems with eye redness in each eye are randomly selected for the study. For each subject, an eye is randomly selected to be treated with the new drops, and the other eye is treated with the standard drops. At the end of the treatment schedule, the redness in each eye is measured using a quantitative scale.

Design Considerations for a Paired *t*-Test

Pairing Observations May Increase the Ability to Detect Differences

A paired *t*-test is appropriate when variability between groups may be sufficiently large to mask any mean differences that might exist between the groups. Pairing is a method of obtaining a more direct measurement on the difference being examined. For example, in the diet example above, one method of assessing the performance of the diet would be to select 30 subjects and randomly assign 15 to go on the diet and 15 to eat regularly for the next month (i.e., the control group). At the end of the month, the weights of the subjects on the diet could be compared with those in the control group to determine whether there is evidence of a difference in average weights. Clearly, this is not a desirable design since the variability of weights of subjects within the two groups will likely mask any differences that might be produced by one month on the diet. A better design would be to select 15 subjects and measure the weights of these subjects before and after the month on the diet. The 15 differences between the before and after weights for the subjects provide much more focused measurements of the effect of the diet than would independent samples.

Paired t-Test Analysis Is Performed on the Difference Scores

The data to be analyzed in a paired *t*-test are the differences between pairs (e.g., the before minus after weight for each subject in a diet study or differences between matched pairs in the study of teaching methods). The difference scores are then analyzed using a one-sample *t*-test.

The Paired t-Test Assumes Normality of the Differences

The basic assumption for the paired *t*-test to be valid when you have small sample sizes is that the difference scores are normally distributed and that the observed differences represent a random sample from the population of differences. (See the section on testing for normality, "Describing Quantitative Data," in Chapter 2.)

Hypotheses for a Paired *t*-Test

The hypotheses to be tested in a paired *t*-test are similar to those used in a two-sample *t*-test. In the case of paired data, μ_1 and μ_2 refer to the population means of the before and after measurements on a single group of subjects or to the first and second pair in the case of matched subjects. The null hypotheses may be stated as H_0: $\mu_1 = \mu_2$. However, in the case of paired data, it is common practice to make use of the fact that the difference between the two population means (i.e., $\mu_1 - \mu_2$) is equal to the population mean of the difference scores, denoted μ_d. In this case, the hypotheses are written as follows:

H_0: $\mu_d = 0$ (the population mean of the differences is zero).

H_a: $\mu_d \neq 0$ (the population mean of the differences is not zero).

EXAMPLE 3.4: Paired *t*-Test

Consider the diet example described above. The data for this example include two variables reporting before and after weights for 15 randomly selected subjects who participated in a test of a new diet for a 1-month period. Figure 3.6 illustrates the data format, where it can be seen that the before and after weights for a subject are entered on the same row. In this case, we want to determine whether there is evidence that the diet works. That is, if we calculate differences as d_i = "*before*" *weight minus* "*after*" *weight*, then we should test the following hypotheses:

H_0: $\mu_d = 0$ (the mean of the differences is zero; i.e., the diet is ineffective).

H_a: $\mu_d > 0$ (the mean of the differences is positive; i.e., the diet is effective).

The first step in the analysis is to simply observe the distribution of the differences using a boxplot. Figure 3.7 shows the plot for the diet data.

This plot shows that the distribution of the differences is fairly symmetric and that the assumption of normality seems reasonable. Also, it can be seen that only a small percentage of the differences were below 0 (no weight loss or negative weight loss).

To analyze the data using a statistical test, we examine the output in the "Paired Samples Test" shown in Table 3.6.

Table 3.6   Paired *t*-Test Output for EXAMPLE 3.4

Paired Samples Test

		Paired Differences							
					95% Confidence Interval of the Difference				
		Mean	Std. Deviation	Std. Error Mean	Lower	Upper	t	df	Sig. (2-tailed)
Pair 1	before - after	3.533	5.330	1.376	.582	6.485	2.567	14	.022

	subject	before	after	var	var	var	var
1	1	210	204				
2	2	207	205				
3	3	183	182				
4	4	195	196				
5	5	187	177				
6	6	201	193				
7	7	158	152				
8	8	180	182				
9	9	173	165				
10	10	198	186				
11	11	225	218				
12	12	243	237				
13	13	168	174				
14	14	177	178				
15	15	196	199				
16							
17							

Figure 3.6   SPSS Editor Showing Diet Data

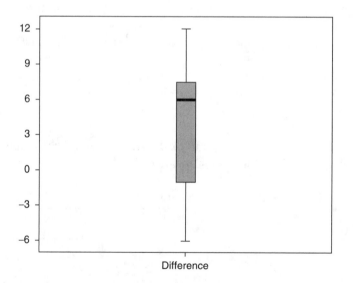

Figure 3.7   Boxplot of the Differences for EXAMPLE 3.4

In this output, it can be seen that the sample mean of the difference scores is 3.533, with a standard deviation of the differences given by 5.330. The calculated *t*-statistic (with 14 *df*) is given by 2.567, which has a *p*-value of 0.022. When interpreting these results, you should notice that the mean of the "*before minus after*" differences is positive, which is supportive of the alternative hypothesis that $\mu_d > 0$. Since this experiment from its inception was only interested in detecting a weight loss, it can be viewed as a one-sided test. Thus, for a one-sided hypothesis test, the reported *p*-value should be one-half of the *p*-value given in the computer output (i.e., $p = 0.011$). That is, at the $\alpha = .05$ level, we reject H_0 and conclude that the diet is effective. The output also includes a 95% confidence interval on the mean difference. It should be noted that this confidence interval is a two-sided confidence interval. In this case, the fact that the confidence interval (0.58, 6.49) contains only positive values suggests that $\mu_d > 0$ (i.e., that the diet is effective).

Reporting the Results for EXAMPLE 3.4: Paired t-Test

The following sample write-ups illustrate how you might report this paired *t*-test in publication format.

Narrative for the Methods Section

"A paired *t*-test was performed to ascertain whether the diet was effective."

Narrative for the Results Section

"There is evidence that the mean weight loss is positive, that is, that the diet is effective in producing weight loss, $t(14) = 2.567$, one-tailed $p = 0.01$."

Or, more completely,

"The mean weight loss ($M = 3.53$, $SD = 5.33$, $N = 15$) was significantly greater than zero, $t(14) = 2.567$, one-tailed $p = 0.01$, providing evidence that the diet is effective in producing weight loss."

SPSS Step-by Step. EXAMPLE 3.4: Paired t-Test

It should be noted that SPSS can be used to perform a paired *t*-test in two different ways.

Using the Data Pairs

1. Open the data set DIET.SAV and select **Analyze/Compare Means/ Paired-Samples T Test.** . . .

2. Select the two variables for which you want the difference to be taken. In this case, click on *Before* and *After* and select them as the paired variables (click on right arrow). The difference "*Before – After*" is used in the analysis.

3. Click OK, and Table 3.6 is displayed.

Programming Notes. It should be noted that the default order of the difference (i.e., in this case, "*Before – After*") is determined by the order in which the variables are entered into the database. That is, using the paired *t*-test option and the data in the data set DIET.SAV, SPSS will by default calculate the difference "*Before – After*." Calculation of the difference "*After – Before*" can be obtained by directly calculating the difference and performing a one-sample *t*-test on the difference scores, as illustrated in the next example.

Using the Difference Scores

The same results as those obtained in Table 3.6 can be obtained by directly computing the "before – after" differences and performing a one-sample *t*-test on the differences. (See the section "Creating a New Variable Using Computation" in Appendix A.) After creating a new variable named *difference,* a one-sample test will produce the output shown in Table 3.7.

Table 3.7   Paired *t*-Test Results Obtained Using a Calculated Difference Variable

One-Sample Test

	Test Value = 0					
					95% Confidence Interval of the Difference	
	t	df	Sig. (2-tailed)	Mean Difference	Lower	Upper
Difference	2.567	14	.022	3.53333	.5816	6.4850

The reported difference is 3.53333 (and the *p*-value for the test is $p = 0.022$). These results are consistent with those obtained earlier. If it were desirable, you could have calculated the differences using the formula "after – before." In this case, the mean difference would be –3.53 and the *t*-value would be –2.567, but the *p*-value would remain the same.

SPSS Step-by-Step. EXAMPLE 3.4:
Paired t-Test Using Difference Scores

To perform the one-sample *t*-test on the new variable called *difference* that exists in the data set DIET_WITH_DIFFERENCE.SAV, follow these steps:

1. Open the data set DIET_WITH_DIFFERNCE.SAV and select **Analyze/ Compare Means/One-Sample T Test. . . .**

2. Select *Difference* as the test variable and specify 0 as the test value.

3. Click OK, and Table 3.7 is displayed.

4. To display the boxplot of the difference scores in Figure 3.7, select **Analyze/Descriptive Statistics/Explore,** add *Difference* to the Dependent List, click on the Plots radio button at the bottom left of the dialog box, and click OK.

Summary

The *t*-test is one of the most widely used statistical procedures. It comes in three basic varieties: the single-sample *t*-test, the two-sample *t*-test, and the paired *t*-test. This chapter presents a concise, but not exhaustive, description of how to perform, interpret, and report the results of *t*-tests.

References

Moore, D., & McCabe, G. (2006). *Introduction to the practice of statistics* (4th ed.). New York: Freeman.

Posten, H. O. (1978). The robustness of the two-sample *t*-test over the Pearson system. *Journal of Statistical Computation and Simulation, 6,* 195–311.

Watkins, A., Scheaffer, R., & Cobb, G. (2004). *Statistics in action: Understanding a world of data.* Emeryville, CA: Key College Publishing.

4

Correlation and Regression

Have you ever noticed that, on the average, the more money people earn, the more expensive the car they drive? I drive a 9-year-old Toyota. Does that tell you anything? You might refer to the association between income and type of car using the term *correlation*. In statistical terms, a correlation is a mathematical measure of the strength of association between two quantitative variables—in this case, between income and value of the car.

A closely related cousin of correlation analysis is regression analysis. In a classic study, the statistician Karl Pearson compiled the heights of 1,078 fathers and sons where the son had reached full height. As would be expected, a scatterplot of the data shows that taller fathers tend to have taller sons while shorter fathers tend to have shorter sons, as shown in Figure 4.1. A correlation analysis involves measuring the extent to which the points in the scatterplot tend to swarm about a line. Suppose, however, that you want to know how well you can predict the height of a son if you know the height of his father. Using the data, you can come up with a regression line (equation) for performing the prediction. In regression analysis, we are interested in using the relationship between the two variables to predict the value of one of the variables given a value of the other variable.

This chapter describes when and how to use correlation and regression analyses. Specifically, these topics are covered:

- *Correlation:* measuring the linear association between two variables
- *Simple linear regression:* used to examine the relationship between a single predictor and a response variable

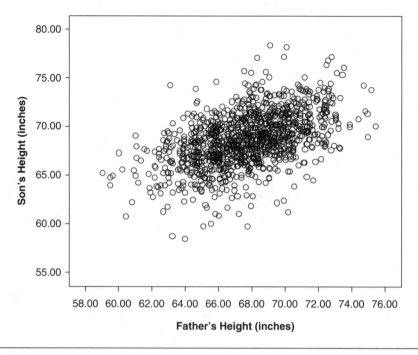

Figure 4.1   Pearson's Scatterplot of Heights of Fathers and Sons

- *Multiple linear regression:* used to examine the relationship between two or more predictor variables with a response variable
- *Bland-Altman analysis:* used to assess the level of agreement between two ways of measuring the same characteristic

Chapter 8 will deal with a specialized type of regression called logistic regression.

Correlation Analysis

A statistic that is often used to measure the strength of a linear association between two variables is the correlation coefficient. Specifically, the correlation covered in this chapter is called Pearson's correlation coefficient (yes—it's the same Pearson who measured the fathers and sons). In this section, we refer to Pearson's correlation coefficient as simply the "correlation coefficient." The theoretical correlation coefficient is often expressed using the Greek letter *rho* (ρ) while its estimate from a set of data is usually denoted by r.

Unless otherwise specified, when we say "correlation coefficient," we mean the estimate (r) calculated from the data. The correlation coefficient is always between -1 and $+1$, where -1 indicates that the points in the scatterplot of the two variables all lie on a line that has negative slope (a perfect negative correlation), and a correlation coefficient of $+1$ indicates that the points all lie on a line that has positive slope (a perfect positive correlation). In general, a positive correlation between two variables indicates that as one of the variables increases, then the other variable also tends to increase. If the correlation coefficient is negative, then as one variable increases, the other variable tends to decrease and vice versa.

A correlation coefficient close to $+1$ (or -1) indicates a strong linear relationship (i.e., that the points in the scatterplot are closely packed around a line). However, the closer a correlation coefficient gets to 0, the weaker the linear relationship and the more scattered the swarm of points in the graph. Most statistics packages quote a t-statistic along with the correlation coefficient for purposes of testing whether the correlation coefficient is significantly different from zero. A scatterplot is a very useful tool for viewing the relationship and determining whether a relationship is indeed linear in nature.

Appropriate Applications for Correlation Analysis

The correlation coefficient might be used to determine whether there is a linear relationship between the following pairs of variables:

- *What Is the Relationship Between Grades in English Rhetoric and Introductory Statistics?* A sample of first-year students was selected at a certain university, and their scores in English rhetoric and introductory statistics are compared.
- *How Do Internet Sales Relate to Advertising Costs?* The monthly amount spent on Google ads and monthly amount received in orders from an Internet store site are compared.
- *Fatigue Versus Performance.* Managers track the number of overtime hours worked and the daily cost of mistakes made at a chemical production facility.

Design Considerations for Correlation Analysis

1. *The correlation coefficient measures the strength of a linear relationship between the two variables.* That is, the relationship between the two variables measures how closely the two points in a scatterplot (X-Y plot) of the two variables cluster about a straight line. If two variables are related but the relationship is not linear, then the correlation coefficient may not be able to detect a relationship.

2. *Observations should be quantitative (numeric) variables.* The correlation coefficient is not appropriate for qualitative (categorical) variables, even if they are numerically coded. In addition, tests of significance of the correlation coefficient assume that the two variables are approximately normally distributed.

3. *The pairs of data are independently collected.* Whereas, for example, in a one-sample *t*-test, we make the assumption that the observations represent a random sample from some population, in correlation analysis, we assume that observed pairs of data represent a random sample from some bivariate population.

Hypotheses for Correlation Analysis

The usual hypotheses for testing the statistical significance of a Pearson's correlation coefficient are the following:

H_0: $\rho = 0$ (there is no linear relationship between the two variables).

H_a: $\rho \neq 0$ (there is a linear relationship between the two variables).

These hypotheses can also be one-sided when appropriate. This null hypothesis is tested in statistics programs using a test statistic based on Student's *t*. (SPSS doesn't actually give the *t* value—just the associated *p*-value for the two-sided test.) If the *p*-value for the test is small, then you reject the null hypothesis and conclude that ρ is not 0. A researcher will then have to make a professional judgment to determine whether the observed association has "practical" significance. A correlation coefficient of $r = 0.25$ may be statistically significant (i.e., we have statistical evidence that it is nonzero), but it may be of no practical importance if that level of association is not of interest to the researcher.

Tips and Caveats for Correlation Analysis

One-Sided Tests

The two-sided *p*-values for tests about a correlation reported by most statistics programs can be divided by two for one-sided tests if the calculated correlation coefficient has the same sign as that specified in the alternative hypothesis.

Variables Don't Have to Be on the Same Scale

The correlation coefficient is unitless. For example, you can correlate height (inches) with weight (pounds). In addition, given a set of data on heights and weights, it does not matter whether you measure height in inches, centimeters, feet, and so on and weight in pounds, kilograms, and so on. In all cases, the resulting correlation coefficient will be the same.

Correlation Does Not Imply Cause and Effect

A conclusion of cause and effect is often improperly inferred based on the finding of a significant correlation. Only in the case where research is properly designed as a prospective study can cause and effect be concluded.

Correlations Provide an Incomplete Picture of the Relationship

Suppose, for example, that you have found that for first-year students at a certain university, there is a very strong positive correlation between grades (from 0–100) in rhetoric and statistics. Simply stating this finding would lead one to believe that rhetoric and statistics grades are very similar (i.e., that a student's score in rhetoric will be very close to his or her score in statistics). However, you should realize that you would get a strong positive correlation if the statistics grade for each student tended to be about 20 points lower than his or her rhetoric grade. (We're not claiming that this is the case—it's just a hypothetical example!) For this reason, when reporting a correlation between two variables, it is good practice to not simply report a correlation but also to report the mean and standard deviation of each of the variables. In addition, a scatterplot provides useful information that should be given in addition to the simple reporting of a correlation. This is addressed in the following.

Examine Relationship With a Scatterplot and Watch for Outliers

Always confirm the linear nature of the correlation with a scatterplot (X-Y plot) because it is possible for a correlation coefficient to appear important when examination of the data themselves suggest otherwise. Figure 4.2 shows several examples of scatterplots, all of which have a computed correlation coefficient of about 0.72. The upper left scatterplot has the typical appearance of points swarming about a line with a correlation of about 0.72. In the upper right scatter diagram, the apparent linear correlation is nearly entirely due to the extreme value or outlier in the upper right-hand corner of the plot. Without that value, there is no apparent relationship between the two variables. This is an example of what is sometimes referred to as the lollipop effect. (Can you see the lollipop?) In the middle left scatterplot, there seems to be a strong linear relationship between the two variables (much stronger than 0.72). However, notice that there is one data value in the lower right-hand corner of the plot that does not fit this correlation structure. This

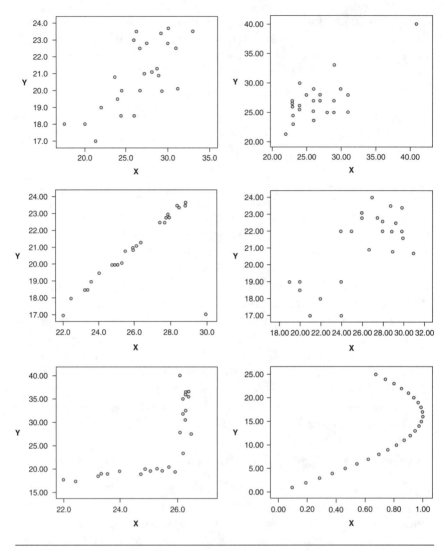

Figure 4.2   Example Scatterplots Associated With $r = .72$

data value dramatically reduces the computed correlation coefficient. Note that this unusual point would not be picked up as an outlier by looking at the univariate (one variable at a time) techniques in Chapter 2 because it is within an acceptable range of both variables. As always, whenever you see unusual or extreme values in your data set, you should investigate whether these values are "real." Even if the outlying values in the upper right or middle left scatterplots are real, their effect on the correlation and resulting test of significance should be noted. In the middle right scatterplot, there appear to be two groupings of data. These groups may correspond to subpopulations, and it should be noted that there appears to be little or no linear relationship between the two variables within each group. In the lower left scatterplot, the points follow a line with very small slope for x between 22 and 26 and follow a different and much steeper linear pattern for x greater than 26. In the lower right scatterplot, the variables appear to be very strongly (maybe functionally) related, but the relationship is nonlinear.

Don't Assume That Linear Relationships Observed Over Certain Ranges of the Variables Will Continue to Exist if the Ranges Are Extended

Consider the case in which two variables have a strong linear relationship over a certain range of variables. If the range on one or both of the variables is expanded, then the linear relationship observed previously may or may not continue to exist. Over an expanded range, the relationship may become nonlinear or may disappear altogether. See, for example, the bottom left graph in Figure 4.2. This is related to the advice against extrapolation that we give related to linear regression analysis.

If Variables Are Not Normally Distributed

If you cannot assume normality of the X or Y variable, then you should use Spearman's correlation to measure agreement between the two variables. See Chapter 7: Nonparametric Analysis Procedures for information on this topic.

EXAMPLE 4.1: Correlation Analysis

Describing the Problem

Data collected on 50 different children include the child's age and the times to complete four different hand-eye coordination tasks (labeled *Time1* to *Time4*). The researcher is interested in understanding the extent to which performances on these tasks are associated with the child's age and with one another. In a preliminary analysis, the correlation between *Age* and *Time1* was measured. The correlation coefficient for these two variables is $r = 0.501$ with $p < 0.001$. The scatterplot shown in Figure 4.3 confirms that there is a mild increase in *Time1* as *Age* increases. This scatterplot is similar in appearance to the father-son data in Figure 4.1, and in both cases, the correlation is approximately $r = 0.5$.

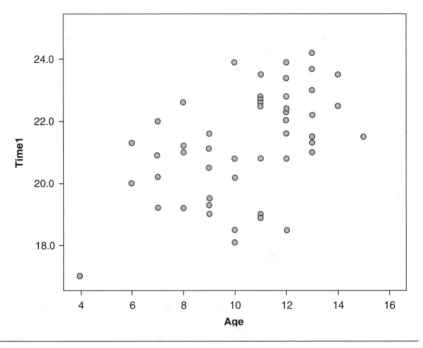

Figure 4.3   Scatterplot of *Time1* by *Age*

Because there are five quantitative variables involved (i.e., *Age, Time1*, . . . , *Time4*), it might be useful to examine them all at once. A matrix of correlation coefficients is displayed in Table 4.1. The top number in each cell is *r*, the calculated correlation coefficient between the two variables under consideration. The second number in each cell is the *p*-value, and the third number is the sample size (i.e., the number of valid pairs that were observed). In this case, all correlations are statistically significant because all *p*-values are less than 0.05. The matrix is symmetric about the diagonal because, for example, the correlation coefficient between *Age* and *Time1* (0.501) in the first row and second column is the same as the correlation coefficient between *Time1* and *Age* in the second row and first column. Note also that, for example, there is a perfect correlation (i.e., $r = 1$) between *Age* and itself in the first diagonal element. The correlation coefficients range from $r = .381$ to $r = .834$ (ignoring the diagonal).

It is also useful to examine a scatterplot matrix (i.e., a matrix of scatterplots) for these data to visualize the nature of the relationships. Figure 4.4 shows a matrix of scatterplots for these variables.

Table 4.1   Matrix of Correlation Coefficients

Correlations

		AGE	TIME1	TIME2	TIME3	TIME4
AGE	Pearson Correlation	1	.501**	.381**	.450**	.488**
	Sig. (2-tailed)		.000	.006	.001	.000
	N	50	50	50	50	50
TIME1	Pearson Correlation	.501**	1	.764**	.686**	.826**
	Sig. (2-tailed)	.000		.000	.000	.000
	N	50	50	50	50	50
TIME2	Pearson Correlation	.381**	.764**	1	.834**	.573**
	Sig. (2-tailed)	.006	.000		.000	.000
	N	50	50	50	50	50
TIME3	Pearson Correlation	.450**	.686**	.834**	1	.649**
	Sig. (2-tailed)	.001	.000	.000		.000
	N	50	50	50	50	50
TIME4	Pearson Correlation	.488**	.826**	.573**	.649**	1
	Sig. (2-tailed)	.000	.000	.000	.000	
	N	50	50	50	50	50

**. Correlation is significant at the 0.01 level (2-tailed).

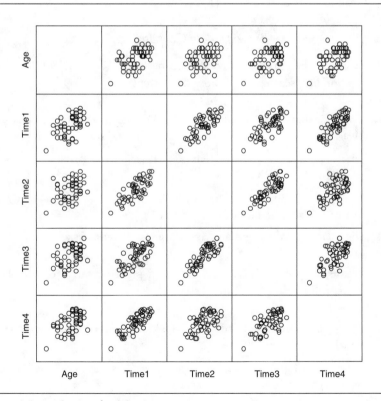

Figure 4.4   Scatterplot Matrix

Reporting the Results for a Pearson's Correlation

The following example illustrates how you could report the results of a correlation analysis using the variables *Age* and *Time1*. Note that the degrees of freedom for the *t*-test of the correlation hypothesis is $N - 2$ (number of cases minus 2).

Narrative for the Methods Section

"An evaluation of the linear relationship between the child's age and the score on the *Time1* coordination exercise was measured using Pearson's correlation."

Narrative for the Results Section

"An analysis using Pearson's correlation coefficient indicated that there is a significant linear relationship between age and performance on *Time1*, $r(48) = 0.50$, $p < 0.001$. For these data, the mean (*SD*) for *Age* was 10.46 (2.43) and for *Time1* was 21.27 (1.72)."

SPSS Step-by-Step. EXAMPLE 4.1: Correlation Analysis

To calculate the correlation coefficient between *Age* and *Time1* and plot the corresponding scatterplot, follow these steps:

1. Open the data set CORRELATION.SAV and select **Analyze/Correlate/Bivariate.**

2. Select *Age* and *Time1* as variables. Make sure the Pearson checkbox is selected and click OK.

3. To display a scatterplot of the variables as in Figure 4.3, select **Graphs/Scatter/Dot . . . /Simple Scatter** and click Define.

4. Select *Time1* as the *y*-axis and *Age* as the *x*-axis variables and click OK.

To create the output in Table 4.1 that displays a matrix of correlation coefficients, follow these additional steps:

1. Using the data set CORRELATION.SAV, select **Analyze/Correlate/Bivariate.**

2. Select *Age*, *Time1*, *Time2*, *Time3*, and *Time4* as variables. Make sure the Pearson checkbox is selected and click OK.

3. To display a scatterplot matrix of the same variables, select **Graphs/ Scatter/Dot . . . /Matrix Scatter** and click Define.

4. Select *Age, Time1, Time2, Time3,* and *Time4* as variables and click OK. The output shown in Figure 4.4 is displayed.

(Note: To produce the scatterplot of the fathers' and sons' heights shown in Figure 4.1, use the same procedure outlined in Steps 1 to 4 above with the data set named PEARSON.SAV.)

Simple Linear Regression

Simple linear regression (SLR) is a statistical tool used to examine the relationship between one predictor (independent) variable and a single quantitative response (dependent) variable. Simple linear regression analysis produces a regression equation that can be used in prediction. A typical experiment involves observing a sample of paired observations in which the independent variable (X) may have been fixed at a variety of values of interest and the dependent variable has been observed. This resulting set of observations is sometimes referred to as a training sample. This sample is then used to create an equation that can be used to predict the dependent variable given a value of the independent variable.

Appropriate Applications for Simple Linear Regression

- *How Good Is a New Medical Test?* A new (less expensive) medical test is developed to potentially replace a conventional (more expensive) test. A regression equation is developed to determine how well the new test (independent variable) predicts the results of the conventional test (dependent variable).
- *Systolic Blood Pressure and Smoking.* A medical researcher wants to understand the relationship between weight (independent variable) and systolic blood pressure (dependent variable) in males older than 40 years of age who smoke. A regression equation is obtained to determine how well the blood pressure reading can be predicted from weight for males older than age 40 who smoke.
- *Should I Spend More on Advertising?* The owner of a Web site wants to know if the weekly costs of advertising (independent variable) on a cable channel are related to the number of visits to his site (dependent variable). In the data

collection stage, the advertising costs are allowed to vary from week to week. A regression equation is obtained from this training sample to determine how well number of visits to the site can be predicted from advertising costs.

Design Considerations for Simple Linear Regression

There Is a Theoretical Regression Line

The regression line calculated from the data is a sample-based version of a theoretical line describing the relationship between the independent variable (X) and the dependent variable (Y). The theoretical line has the form

$$Y = \alpha + \beta X + \varepsilon$$

where α is the y-intercept, β is the slope, and ε is an error term with zero mean and constant variance. Notice that $\beta = 0$ indicates that there is no linear relationship between X and Y.

The Observed Regression Equation Is Calculated From the Data Based on the Least Squares Principle

The regression line that is obtained for predicting the dependent variable (Y) from the independent variable (X) is given by

$$\hat{Y} = a + bX$$

and it is the line for which the sum-of-squared vertical differences from the points in the X-Y scatterplot to the line is a minimum. In practice, $\hat{Y}$ is the prediction of the dependent variable given that the independent variable takes on the value X. We say that the values a and b are the least squares estimates of α and β, respectively. That is, the least squares estimates are those for which the sum-of-squared differences between the observed Y values and the predicted Y values are minimized. To be more specific, the least squares estimates a and b are the values of a and b for which the sum of the quantities $(Y_i - a - bX_i)^2$, $i = 1, \ldots, N$ is minimized.

Several Assumptions Are Involved

These include the following:

1. *Normality.* The population of Y values for each X is normally distributed.

2. *Equal variances.* The populations in Assumption 1 all have the same variance.

3. *Independence*. The dependent variables used in the computation of the regression equation are independent. This typically means that each observed X-Y pair of observations must be from a separate subject or entity.

You will often see the assumptions above stated in terms of the error term ε. Simple linear regression is robust to moderate departures from these assumptions, but you should be aware of them and should examine your data to understand the nature of your data and how well these assumptions are met.

Hypotheses for a Simple Linear Regression Analysis

To evaluate how well a set of data fits a simple linear regression model, a statistical test is performed regarding the slope (β) of the theoretical regression line. The hypotheses are as follows:

H_0: $\beta = 0$ (the slope is zero; there is no linear relationship between the variables).

H_a: $\beta \neq 0$ (the slope is not zero; there is a linear relationship between the variables).

The null hypothesis indicates that there is no linear relationship between the two variables. One-sided tests (specifying that the slope is positive or negative) can also be performed. A low *p*-value for this test (less than 0.05) would lead you to conclude that there is a linear relationship between the two variables and that knowledge of X would be useful in the prediction of Y.

The statistical test for the hypothesis that the slope is zero in a simple linear regression is mathematically equivalent to the test in correlation analysis that $\rho = 0$.

Tips and Caveats for Simple Linear Regression

Don't Extrapolate

Once a regression line is obtained and it is concluded that there is indeed a significant linear relationship upon which to base the predictions, you can use the line for predicting Y values for a given value X. However, the linear relationship that is established applies only to the range of X values used in developing the regression line. Based on the analysis leading to the regression equation, you have no way of knowing whether the observed linear relationship exists beyond the range of the observed X values. For example, consider the data shown in the bottom left scatterplot in Figure 4.2. Suppose you have access to only the data for which $X \leq 26$ and you find the regression line for predicting Y from X. It can be seen that this line will do a good job of predicting Y for X between 22 and 26. However, if you use this line to predict the value of Y when $X = 26.4$, it is clear that the predicted Y will be much lower than the actual Y because the nature of the relationship between X and Y changed at about $X = 26$. The regression line you obtained applies only to the range of X values used in its computation. Using the regression line to predict Y for a value of X that is outside the range of X values observed is called extrapolation. Don't do it!

Analyze Residual Plots

Residuals are calculated as $e = Y - \hat{Y}$ for each pair of observations in the data set, where $\hat{y}$ is the prediction obtained from the regression line and Y is the original data value. Note that for each X-Y pair in the data set, a residual is computed, and a scatterplot of these residuals is often plotted with the independent variable on the horizontal axis and the residuals on the vertical axis. If the assumptions are met, then this scatterplot should appear as random points centered at zero. It may also be useful to plot the residuals using run-order as the horizontal axis. (Run-order is the order in which the observations were observed.)

Examination of residual plots can help you determine whether the assumptions are met. For example, if the residuals follow some sort of nonlinear curve, then this may be an indication that a linear regression is not appropriate. If the spread of the points around the center line tends to change across the range of the independent variable, this may be an indication that the assumption of equal variances is not appropriate. If a pattern appears in a run-order residual plot, you should determine if there was some type of change over time (e.g., fatigue) that influenced the data values.

Sometimes, standardized residuals (residuals divided by their standard error) are plotted. In this case, the basic patterns to be examined are the same, but the standardizing makes it easier to identify outliers. If a standardized residual is larger than 2 or 3 in absolute value, it may indicate an outlier or at least a data point of some interest. For more discussion of residual analysis, see Kleinbaum, Kupper, Muller, and Nizam (1997), and for more on outlier detection, see Barnett and Lewis (1994).

Transformations

If the residuals do not appear to be random in the residual plot, you may consider applying a transformation to one or both of the variables to help eliminate the problem. Common transformations include the logarithm and the square root. Depending on the type of nonlinearity observed, you may want to apply this transformation to the independent variable, the dependent variable, or both. Information on how to transform data to create new variables in SPSS is given in Appendix A: A Brief Tutorial for Using SPSS for Windows. A good reference for learning more about transformations is Kleinbaum et al. (1997).

Other tips and caveats similar to those in correlation analysis include the following:

- Variables need not be on the same scale.
- A *p*-value less than 0.05 indicates only that there is *some* predictive value when using X to predict Y.
- The finding of a significant predictive relationship does not imply cause and effect.
- The two-sided *p*-values associated with the test for slope given by most statistics programs can be divided by two for one-sided tests if the slope estimate has the same sign as that specified in the alternative hypothesis.
- Relationships should be examined using scatterplots.

Interval Estimates

There are several interval estimates used in simple linear regression.

- *Confidence Interval for* β. You can obtain confidence intervals on the parameter β related to the hypothesis test mentioned above. If the resulting 95% confidence interval contains zero, then there is not sufficient evidence to conclude that the theoretical slope is nonzero (i.e., there is not significant evidence of a linear relationship).
- *Confidence Interval for Mean of* Y *for Given Value of* X. This is really a collection of confidence intervals, one for each value of the independent variable. The upper and lower limits of these confidence intervals are typically drawn as curves across the range of observed values X (see Figure 4.5).
- *Prediction Interval for Future Value of* Y *Given* X. This interval is technically not a confidence interval. The interpretation of a 95% prediction interval for Y given X is as follows. Suppose we randomly select a new data pair for which the independent variable takes on the value X. We are 95% sure that the corresponding value of Y will fall in this prediction interval. This interval is similar to the confidence interval on the mean value of Y for a given value X but is somewhat wider.

EXAMPLE 4.2: Simple Linear Regression

Describing the Problem

A random sample of 14 students is selected from an elementary school, and each student is measured on a creativity score (*Create*) using a new testing instrument and on a task score (*Task*) using a standard instrument. The

Task score is the mean time taken to perform several hand-eye coordination tasks. Because the test for the creativity test is much cheaper, it is of interest to know whether you can substitute it for the more expensive *Task* score. That is, can you create a regression equation that will effectively predict a *Task* score (the dependent variable) from the *Create* score (the independent variable)? In Figure 4.5, we show a scatterplot of these two variables along with the regression line and the confidence intervals for Y given X. In the plot, we use the standard practice of plotting the independent variable (*Create*) on the x-axis and the dependent variable (*Task*) on the y-axis. By observing the scatterplot (try to ignore the line and interval estimates for now), it can be seen that there is a positive correlation between the two variables (in this case, $r = .74$), and it appears that knowing *Create* should help in predicting *Task*. It is also clear that knowing *Create* does not in any way perfectly predict *Task*.

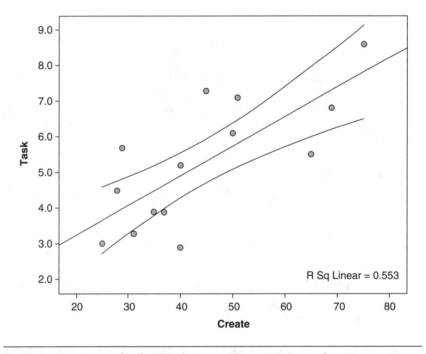

Figure 4.5   Scatterplot for Simple Linear Regression Example

Regression analysis results are shown in Table 4.2. The "create" line gives the results of the two-sided hypothesis test that the theoretical slope of the regression line for predicting *Task* from *Create* is 0. In this case, $p = 0.002$

Table 4.2   Results of Simple Linear Regression Analysis

Coefficients[a]

Model		Unstandardized Coefficients		Standardized Coefficients	t	Sig.
		B	Std. Error	Beta		
1	(Constant)	1.599	1.008		1.586	.139
	create	.083	.022	.744	3.856	.002

a. Dependent Variable: task

indicates that you should reject the null hypothesis and conclude that there is a statistically significant linear relationship between the two variables and, therefore, that *Create* should be useful in predicting *Task*.

Note that the *p*-value associated with the "Constant" term is for testing H_0: $\alpha = 0$ (i.e., that the theoretical *y*-intercept is zero). In most cases, this will not be of interest to you. That is, usually the only *p*-value of interest will be the one associated with the independent variable (i.e., the one used for testing whether the slope is significantly different from zero).

The sample regression equation is created from the "Unstandardized Coefficients" in the coefficients table. Thus, the regression equation for predicting *Task* from *Create* is

$$\text{Predicted Task} = 1.599 + 0.083\text{Create}$$

or, in words, you predict the *Task* value by multiplying *Create* by 0.083 and adding 1.599. Figure 4.5 shows the scatterplot along with the regression line, which seems to provide reasonable estimates for *Task* for each value of *Create*. For a new student who has a *Create* score of 52, you would predict a *Task* score using the following equation:

$$\text{Predicted Task} = 1.599 + 0.083(52) = 5.915$$

which is visually consistent with the regression line in Figure 4.5 at $X = 52$. A visual inspection of the scatterplot indicates, however, that although the relationship is (strongly) statistically significant, the scatter of points around the prediction line is not extremely tight. Therefore, although statistically significant, these results may or may not lead you to conclude that the *Create* test results can be adequately predicted using *Task*. This is a decision that

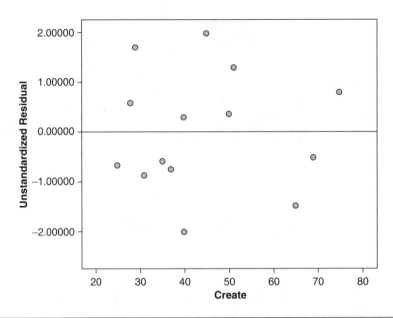

Figure 4.6   Residual Plot for Simple Linear Regression Example

you will have to make based on your professional knowledge of the subject matter. For example, you must determine whether you are willing to accept the size of possible errors in estimates of *Task* obtained from the regression line. Examining Figure 4.5, you can see that some values of *Task* are as much as 2 units away from the fitted regression line. If making this magnitude of a predictive error is life threatening or costly in some other way, you may feel that the predictive capability of the equation, although statistically significant, is not strong enough to be adopted for actual use.

A residual plot is shown in Figure 4.6. This plot suggests that the underlying assumptions are met because it shows a random scatter of points above and below the zero line. With so few points, it is difficult to determine whether there is any pattern of concern.

SPSS Step-by-Step. EXAMPLE 4.2: Simple Linear Regression

To perform the simple linear regression analysis in this example, use the following steps in SPSS:

1. Open the file REGSIMP.SAV and select **Analyze/Regression/Linear**.

2. Select *Task* as the dependent variable and *Create* as the independent variable and click OK. The output tables for the analysis, including Table 4.2, will be displayed.

3. To produce a scatterplot of the data as shown in Figure 4.5, select **Graphs/Scatter/Dot/Simple Scatter** and Define. Select *Task* as the *y*-axis and *Create* as the *x*-axis and click OK.

4. To draw the regression line on the plot, once the scatterplot appears, double-click on it to enter the SPSS Chart Editor:
   - From the Chart Editor menu, select **Elements/Fit Line at Total.**
   - Click the Fit Line tab and select Linear as the fit method.
   - In the Confidence Interval box, select Mean.
   - Click Apply and Close.

5. Close the chart editor (File/Close). The plot in Figure 4.5 is displayed.

6. To obtain the residual plot in Figure 4.6, select **Analyze/Regression/Linear,** selecting the independent and dependent variables as before, and then do the following:
   - Check the Save box and select unstandardized residuals.
   - Click Continue and OK. (Note: This has placed a new variable, *Unstandardized Residual(Res_1)*, in the data file.)
   - Select the **Graphs/Scatter/Dot/Simple Scatter** and select *Unstandardized Residual* as the *y*-axis and *Create* as the *x*-axis and click OK.

7. To place a horizontal line at $Y = 0$, once the scatterplot appears, double-click on it to enter the SPSS Chart Editor:
   - From the Chart Editor menu, select Options/Y Axis Reference Line.
   - Indicate the *y*-axis position as 0.
   - Click Apply and Close.
   - Close the chart editor (File/Close).

Multiple Linear Regression

Multiple linear regression is an extension of simple linear regression in which there is a single dependent (response) variable (Y) and k independent (predictor) variables X_i, $i = 1, \ldots, k$. In multiple linear regression, the dependent variable is a quantitative variable while the independent variables may be quantitative or indicator (0, 1) variables. The usual purpose of a multiple regression analysis is to create a regression equation for predicting the dependent variable from a group of independent variables. Desired outcomes of such an analysis may include the following:

1. Screen independent variables to determine which ones are good predictors and thus find the most effective (and efficient) prediction model.

2. Obtain estimates of individual coefficients in the model to understand the predictive role of the individual independent variables used.

Appropriate Applications of Multiple Linear Regression

- *How Can the Selling Price of a House Be Predicted?* A large city is broken down into 50 "neighborhoods," and for each neighborhood, the following variables are collected: average selling price per square foot of houses in the neighborhood (AST), population density, yearly crime rate, proportion of nonbusiness acres, proportion of lots over 25,000 square feet, average square footage for residential dwellings, distance to downtown, and average family income. It is desired to see how well AST can be predicted using the other variables and which of the other variables are useful in predicting AST.
- *Does Tutoring Help?* To assess the effectiveness of tutorial help in a psychology course, the instructor wants to know how well the grade achieved on the final exam can be predicted using all or a subset of the following variables: amount of time spent on Web tutorials, time spent in small tutorial classes, the time spent in one-on-one tutorial meetings, and student gender.
- *Can Emergency Room Costs Be Predicted by Observing Initial Injury Measures?* Administrators at a hospital want to know how well the cost of a visit to the emergency room can be predicted using all or a subset of the following variables: evidence of intoxication, AIS score (injury severity), gender, type of injury (blunt, burn, or penetrating), GCS (Glasgow Coma Scale) score, and initial systolic blood pressure.

Design Considerations for Multiple Linear Regression

A Theoretical Multiple Regression Equation Exists That Describes the Relationship Between the Dependent Variable and the Independent Variables

As in the case of simple linear regression, the multiple regression equation calculated from the data is a sample-based version of a theoretical equation describing the relationship between the k independent variables and the dependent variable Y. The theoretical equation is of the form

$$Y = \alpha + \beta_1 X_1 + \beta_2 X_2 + \ldots + \beta_k X_k + \varepsilon$$

where α is the intercept term and β_i is the regression coefficient corresponding to the ith independent variable. Also, as in simple linear regression, ε is an error term with zero mean and constant variance. Note that if $\beta_i = 0$, then in this setting, the ith independent variable is not useful in predicting the dependent variable.

*The Observed Multiple Regression
Equation Is Calculated From the Data
Based on the Least Squares Principle*

The multiple regression equation that is obtained from the data for predicting the dependent variable from the k independent variables is given by

$$\hat{Y} = a + b_1 X_1 + b_2 X_2 + \ldots + b_k X_k.$$

As in the case of simple linear regression, the coefficients $a, b_1, b_2, \ldots$, and b_k are least squares estimates of the corresponding coefficients in the theoretical model. That is, as in the case of simple linear regression, the least squares estimates a and $b_1, \ldots, b_k$ are the values for which the sum-of-squared differences between the observed y values and the predicted y values are minimized.

Several Assumptions Are Involved

These include the following:

1. *Normality.* The population of Y values for each of combination of independent variables is normally distributed.

2. *Equal Variances.* The populations in Assumption 1 all have the same variance.

3. *Independence.* The dependent variables used in the computation of the regression equation are independent. This typically means that each observed y value must be from a separate subject or entity.

Hypotheses for Multiple Linear Regression

In multiple regression analysis, the usual procedure for determining whether the ith independent variable contributes to the prediction of the dependent variable is to test the following hypotheses:

H_0: $\beta_i = 0$

H_a: $\beta_i \neq 0$

for $i = 1, \ldots, k$. Each of these tests is performed using a t-test. There will be k of these tests (one for each independent variable), and most statistical packages report the corresponding t-statistics and p-values. Note that if there was no linear relationship whatsoever between the dependent variable and the independent variables, then all of the β_is would be zero. Most programs also report an F-test in an analysis of variance output that provides a single test of the following hypotheses:

H_0: $\beta_1 = \beta_2 = \ldots = \beta_k = 0$ (there is no linear relationship between the dependent variable and the collection of independent variables).

H_a: At least one of the β_i s is nonzero (there is a linear relationship between the dependent variable and at least one of the independent variables).

The analysis-of-variance framework breaks up the total variability in the dependent variable (as measured by the total sum of squares) by that which can be explained by the regression using X_1, X_2, . . . , X_k (the regression sum of squares) and that which cannot be explained by the regression (the error sum of squares). It is good practice to check the p-value associated with this overall F-test as the first step in the testing procedure. Then, if this p-value is less than 0.05, you would reject the null hypothesis of no linear relationship and proceed to examine the results of the t-tests. However, if the p-value for the F-test is greater than 0.05, then you have no evidence of any relationship between the dependent variable and any of the independent variables, so you should not examine the individual t-tests. Any findings of significance at this point would be questionable.

> Most statistics programs also give the t-statistic and associated p-value for testing the null hypothesis H_0: $\alpha = 0$. As in the case of simple linear regression, you will usually not be interested in testing whether the y-intercept is zero.

R-Square

Another measure that assesses the performance of the multiple regression is the R^2 (R-squared) statistic. This statistic reports the strength of the relationship between the set of independent variables and the dependent variable. R^2 ranges from 0 (meaning no linear relationship) to 1.0 (meaning perfect linear relationship). R^2 is the ratio of the regression sum of squares divided by the total sum of squares and measures the proportion of the variation in the dependent variable that is accounted for by the regression. For example, an R^2 of 0.89 would typically be described by reporting that 89% of the variability in the dependent variable is accounted for by the regression.

Model Selection Procedures for Multiple Linear Regression

It is often the case in working with multiple linear regression that there are a number of candidate independent variables, and the goal is to create a model that contains some group of these variables that will best and most efficiently predict the dependent variable. Based on the discussion above concerning testing hypotheses in a multiple regression, it is tempting to conclude that the best way to proceed is to enter all of the independent variables of possible interest into the multiple regression equation and choose the ones for which the corresponding p-values are less than 0.05. However, this may not produce desirable results, often because of collinearity among the independent variables.

Collinearity occurs when independent variables are themselves highly correlated or when one independent variable is nearly a linear combination of two or more independent variables. The presence of collinearity among the independent variables can cause problems in interpretation of the resulting multiple regression equations. If there are strong interrelationships among the independent variables, then coefficient estimates cannot be trusted to be meaningful. For example, if an independent variable is by itself positively related to the dependent variable, then you would expect the coefficient associated with this variable to be positive.

Suppose that you have two independent variables that are each positively correlated with the dependent variable and also strongly positively correlated with each other. Because the two variables are highly positively correlated with each other, they are introducing very similar information into the regression equation for predicting the dependent variable, and it will often be the case that only one of these independent variables is needed. However, if these two variables are simultaneously placed into the regression equation, this may result in confusing results such as one variable having a positive coefficient and the other a negative coefficient, one or both variables appearing to be insignificant, and so on.

One solution may be to create new variables that are themselves linear combinations of the existing independent variables. Also, several techniques have been developed for deciding which of a group of candidate independent variables should be used in a final model. Among these are the following:

1. *Forward Selection.* This procedure enters variables in a stepwise manner using an entry criterion for selecting the next variable to be entered. At each step, an associated p-value is checked to determine whether the selected variable contributes enough to be included.

2. *Backward Elimination.* All independent variables are initially entered into the equation. At each step, there is a removal criterion for selecting the next variable to be removed from the model and an associated *p*-value to determine whether the selected variable should be removed.

3. *Stepwise Entry.* This procedure adds independent variables one at a time as in forward selection. However, at each step, a backward elimination procedure is used to see whether any variables should be removed.

4. *Best Subset Regression.* This strategy reports the multiple regression based on a subset of a specified number, say, *m,* of independent variables for which R^2 (or some other criterion) is maximized among all possible subsets of *m* independent variables. Note: This option is not available in SPSS but is available in statistics programs such as SAS (SAS Institute, 2003) and WINKS (TexasSoft, 2004).

5. *Other Techniques.* Some researchers use hierarchical regression, which is a technique in which the researcher decides on the order of entry of independent variables. These variables may be entered individually or in blocks.

A few other issues that should be considered when selecting variables:

- *Include Only Variables That Make Sense.* Variables selected for inclusion in a prediction model should make sense in the context of the analysis. If it is not clear why a variable should be predictive, it may be best to not include it in your model, even if the selection criterion chooses it.
- *Force Important Variables Into a Model.* You may sometimes want to force variables of obvious importance to be included in a final model even if the selection procedures do not choose it.
- *Be Wary of Variable Selection Results.* It is interesting to note that the various selection procedures described above may lead to different final models. It is good practice to use several of these techniques and to compare the final models. (The stepwise and forward selection procedures are similar. If one of these is being used, then also try backward elimination.) Some researchers argue that backward elimination procedures are preferable to the forward selection and stepwise procedures. Among other issues, it has been shown that in forward selection and stepwise approaches, the R^2 values are biased high, and the resulting *p*-values do not have proper meaning. These problems are not as severe in backward elimination methods (see Mantel, 1970). Our advice is that you should not let any automated variable selection procedure be the sole criterion by which your final model is chosen.

Tips and Caveats for Multiple Linear Regression

Besides the tips and caveats described in the previous simple linear regression section above, here are some additional considerations:

Using Indicator Variables

Your independent variables may include a categorical variable with two or more categories. Examples might be race, location of hospital, brand of milling machine, and so on. To include these variables in the equation, indicator variables must be used. For example, if you have a variable called *Race* that includes the categories White, African American, Hispanic, and Other (four categories), you would need to create three indicator variables (i.e., the variables take on the values 0 and 1) to account for these categories. These new variables might be named *White*, *AA*, and *Hispanic* and can be constructed as follows: If a subject is "White," the variables take on the following values: *White* = 1, *AA* = 0, and *Hispanic* = 0. If a subject is African American, the variables take on the following values: *White* = 0, *AA* = 1, *Hispanic* = 0, and so forth. Note that if the subject is "Other," the variables take on the following values: *White* = 0, *AA* = 0, and *Hispanic* = 0. Thus, these three indicator variables can uniquely account for all four categories using 0, 1 indicator variables. In this case, all three variables (*White*, *AA*, and *Hispanic*) would be used as independent variables in the multiple regression equation. Thus, a general rule is that the number of independent variables required to account for a categorical variable is the number of categories minus one.

Don't Extrapolate

As with simple linear regression, predictions obtained using the multiple regression equation should be used only for independent variables that are (as a group) within the range of independent variables used in the computation of the regression equation.

Too Many Predictors?

The number of independent variables that should be used in your final model is limited by the number of observations. A rule of thumb used by some researchers is to limit the number of independent variables to one independent variable for every 10 observations. Thus, if you have 50 observations, this rule would indicate that you should limit your final regression model to a maximum of five independent variables.

Model Interpretation and Evaluation for Multiple Linear Regression

Model evaluation is performed using graphs and statistical tests. Some commonly used procedures for assessing the performance of a multiple regression model are discussed here. These include the following:

- *Compare Competing* R^2 *Values.* Compare the R^2 values of competing models to see if there is one that results in a larger R^2 value than the others. However, you should be aware that if you start with a multiple regression with three variables and add a fourth variable to this list, then the R^2 value will nearly always increase and will never decrease. Thus, simple increase in R^2 is not sufficient evidence for deciding to include an additional variable. Comparison of R^2 values thus makes the most sense when you are comparing candidate models with the same number of independent variables.
- *Analyze Residual Plots.* Plots of residuals similar to those discussed in the section on simple linear regression are also useful in multiple regression. In multiple regression, the residuals are again calculated as the difference between an actual Y value and its corresponding predicted value. Again, these plots should show a random behavior with no real pattern. As in simple linear regression, if a standardized residual is larger than 2 or 3, it may indicate an outlier or at least a data point of some interest. In multiple regression, you can plot separate residual plots for each of the independent variables on the horizontal axis. It is also common practice to plot residuals versus the predicted Y values or against run-order.

EXAMPLE 4.3: Multiple Linear Regression Analysis

Describing the Problem

An employer wants to be able to predict how well applicants will do on the job once they are hired. He devises four tests (*Test1* to *Test4*) that are designed to measure the skills required for the job. Current employees are selected at random from a group of current workers and given the four tests. These workers are then evaluated by a supervisor, who gives each employee a job proficiency score (*Jobscore*). From the "training data," we wish to develop a multiple regression equation for predicting *Jobscore* from all or a subset of the four test scores.

From the matrix of scatterplots in Figure 4.7, you can see that there appears to be a linear relationship between *Jobscore* and *Test1*. The association between *Jobscore* and the other variables is unclear.

To select the collection of independent variables to be used in the final model, we investigate the use of variable selection methods. These automated methods are not foolproof, and as mentioned previously, you should not rely on one method to find the best set of predictors.

Using a stepwise procedure, the variables *Test1* and *Test3* are entered into the equation using the stopping rule that says that in order to be entered into the equation, an entry p-value less than 0.05 is required while a p-value greater than 0.10 is required for a variable to be removed. These results are shown in Table 4.3, where it can be seen that (not surprisingly) *Test1* was

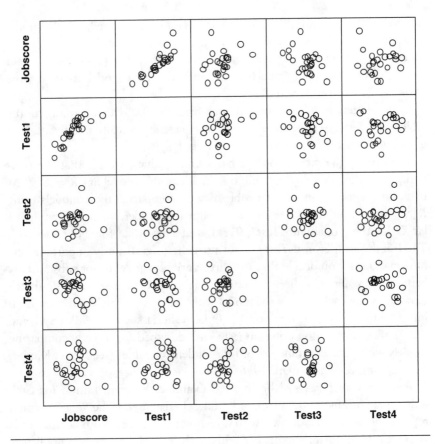

Figure 4.7   Matrix of Scatterplots for *Jobscore* Data

Table 4.3   Output for Stepwise Model Selection

Coefficients[a]

Model		Unstandardized Coefficients		Standardized Coefficients	t	Sig.
		B	Std. Error	Beta		
1	(Constant)	-87.136	26.383		-3.303	.003
	test1	2.575	.317	.861	8.124	.000
2	(Constant)	-11.922	38.641		-.309	.761
	test1	2.406	.295	.805	8.168	.000
	test3	-.768	.311	-.244	-2.475	.022

a. Dependent Variable: jobscore

selected as the first variable to be entered, *Test3* was entered into the model next, and no further variables satisfied the entry criterion.

When a second method, backward elimination, is used on the same data (with the same stopping rule for removal), the final model contained the variables *Test1, Test3,* and *Test4.*

Both models have a strong model fit ($p < 0.001$), according to the ANOVA *F*-tests, so either one can be considered statistically significant. You must choose between these two competing models.

Comparing the models on the basis of R^2 values, we see that the two-variable model has $R^2 = .798$, and the three-variable model has $R^2 = .827$. As mentioned earlier, one of the problems with comparing these models using R^2 values is that simply from mathematical considerations, R^2 should be larger for the model with *Test1, Test3,* and *Test4* than for the model with *Test1* and *Test3,* even if *Test4* is not providing significantly important new information. If you decide that the three-variable model is not substantially better, then you might choose the two-variable model based on the desire for parsimony (i.e., selection of the model with the fewest variables if there is no important difference in the models). Other criteria such as Mallows C_p and the Akaike information criterion (AIC) are designed for directly comparing models with different numbers of independent variables (see Neter, Kutner, Nachtsheim, & Wasserman, 1996).

Another way to assess the fit is to examine the contribution for each individual variable in the proposed model. In Table 4.3, the "Sig." column reports the *p*-value associated with a test that the associated β coefficient is zero for each of the predictors currently in the model. For the two predictors *Test1* and *Test3* in Model 2 of the table, these *p*-values are both less than 0.05. If either of these *p*-values were large, it would suggest that the variable was not providing important information to the equation and should possibly be dropped.

When faced with several model candidates, you must decide not only which one best fits the data but also which one makes the most sense in the context of your research and which one uses the fewest variables to create an acceptable model. For example, if each test costs $25 to administer and there are potentially 1,000 candidates, eliminating a single unneeded test would save $25,000.

Based on these considerations, let's use the model with the two independent variables (*Test1* and *Test3*). The corresponding regression equation for predicting *Jobscore* is given by

$$\text{Predicted } Jobscore = -11.922 + 2.406\ Test1 - 0.768\ Test3$$

If the model is adequate, it should be helpful in using these two tests to predict how new employees will perform on the job.

Residual Analysis

Figure 4.8 shows a plot of unstandardized residuals plotted against the predicted *Jobscore* variable. Notice that the points are spread randomly around the zero line, with 1 point for a predicted *Jobscore* of about 200 somewhat out of place. In addition, there is the appearance of a possible increase in variability as the predicted *Jobscore* increases.

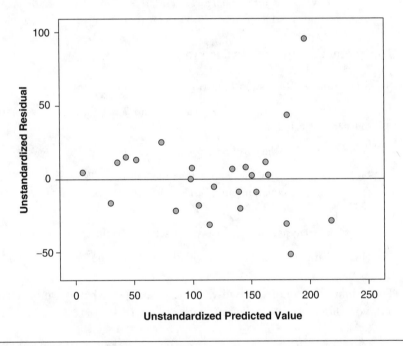

Figure 4.8   Residual Plot for JOBSCORE.SAV Data

The "Casewise Diagnostics" table in the output (not shown here) indicates that the record with the large residual (i.e., with a residual of approximately 100) is a potential outlier since it has a standardized residual greater than 3. The program identifies this as case number 7. You should investigate this case to see if there is something unusual about this subject. Perhaps it is a superstar employee who would be hard to predict using the developed model. You might consider rerunning the analysis without this unusual value to see how that might influence your model.

SPSS Step-by-Step. EXAMPLE 4.3: Multiple Linear Regression Analysis

To examine a matrix of scatterplots of all the variables in the JOB-SCORE.SAV data set as shown in Figure 4.7, use these steps:

1. Open the data set JOBSCORE.SAV and select **Graphs/Scatter/Dot/Matrix Scatter** and click Define.

2. Select the variables *Jobscore, Test1, Test2, Test3,* and *Test4* as the matrix variables and click OK. Figure 4.7 shows the resulting matrix of scatterplots.

To perform the variable selection procedure:

3. Select **Analyze/Regression/Linear. . . .**

4. Select *Jobscore* as the dependent variable and *Test1* through *Test4* as the independent variables.

5. Select Stepwise as the entry criterion and click OK.

6. From this initial analysis, notice that the variables *Test1* and *Test3* are entered into the equation, and *Test2* and *Test4* are excluded, as shown in Table 4.3.

7. Rerun the analysis, this time selecting Backward as the entry criterion.

8. Notice that this method ends up with *Test1, Test3,* and *Test4* in the model.

To evaluate the fit of the two-variable model (or whatever model you select), you should examine the residuals. Follow these steps:

9. Select **Analyze/Regression/Linear,** selecting *Jobscore* as the dependent variable, *Test1* and *Test3* as the independent variables, and Enter as the entry criterion.

10. Check the Save box and select Unstandardized Predicted Values and Unstandardized Residuals and click Continue. Note: This has placed new variables, *Unstandardized Predicted Value(Pre_1)* and *Unstandardized Residual (Res_1),* in the data file.

11. To select casewise diagnostic analysis, check the Statistics checkbox and select Casewise Diagnostics. Click Continue and OK. This gives you the information that subject number 7 has an unusually large residual.

12. To obtain the residual plot in Figure 4.8, select **Graphs/Scatter/Dot/Simple Scatter** and select *Unstandardized Predicted Value* as the *x*-axis variable and *Unstandardized Residual* for the *y*-axis variable and click OK.

13. Double-click on the graph to enter the SPSS Chart Editor. Add a reference (**Options/Y Axis Reference Line**) line at 0. Click Apply and Close.

Bland-Altman Analysis

The Bland-Altman analysis is a different type of animal. From the beginning, you should realize that is it not a statistical test measured with a *p*-value. Instead, it is a subjective process used to assess agreement between two methods of measurement. That is, can the two different measures be used interchangeably (Bland & Altman, 1986, 2003)? An important requirement of the Bland-Altman method for measuring agreement is that the two methods for measuring the same characteristic use the same scale of measurement. This implies that when plotted, the points should line up along the line $y = x$ (line of identity).

This analysis does not depend on either method being a "gold standard" but only that they measure the same characteristic consistently. It is possible for two measures to have strong linear agreement using a Pearson's correlation (r) when they are not measuring the same quantity because, as mentioned previously, a correlation analysis does not require that the two measurements be on the same scale or to even be measurements of the same characteristic.

As mentioned above, there is no specific hypothesis test associated with a Bland-Altman analysis. Instead, the analysis is based on examination of two plots:

- *Plot of Identity*. This plot is a scatterplot of the two measurements along with the line $y = x$. If the measurements are in basic agreement, then the points in the scatterplot will line up closely to the line $y = x$.
- *Bland-Altman Plot*. For this plot, two new variables are created: the average between the two measurements and the difference between the two measurements. The Bland-Altman plot is a scatterplot of these new variables, with the means plotted on the horizontal axis and the differences plotted on the vertical axis. This plot shows the amount of disagreement between the two measures (via the differences) and lets you see how this disagreement relates to the magnitude of the measurements. This plot includes approximate 95% limits (based on an assumption of normal differences). If differences observed in this plot are not deemed scientifically (or clinically) important (according to the researcher's own expertise), then this is a confirmation of agreement. (The

decision as to what constitutes a clinically important difference should be made in advance of the analysis.)

Design Considerations for a Bland-Altman Analysis

- The two different methods of measurement should be measuring the same variable on the same scale.
- The mean and standard deviation (*SD*) of the differences should be constant throughout the range of measurements, and the differences should be approximately a normal distribution (Bland & Altman, 2003).

EXAMPLE 4.4: Bland-Altman Analysis

Describing the Problem

Using an example from Bland and Altman (1986), suppose two measurements of peak expiratory flow rate (PEFR) are compared. One of these measurements uses a "large" meter and the other a "mini" meter. The research question of interest is whether these two techniques are measuring the same phenomenon. We first examine the plot of identity shown in Figure 4.9.

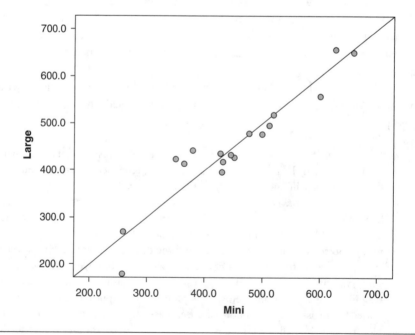

Figure 4.9   Plot of Identity

It should be noted that the line drawn here is the line $y = x$, not the regression line. If the scatter of points in this plot lies near the line, it indicates that the two ways of measuring PEFR are similar. From the plot of identity in Figure 4.9, you can see that the scatterplot falls close to the line, which suggests that the two machines are measuring the same characteristic.

The Bland-Altman plot is shown in Figure 4.10. This plot is a scatterplot of the average of the two measurements against the difference (large minus mini) between measurements for each subject. This plot is a visual check that the magnitudes of the differences are essentially constant throughout the range of measurement. We also show 95% limit lines.

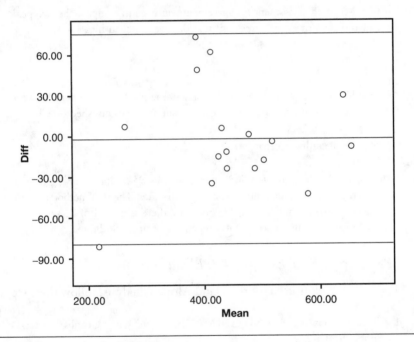

Figure 4.10   Bland-Altman Plot

If the differences are approximately normally distributed, then you would expect about 5% of the points to lie outside the limit lines, and this seems to be the case in Figure 4.10. However, it should be noticed that the 95% limit lines are at about ± 75 for the differences between readings, and the graph shows a few differences outside or close to the limit lines, that is, differences in the neighborhood of ± 75 (the actual limits are −75.4 and 79.6). Bland and Altman (1986) argue that such large differences are *clinically important* (a decision not based on any *p*-value) and therefore conclude that the two devices do not show sufficient agreement to be used interchangeably. It is important to note that this lack of agreement is not apparent in Figure 4.9 (see Bland & Altman, 1986).

Reporting the Results of a Bland-Altman Analysis

The following example illustrates how you might report the results of a Bland-Altman analysis in publication format.

Narrative for Methods Section

"A Bland-Altman assessment for agreement was used to compare the two peak flow methods. A range of agreement was defined as mean bias ± 2 *SD*."

or

"A Bland-Altman analysis was used to assess the level of agreement between the two methods to compare the new technique to the established one."

Narrative for Results Section

"The Bland-Altman analysis indicates that the 95% limits of agreement between the two methods ranged from –75.4 to 79.6. The two methods do not consistently provide similar measures because there is a level of disagreement that includes clinically important discrepancies of up to 80 l/min."

SPSS Step-by-Step. EXAMPLE 4.4: Bland-Altman Analysis

To create the plots used for the Bland-Altman analysis, follow these steps:

1. Open the data set BLAND_ALTMAN.SAV and select **Graphs/Scatter/Dot/ Simple Scatter.**

2. Select *Mini* for the *x*-axis and *Large* for the *y*-axis. Click OK.

3. When the plot appears, double-click on it to bring up the SPSS Editor.

4. From the Chart menu, select **Edit/Select X Axis.**

5. Click the Scale tab, uncheck "Auto" for minimum and maximum, and specify 200 as the minimum and 700 for maximum values. Click Apply and Close.

6. Set the same minimum and maximum values for the *y*-axis (**Edit/Select Y Axis**).

7. Add a line of identity by selecting **Options/Reference Line From Equation.** In the Properties dialog box, indicate an intercept of 0 and the slope of 1. Click Apply and Close.

8. Exit the Chart Editor. The plot shown in Figure 4.9 is displayed.

To create the Bland-Altman plot in SPSS, you must first perform a few calculations.

1. Using the BLAND_ALTMAN.SAV data set, compute the difference between the two measures. This can be done by selecting **Transform/Compute** and computing a new variable called *Diff* from the equation *Large − Mini*.

2. Compute the average of the two variables in the same way using *Mean* for the variable name and the equation *(Large + Mini)/2*.

3. Determine the mean and standard deviation of *Diff* using **Analyze/ Descriptive Statistics/Descriptives.** The mean difference is −2.1176, and $SD = 38.76513$.

4. Create a scatterplot (**Graphs/Scatter/Dot/Simple Scatter**) with *Mean* as the x-axis and *Diff* as the y-axis.

5. Double-click on the graph to enter the SPSS Chart Editor. Add a reference (**Options/Y Axis Reference Line**) line at $-2.1176 + 2*38.76513 = 75.41$ (Reference Line tab) and select a dashed-line style (Lines tab). Click Apply and Close.

6. Add another reference line (**Options/Y Axis Reference Line**) at $-2.1176 - 2*38.76513 = -79.65$ using the same technique.

7. Finally, add a third reference line (**Options/Y Axis Reference Line**) at −2.1176, making this dashed-line style solid.

8. Close the Chart Editor, and the Bland-Altman plot is displayed as shown in Figure 4.10.

Summary

Correlation and regression are statistical techniques used to examine associations between numeric variables and to create predictive equations. Simple and multiple regression techniques can be used to develop a model that explains in a mathematical formula how one or more variables can be used to predict the value of an outcome variable. However, correlations and regression equations do not necessarily suggest cause and effect.

References

Barnett, V., & Lewis, T. (1994). *Outliers in statistical data* (3rd ed.). New York: John Wiley.

Bland, J. M., & Altman, D. G. (1986, February). Statistical methods for assessing agreement between two methods of clinical measurement. *Lancet,* pp. 307–310.

Bland, J. M., & Altman, D. G. (2003). Applying the right statistics: Analyses of measurement studies. *Ultrasound in Obstetrics and Gynecology, 22,* 85–93.

Kleinbaum, D. G., Kupper, L. L., Muller, K. E., & Nizam, A. (1997). *Applied regression analysis and other multivariate methods* (3rd ed.). North Scituate, MA: Duxbury.

Mantel, N. (1970). Why stepdown procedures in variable selection. *Technometrics, 12,* 621–625.

Neter, J., Kutner, M. H., Nachtsheim, C. J., & Wasserman, W. (1996). *Applied linear statistical models* (4th ed.). Chicago: Irwin.

SAS Institute. (2003). *SAS/STAT software: Reference, Version 9.1.* Cary, NC: Author.

TexasSoft. (2004). *WINKS statistical software.* Cedar Hill, TX: Author.

5

Analysis of Categorical Data

People like to clump things into categories. Virtually every research project categorizes some of its observations into neat, little distinct bins: male or female; marital status; broken or not broken; small, medium, or large; race of patient; with or without a tonsillectomy; and so on. When we collect data by categories, we record counts—how many observations fall into a particular bin. Categorical variables are usually classified as being of two basic types: nominal and ordinal. Nominal variables involve categories that have no particular order such as hair color, race, or clinic site, while the categories associated with an ordinal variable have some inherent ordering (categories of socioeconomic status, etc.). Unless otherwise stated, the procedures discussed here can be used on any type of categorical data. There are some specific procedures for ordinal data, and they will be briefly discussed later in the chapter.

Statisticians have devised a number of ways to analyze and explain categorical data. This chapter presents explanations of each of the following methods:

- A contingency table analysis is used to examine the relationship between two categorical variables.
- McNemar's test is designed for the analysis of paired dichotomous, categorical variables to detect disagreement or change.
- The Mantel-Haenszel test is used to determine whether there is a relationship between two dichotomous variables controlling for or within levels of a third variable.

113

- Interrater reliability (kappa) tests whether two raters looking at the same occurrence (or condition) give consistent ratings.
- A goodness-of-fit test measures whether an observed group of counts matches a theoretical pattern.
- A number of other categorical data measures are also briefly discussed.

To get the most out of this chapter, you should first verify that your variables are categorical and then try to match the hypotheses you are testing with the ones described in this chapter. If it is not clear that the hypotheses you are testing match any of these given here, we recommend that you consult a statistician.

Contingency Table Analysis ($r \times c$)

Contingency table analysis is a common method of analyzing the association between two categorical variables. Consider a categorical variable that has r possible response categories and another categorical variable with c possible categories. In this case, there are $r \times c$ possible combinations of responses for these two variables. The $r \times c$ crosstabulation or contingency table has r rows and c columns consisting of $r \times c$ cells containing the observed counts (frequencies) for each of the $r \times c$ combinations. This type of analysis is called a contingency table analysis and is usually accomplished using a chi-square statistic that compares the observed counts with those that would be expected if there were no association between the two variables.

Appropriate Applications of Contingency Table Analysis

The following are examples of situations in which a chi-square contingency table analysis would be appropriate.

- A study compares types of crime and whether the criminal is a drinker or abstainer.
- An analysis is undertaken to determine whether there is a gender preference between candidates running for state governor.
- Reviewers want to know whether worker dropout rates are different for participants in two different job-training programs.
- A marketing research company wants to know whether there is a difference in response rates among small, medium, and large companies that were sent a questionnaire.

Design Considerations for a Contingency Table Analysis

Two Sampling Strategies

Two separate sampling strategies lead to the chi-square contingency table analysis discussed here.

1. *Test of Independence.* A single random sample of observations is selected from the population of interest, and the data are categorized on the basis of the two variables of interest. For example, in the marketing research example above, this sampling strategy would indicate that a single random sample of companies is selected, and each selected company is categorized by size (small, medium, or large) and whether that company returned the survey.

2. *Test for Homogeneity.* Separate random samples are taken from each of two or more populations to determine whether the responses related to a single categorical variable are consistent across populations. In the marketing research example above, this sampling strategy would consider there to be three populations of companies (based on size), and you would select a sample from each of these populations. You then test to determine whether the response rates differ among the three company types.

The two-way table is set up the same way regardless of the sampling strategy, and the chi-square test is conducted in exactly the same way. The only real difference in the analysis is in the statement of the hypotheses and conclusions.

Expected Cell Size Considerations

The validity of the chi-square test depends on both the sample size and the number of cells. Several rules of thumb have been suggested to indicate whether the chi-square approximation is satisfactory. One such rule suggested by Cochran (1954) says that the approximation is adequate if no expected cell frequencies are less than one and no more than 20% are less than five.

Combining Categories

Because of the expected cell frequency criterion in the second sampling strategy, it may be necessary to combine similar categories to lessen the number of categories in your table or to examine the data by subcategories. See the section that follows later in this chapter on Mantel-Haenszel comparisons for information on one way to examine information within categories.

Hypotheses for a Contingency Table Analysis

The statement of the hypotheses depends on whether you used a test of independence or a test for homogeneity.

Test of Independence

In this case, you have two variables and are interested in testing whether there is an association between the two variables. Specifically, the hypotheses to be tested are the following:

H_0: There is no association between the two variables.

H_a: The two variables are associated.

Test for Homogeneity

In this setting, you have a categorical variable collected separately from two or more populations. The hypotheses are as follows:

H_0: The distribution of the categorical variable is the same across the populations.

H_a: The distribution of the categorical variable differs across the populations.

Tips and Caveats for a Contingency Table Analysis

Use Counts—Do Not Use Percentages

It may be tempting to use percentages in the table and calculate the chi-square test from these percentages instead of the raw observed frequencies. This is incorrect—don't do it!

No One-Sided Tests

Notice that the alternative hypotheses above do not assume any "direction." Thus, there are no one- and two-sided versions of these tests. Chi-square tests are inherently nondirectional ("sort of two-sided") in the sense that the chi-square test is simply testing whether the observed frequencies and expected frequencies agree without regard to whether particular observed frequencies are above or below the corresponding expected frequencies.

Each Subject Is Counted Only Once

If you have n total observations (i.e., the total of the counts is n), then these n observations should be independent. For example, suppose you have a categorical variable *Travel* in which subjects are asked by what means they commute to work. It would not be correct to allow a subject to check multiple responses (e.g., car and commuter train) and then include all of these responses for this subject in the table (i.e., count the subject more than once). On such a variable, it is usually better to allow only one response per variable. If you want to allow for multiple responses such as this, then as you are tallying your results, you would need to come up with a new category, "car and commuter train." This procedure can lead to a large number of cells and small expected cell frequencies.

Explain Significant Findings

Unlike many other tests, the simple finding of a significant result in a contingency table analysis does not explain why the results are significant. It is important for you to examine the observed and expected frequencies and explain your findings in terms of which of the differences between observed and expected counts are the most striking.

Contingency Table Examples

The following two examples of contingency table analysis illustrate a variety of the issues involved in this type of analysis.

EXAMPLE 5.1: $r \times c$ Contingency Table Analysis

Describing the Problem

In 1909, Karl Pearson conducted a now classic study involving the relationship between criminal behavior and the drinking of alcoholic beverages. He studied 1,426 criminals, and the data in Table 5.1 show the drinking patterns in various crime categories. (The term *coining* in the table is a term for counterfeiting that is no longer in common usage.) This table is made up of counts in 6 × 2 cells, and, for example, 300 subjects studied were abstainers who had been convicted of stealing.

The hypotheses of interest are as follows:

H_0: There is no association between type of crime and drinking status.

H_a: There is an association between type of crime and drinking status.

In Table 5.2, we show output for these data where we see not only the cell frequencies shown in Table 5.1 but also the expected cell frequencies and the row percentages. That is, for each cell, the table gives the percentage of the row total that this cell count represents. For example, there were

Table 5.1   Pearson's Crime Analysis Data

Crime	Drinker	Abstainer	Total
Arson	50	43	93
Rape	88	62	150
Violence	155	110	265
Stealing	379	300	679
Coining	18	14	32
Fraud	63	144	207
Total	753	673	1426

93 arsonists, and 50 of these said they were drinkers. The row percentage in this case tells us that 50 is 53.8% of 93. From the bottom of the table, it can be seen that slightly more than half (i.e., 753 out of 1,426 or 52.8%) of the subjects were drinkers.

If this pattern turns out to be consistent among all crime categories (i.e., if about 52.8% were drinkers in each crime category), then this would be evidence against an association between type of crime and drinking status, and we would thus not expect to reject the null hypothesis.

However, examination of the table reveals the interesting result that while every other crime category has a few more drinkers than abstainers, the crime category of "Fraud" shows a strong preponderance of abstainers. Note that if there were no association between the two variables, then we would expect, for example, that about 52.8% of the 93 arson subjects (i.e., 49.1) would be drinkers and that about 47.2% of these 93 subjects (i.e., 43.9) would be abstainers. In the case of arson, for example, the observed frequencies are quite similar to these "expected" frequencies. In contrast, for the criminals involved in fraud, the observed frequencies are very different from the expected frequencies. Notice that while the expected count for abstainers involved in fraud is 97.7, the observed count is 144—clearly a large and unanticipated difference if there is no association between crime and drinking status.

In Table 5.3, we show the statistical results related to the analysis of these data. The value of the chi-square statistic is 49.731, with 5 degrees of freedom and $p = 0.000$ (this would be reported as $p < 0.001$), and thus we reject the null hypothesis of no association and conclude that there is a relationship between crime and drinking status. As previously mentioned, this relationship

Table 5.2   Output for Crime Data

Crosstab

			Drinker		Total
			Drinker	Abstainer	
Crime	Arson	Count	50	43	93
		Expected Count	49.1	43.9	93.0
		% within Crime	53.8%	46.2%	100.0%
	Rape	Count	88	62	150
		Expected Count	79.2	70.8	150.0
		% within Crime	58.7%	41.3%	100.0%
	Violence	Count	155	110	265
		Expected Count	139.9	125.1	265.0
		% within Crime	58.5%	41.5%	100.0%
	Stealing	Count	379	300	679
		Expected Count	358.5	320.5	679.0
		% within Crime	55.8%	44.2%	100.0%
	Coining	Count	18	14	32
		Expected Count	16.9	15.1	32.0
		% within Crime	56.3%	43.8%	100.0%
	Fraud	Count	63	144	207
		Expected Count	109.3	97.7	207.0
		% within Crime	30.4%	69.6%	100.0%
Total		Count	753	673	1426
		Expected Count	753.0	673.0	1426.0
		% within Crime	52.8%	47.2%	100.0%

is primarily due to the unusual fact that about 70% of the criminals convicted of fraud were abstainers. (One wonders if there was some "fraud" involved in these criminals' answers to this question.) It can also be seen that the expected frequencies are relatively close to the observed frequencies for each cell except in the cells for fraud. The bar chart in Figure 5.1 provides a visual confirmation that the pattern for fraud crimes is different than the other crimes. All three pieces of information lead you to conclude that the crime of fraud is more common to abstainers and that the other crimes are more common to drinkers.

Before proceeding, it should be noted that the likelihood ratio statistic given in Table 5.3 is an alternative to the Pearson chi-square. While these two test statistics usually give similar results (as they did in this example), most practitioners prefer Pearson's chi-square.

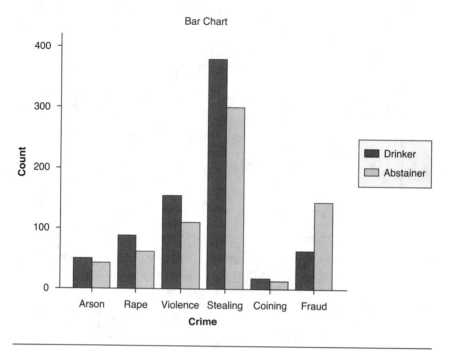

Figure 5.1   Bar Chart for Crime Versus Drinking Analysis

Table 5.3   Chi-Square Tests for Crime Data

Chi-Square Tests

	Value	df	Asymp. Sig. (2-sided)
Pearson Chi-Square	49.731[a]	5	.000
Likelihood Ratio	50.517	5	.000
N of Valid Cases	1426		

a. 0 cells (.0%) have expected count less than 5. The minimum expected count is 15.10.

Reporting the Results of a Contingency Table Analysis

The following illustrates how you might report this chi-square test in a publication format.

Narrative for the Methods Section

"A chi-square test was performed to test the null hypothesis of no association between type of crime and incidence of drinking."

Narrative for the Results Section

"An association between drinking preference and type of crime committed was found, χ^2 (5, N = 1,426) = 49.7, p < 0.001."

Or, to be more complete,

"An association between drinking preference and type of crime committed was found, χ^2 (5, N = 1,426) = 49.7, p < 0.001. Examination of the cell frequencies showed that about 70% (144 out of 207) of the criminals convicted of fraud were abstainers while the percentage of abstainers in all of the other crime categories was less than 50%."

SPSS Step-by-Step. EXAMPLE 5.1: r × c Contingency Table Analysis

While most data sets in SPSS are stored casewise, you can store count data such as that shown in Table 5.1. These data are available (in count form) in file CRIME.SAV. To create this data set, follow these steps:

1. Select **File/New/Data. . . .**

2. This new data set will have three numeric variables: *Crime, Drinker,* and *Count.* In the first column (i.e., for the *Crime* variable), enter the numbers 1 for arson, 2 for rape, 3 for violence, 4 for stealing, 5 for coining, and 6 for fraud. These labels are specified using value labels (see Appendix A: A Brief Tutorial for Using SPSS for Windows if you do not know how to do this). The second column corresponds to the variable *Drinker,* where 1 indicates drinker and 2 indicates abstainer. The third column corresponds to the variable *Count.* For example, the observation 43 for the variable *Count* in the second row of the table is the number of subjects who were arsonists (*Crime* = 1) and abstainers (*Drinker* = 2).

3. Select **Data/Weight Cases . . .** and select the "weight case by" option with *Count* as the Frequency variable.

The contents of CRIME.SAV are shown in Figure 5.2.

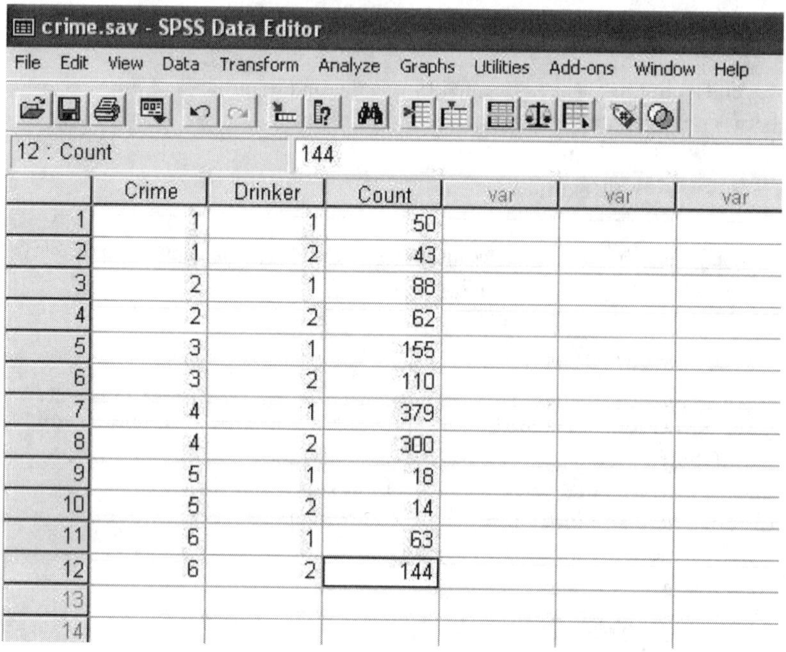

	Crime	Drinker	Count	var	var	var
1	1	1	50			
2	1	2	43			
3	2	1	88			
4	2	2	62			
5	3	1	155			
6	3	2	110			
7	4	1	379			
8	4	2	300			
9	5	1	18			
10	5	2	14			
11	6	1	63			
12	6	2	144			
13						
14						

Figure 5.2 CRIME.SAV Count Form Data Set

Once you have specified this information, you are ready to perform the analysis. Follow these steps:

4. Select **Analyze/Descriptives/Crosstabs.**
5. Choose *Crime* as the row variable and *Drinker* as the column variable.
6. Select the checkbox labeled "Display Clustered Bar Charts."
7. Click the Statistics button and select Chi-Square and Continue.
8. Click the Cells button and select Expected in the Counts box and select Row in the Percentages section and Continue.
9. Click OK, and SPSS creates the output shown in Tables 5.2 and 5.3 along with Figure 5.1.

Program Comments

In this example, we instructed SPSS to print out the table showing the observed and expected frequencies under the Cells option. We can also ask for the row, column, and total percentages. For example, if total percentages were selected, then the percentage that each observed frequency is of the total sample size would be printed in each cell.

EXAMPLE 5.2: 2 × 2 Contingency Table Analysis

A number of experiments involve binary outcomes (i.e., 1 and 0, yes and no). Typically, these occur when you are observing the presence or absence of a characteristic such as a disease, flaw, mechanical breakdown, death, failure, and so on. The analysis of the relationship between two bivariate categorical variables results in a 2 × 2 crosstabulation table of counts. Although the 2 × 2 table is simply a special case of the general $r \times c$ table, the SPSS output for the 2 × 2 tables is more extensive.

Consider an experiment in which the relationship between exposure to a particular reagent (a substance present in a commercial floor cleanser) and the occurrence of a type of reaction (mild skin rash) was studied. Two groups of subjects were studied: One group of 20 patients was exposed to the reagent, and the other group was not. The 40 subjects were examined for the presence of the reaction. The summarized data are shown in Table 5.4.

Table 5.4   Exposure/Reaction Data

	Reaction	No Reaction	
Exposed	13	7	20
Not Exposed	4	16	20
	17	23	40

Table 5.5 shows computer output where the observed and expected frequencies are shown along with row percentages, and Table 5.6 shows typical statistical output for a 2 × 2 table.

These results report a Pearson chi-square of 8.286 with 1 degree of freedom and $p = 0.004$. It should be noted that in the 2 × 2 setting, use of the rule of thumb that no more than 20% of the expected values are less than 5 requires that none of the four expected values should be less than 5. Footnote b reports this fact for these data.

The continuity correction statistic (Yates's correction) is an adjustment of the chi-square test for 2 × 2 tables used by some statisticians to improve the

Table 5.5   Output for 2 × 2 Exposure/Reaction Data

Exposure * Reaction Crosstabulation

| | | | Reaction | | |
			Reaction	No Reaction	Total
Exposure	Exposed	Count	13	7	20
		Expected Count	8.5	11.5	20.0
		% within Exposure	65.0%	35.0%	100.0%
	Not Exposed	Count	4	16	20
		Expected Count	8.5	11.5	20.0
		% within Exposure	20.0%	80.0%	100.0%
Total		Count	17	23	40
		Expected Count	17.0	23.0	40.0
		% within Exposure	42.5%	57.5%	100.0%

Table 5.6   Statistical Output for 2 × 2 Exposure/Reaction Data

Chi-Square Tests

	Value	df	Asymp. Sig. (2-sided)	Exact Sig. (2-sided)	Exact Sig. (1-sided)
Pearson Chi-Square	8.286[b]	1	.004		
Continuity Correction[a]	6.547	1	.011		
Likelihood Ratio	8.634	1	.003		
Fisher's Exact Test				.010	.005
Linear-by-Linear Association	8.079	1	.004		
N of Valid Cases	40				

a. Computed only for a 2×2 table
b. 0 cells (.0%) have expected count less than 5. The minimum expected count is 8.50.

chi-square approximation. This correction has a more dramatic effect when expected values are relatively small. The continuity correction reduces the size of the chi-square value and thus increases the p-value. In this case, the corrected chi-square value is 6.547 with $p = 0.011$. When there are small expected values in the 2 × 2 table, many statisticians recommend reporting the results of Fisher's exact test. This test is based on all possible 2 × 2 tables that have the observed marginal frequencies (i.e., 20 in each of the exposed and nonexposed groups, with 17 having a reaction and 23 not experiencing the reaction).

The probabilities of obtaining each of the possible tables when the null hypothesis is true are obtained, and the p-value is the sum of these probabilities from all tables as rare, or rarer than, the one observed. For these data, the resulting p-value for Fisher's two-sided test is $p = 0.010$. There is no actual test statistic to quote when using Fisher's exact test, and there is a one-sided version if that is desired. All of the results are consistent in leading to rejection of the null hypothesis at the $\alpha = 0.05$ level and thus to the conclusion that there is a relationship between the reagent and reaction. In this case, the exposed subjects had a significantly higher rate of response to the reagent (65% or 13 of 20) than did nonexposed subjects (20% or 4 of 20).

> When there are small expected values in the 2 × 2 table, many statisticians recommend reporting the results of Fisher's exact test.

Reporting the Results of a 2 × 2 Contingency Table Analysis

The following illustrates how you might report this chi-square test in a publication format.

Narrative for the Methods Section

"A chi-square test was performed to test the hypothesis of no association between exposure and reaction."

Narrative for the Results Section

"A higher proportion of the exposed group showed a reaction to the reagent, $\chi^2 (1, N = 40) = 8.29, p = 0.004$."

Or, to be more complete,

"A higher proportion of the exposed group (65% or 13 of 20) showed a reaction to the reagent than did the nonexposed group (20% or 4 of 20), $\chi^2 (1, N = 40) = 8.29, p = 0.004$."

SPSS Step-by-Step. EXAMPLE 5.2: 2 × 2 Contingency Table Analysis

The data in this example are in file EXPOSURE22.SAV as 40 casewise observations on the two variables, *Exposure* (0 = exposed, 1 = not exposed) and *Reaction* (0 = reaction, 1 = no reaction). This data file was created using *Exposure* and *Reaction* as numeric variables with the labels given above. A portion of the data is shown in Figure 5.3.

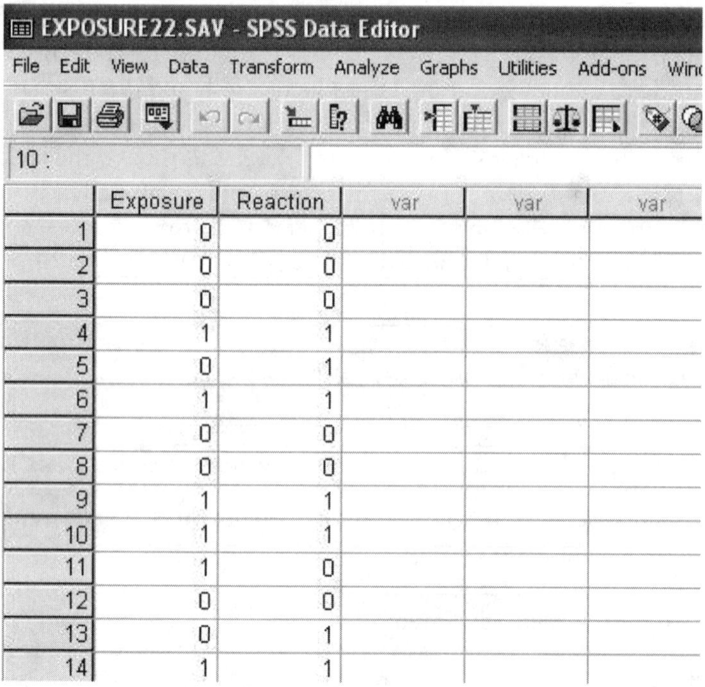

Figure 5.3   First 14 Cases of EXPOSURE22.SAV

To obtain the chi-square results in Table 5.6, open the data set EXPO-SURE22.SAV and do the following:

1. Select **Analyze/Descriptives/Crosstabs**.

2. Choose *Exposure* as the row variable and *Reaction* as the column variable.

3. Click the Statistics button and select Chi Square and Continue.

4. Click the Cells button and select Expected in the Counts box and select Row in the Percentages section and Continue.

5. Click OK.

Analyzing Risk Ratios in a 2 × 2 Table

Another way to analyze a 2 × 2 table is by examining measures of risk. In a medical setting, for example, a 2 × 2 table is often constructed where one variable represents exposure (to some risk factor) and the other represents an outcome (presence or absence of disease). In this case, the researcher is interested in calculating measures of risk. The odds ratio (OR) is used as a measure of risk in a retrospective (case control) study. A case control study is one in which the researcher takes a sample of subjects based on their outcome and looks back in history to see whether they had been exposed. If the study is a prospective (cohort) study, where subjects are selected by presence or absence of exposure and observed over time to see if they come down with the disease, the appropriate measure of risk is the relative risk (RR).

A standard format for risk analysis data is given in Table 5.7. Note that subjects with the outcome of interest are counted in the first column, and those exposed to the risk factor are given in the first row so that "*a*" represents the number of subjects who were exposed to the risk factor and had the outcome of interest.

Table 5.7   Standard Risk Analysis Table

Risk Factor	Outcome		Total
	Present	*Absent*	
Exposed	*a*	*b*	*a + b*
Not Exposed	*c*	*d*	*c + d*
Total	*a + c*	*b + d*	*N = a + b + c + d*

For a retrospective study, the appropriate measure of risk is the odds ratio. In this case, the observed odds of having the outcome when exposed is *a/b,* while the corresponding odds when not exposed is *c/d.* Thus, the odds ratio is estimated to be $(a/b)/(c/d) = ad/bc$. So, for example, if the odds ratio is 3, then this means that the odds of having the outcome of interest are three times larger in the exposed group than in the nonexposed group. Similarly, in a prospective study, we use the relative risk. In this case, it makes sense to say that the estimated risk of having the outcome of interest is $a/(a + b)$ for the exposed group and $c/(c + d)$ for the nonexposed group. Thus, the estimated relative risk is $\frac{a/(a + b)}{c/(c + d)}$, and if, for example, the relative risk is 3, this indicates that the observed risk of having the outcome of interest is three times greater in the exposed group than in the nonexposed group.

When the outcome is rare, the values of the odds ratio and relative risk are approximately equal.

In many retrospective analyses, we are interested in discovering if the odds ratio is (statistically) different than 1. If the OR is shown to be greater than 1, for example, it provides evidence that a risk (measured by the size of OR) exists. An OR that is not different from 1 provides no evidence that a risk exists. If the OR is significantly less than 1, it implies that exposure to the factor provides a benefit.

Appropriate Applications for Retrospective (Case Control) Studies

The following are examples of retrospective (case control) studies in which the odds ratio is the appropriate measure of risk.

- In order to investigate smoking and lung cancer, a group of patients who have lung cancer (cases) are compared to a control group without lung cancer. Each of the subjects in these two groups is then classified as being a smoker (i.e., the exposure) or a nonsmoker.
- In order to assess whether having received the measles, mumps, and rubella vaccine increases the risk of developing autism, a group of autistic children and a control group of nonautistic children are compared on the basis of whether they have previously received the vaccine.

Appropriate Applications for Prospective (Cohort) Studies

- A group of football players with a history of concussion is compared over a 2-year period with a control group of football players with no history of concussion to see whether those with such history are more likely to experience another concussion during that period.
- Samples of 500 subjects with high cholesterol and 500 subjects without high cholesterol are followed for the next 10 years to determine whether subjects in the high-cholesterol group were more likely to have a heart attack during that period.

In the following example, we reexamine the data analyzed in EXAMPLE 5.2 from the perspective of a risk analysis.

EXAMPLE 5.3: Analyzing Risk Ratios for the Exposure/Reaction Data

Consider again the data in Tables 5.4 and 5.5 related to the exposure to a reagent and the occurrence of a particular reaction. Risk analysis output is shown in Table 5.8.

Table 5.8   Risk Analysis Results

Risk Estimate

		95% Confidence Interval	
	Value	Lower	Upper
Odds Ratio for Exposure (Exposed/Not Exposed)	7.429	1.778	31.040
For cohort Reaction = Reaction	3.250	1.278	8.267
For cohort Reaction = No Reaction	.438	.232	.827
N of Valid Cases	40		

In the previous discussion of these data, we intentionally did not specify whether the data were collected for purposes of a prospective or retrospective study. In the following, we discuss both types of analyses.

Analysis as a Retrospective (Case Control) Study

We assume here that 17 subjects experiencing the reaction were selected for study along with 23 subjects who did not experience such a reaction (see Table 5.4). We then look back to determine which of these subjects experienced the particular exposure in question. The calculated odds ratio (odds ratio for exposure) of 7.429 estimates that the odds of having the reaction when exposed is 7.429 times greater than the odds when not exposed. Since the 95% confidence interval of the true odds ratio—that is, (1.778, 31.040)—stays greater than 1, then you can interpret this result as being statistically significant (i.e., you can conclude that the odds of having the reaction when exposed is higher than the odds when not exposed).

Analysis as a Prospective (Cohort) Study

In this setting, we assume that 20 subjects who experienced the particular exposure and 20 who did not were chosen for the study. These subjects were then followed over time to see whether they had the reaction. In this case, the appropriate measure of risk is relative risk, and the value of 3.25, labeled as "For cohort Reaction = Reaction," indicates that the observed risk of having the reaction is 3.25 times greater for the exposed group than for the nonexposed group. The corresponding 95% confidence interval on the true relative risk is (1.278, 8.267), which again stays greater than 1 and thus indicates a significant result.

A savvy researcher will use the confidence interval not only to assess significance but to also determine what practical meaning this risk would entail if the
true value were at the lower or upper end of the interval. Also, it is helpful to
interpret confidence intervals in context with other published studies.

Reporting the Results of a Risk Analysis

The following illustrates how you might report risk analysis results in a publication format.

Narrative for the Methods Section of a Retrospective (Case Control) Study

"To examine the relative risk of having the reaction when exposed, we calculated an odds ratio."

Narrative for the Results Section of a Retrospective (Case Control) Study

"The odds of having the reaction were 7.43 times greater for subjects in the
exposed group than for subjects not exposed to the reagent (OR = 7.4, 95%
CI = 1.8, 31.0). Thus, the odds ratio is significantly greater than 1, suggesting
that the true odds of having the reaction are greater for the exposed group."

Narrative for the Methods Section of a Prospective (Cohort) Study

"To examine the relative risk of having the reaction when exposed, we calculated relative risk."

Narrative for the Results Section of a Prospective (Cohort) Study

"Subjects exposed to the reagent were 3.25 times more likely to have a
reaction as measured by relative risk (RR = 3.25, 95% CI = 1.3, 8.3). Thus,
the relative risk is significantly greater than 1, indicating that the risk of
having the reaction is greater for the exposed group."

SPSS Step-by-Step. EXAMPLE 5.3:
Analyzing Risk Ratios for the Exposure/Reaction Data

In this example, we use the exposure data in EXPOSURE22.SAV. To obtain the risk analysis results, open the data set EXPOSURE22.SAV and do the following:

1. Select **Analyze/Descriptives/Crosstabs.**

2. Choose *Exposure* as the row variable and *Reaction* as the column variable.

3. Click the Statistics button and select the Risk checkbox and Continue.

4. Click OK.

The resulting output is displayed in Table 5.8.

Program Comments

For SPSS to calculate the correct values for the odds ratio, you will need to set up your SPSS data set in a specific way so that the resulting 2×2 output table appears in the standard display format shown in Table 5.7. In this table, notice that subjects at risk are in the first row and subjects not at risk are in the second row of the table. Similarly, those who experience the outcome of interest are placed in column 1. For SPSS to produce this table, you must designate row and column positions alphabetically or in numeric order. That is, in the current example, the risk factor is coded so that 0 = exposed and 1 = not exposed. You could also code them as 1 = exposed and 2 = not exposed. Both of these coding strategies put the exposed subjects in the first row of the table. If, for example, you used the opposite strategy where 0 = not exposed and 1 = exposed, that would place those having the exposure in the second row. This would cause the OR to be calculated as 0.135 (which is the inverse of the actual value OR = 7.429). This coding conundrum is unfortunate since most people intuitively code their data with 1 meaning exposure and 0 meaning no exposure. However, to make the results come out correctly in SPSS, you should use the guidelines listed above.

McNemar's Test

In the section on contingency table analysis, we saw that a test for independence is used to test whether there is a relationship between dichotomous categorical variables such as political party preference (Republican or Democrat) and voting intention (plan to vote or do not plan to vote). Also, in EXAMPLE 5.2, researchers were interested in determining whether there was a relationship between exposure to a risk factor and occurrence of a reaction. While in these cases, it is of interest to determine whether the variables are independent, in some cases, the categorical variables are paired in such a way that a test for independence is meaningless. McNemar's test is designed for the analysis of paired dichotomous, categorical variables in much the same way that the paired *t*-test is designed for paired quantitative data.

Appropriate Applications of McNemar's Test

The following are examples of dichotomous categorical data that are paired and for which McNemar's test is appropriate.

- An electrocardiogram (ECG) and a new scanning procedure are used to detect whether heart disease is present in a sample of patients with known heart disease. Researchers want to analyze the disagreement between the two measures.
- A sample of possible voters is polled to determine how their preferences for the two major political party candidates for president changed before and after a televised debate.
- Consumers are selected for a study designed to determine how their impressions of a particular product (favorable or unfavorable) changed before and after viewing an advertisement.

In each case above, the pairing occurs because the two variables represent two readings of the same characteristic (e.g., detection of heart disease, presidential preference, etc.). You already know that the readings will agree to some extent, and thus testing for independence using a contingency table approach is not really appropriate. What you want to measure is disagreement or change. That is, in what way do the two heart scan procedures differ, how has the debate or the advertisement changed the opinions of the subjects, and so forth?

Hypotheses for McNemar's Test

In situations for which McNemar's test is appropriate, the interest focuses on the subjects for which change occurred. Following up on the third bulleted example above, suppose an advertiser wants to know whether an advertisement has an effect on the impression consumers have of a product. A group of people is selected, and their feelings about the product before and after viewing the advertisement are recorded as favorable or unfavorable. Thus, there are four categories of "before versus after" responses:

- (*i*)   Favorable both before and after viewing the advertisement
- (*ii*) Favorable before and unfavorable after viewing the advertisement
- (*iii*) Unfavorable before and favorable after viewing the advertisement
- (*iv*) Unfavorable both before and after viewing the advertisement

We are interested in determining whether the advertisement changed attitudes toward the product. That is, we concentrate on the subjects in categories (*ii*) and (*iii*). Was it more common for a subject to be in category (*ii*) than in category (*iii*) or vice versa? The hypotheses of interest would be the following:

H_0:   The probability of a subject having a favorable response to the product before viewing the advertisement and an unfavorable response afterward is equal to the probability of having an unfavorable response to the product before viewing the advertisement and a favorable response afterward.

H_a: The probability of a subject having a favorable response to the product before viewing the advertisement and an unfavorable response afterward is not equal to the probability of having an unfavorable response to the product before viewing the advertisement and a favorable response afterward.

Clearly, the goal of the advertisement would be to improve people's attitudes toward the product; that is, there should be more people in category (*iii*) than category (*ii*). The corresponding one-sided hypotheses reflecting this goal are as follows:

H_0:   The probability of a subject having a favorable response to the product before viewing the advertisement and an unfavorable response afterward is equal to the probability of having an unfavorable response to the product before viewing the advertisement and a favorable response afterward.

H_a: The probability of a subject having a favorable response to the product before viewing the advertisement and an unfavorable response afterward is less than the probability of having an unfavorable response to the product before viewing the advertisement and a favorable response afterward.

EXAMPLE 5.4: McNemar's Test

Continuing with the advertising effectiveness illustration, suppose 20 subjects were asked to express their opinions before and after viewing the advertisement. A crosstabulation of the responses is shown in Table 5.9, where it can be seen that 13 of the 20 subjects did not change their opinions of the product after viewing the advertisement. The important issue concerns how the other 7 subjects responded. That is, did those who changed their minds tend to change from favorable before to unfavorable after or from unfavorable before to favorable after (clearly the advertiser's preference)? In the table, we see that 2 subjects changed from a favorable opinion before the advertisement to an unfavorable opinion afterward, while 5 improved their opinion after the advertisement.

Table 5.9   2 × 2 Table for Advertising Effectiveness Data

before * after Crosstabulation

Count

		after		Total
		Unfavorable	Favorable	
before	Unfavorable	4	5	9
	Favorable	2	9	11
Total		6	14	20

Suppose for the moment that the advertiser is simply interested in knowing whether the advertisement changes the perception of the viewer in either direction. In this case, we would test the first set of hypotheses given previously. The results for this analysis are shown in Table 5.10.

Table 5.10   McNemar's Test Results for Advertising Effectiveness Data

Chi-Square Tests

	Value	Exact Sig. (2-sided)
McNemar Test		.453[a]
N of Valid Cases	20	

a. Binomial distribution used.

For this analysis, the test yields a p-value of 0.453. Since this p-value is large, the null hypothesis of equal probabilities is not rejected. That is, there is not enough evidence to say that those who will change their reactions after the advertisement will do so in one direction more than the other.

As mentioned earlier, it is probably the case that the advertiser wants to show that there is a stronger tendency for subjects to improve their opinion after the advertisement; that is, it is more likely to be in category (*iii*) than category (*ii*). In this case, you would want to test the second set of hypotheses given previously (i.e., the one-sided hypotheses). The data support the alternative of interest since 5 people who changed were in category (*iii*) and only 2 were in category (*ii*). Thus, for this one-sided hypothesis, the p-value in the table should be cut in half, but even with this reduction, the results are still not significant. (This negative result could have resulted from a sample size too small to detect a meaningful difference. See the discussion of the power of a test in Chapter 1.)

Reporting the Results of McNemar's Test

The following illustrates how you might report these McNemar test results in a publication format in the setting in which the alternative specifies an improved impression after viewing the advertisement.

Narrative for the Methods Section

"McNemar's test was used to test the null hypothesis that the probability of changing from favorable before to unfavorable after viewing the advertisement is equal to the probability of changing from unfavorable before to favorable after viewing the advertisement."

Narrative for the Results Section

"Using McNemar's test, no significant tendency was found for subjects who changed their opinion to be more likely to have a favorable opinion of the product after viewing the advertisement $(p = 0.23)$."

SPSS Step-by-Step. EXAMPLE 5.4: McNemar's Test

The data set MCNEMAR.SAV contains two variables, labeled *Before* and *After,* in casewise form. The data are all dichotomous, where 0 indicates nonfavorable and 1 indicates favorable. To perform a McNemar's test on these data, open the data set MCNEMAR.SAV and follow these steps:

1. Select **Analyze/Descriptives Statistics/Crosstabs.**

2. Select *Before* as the row variable and *After* as the column variable.

3. Click on the Statistics button and select McNemar and Continue.

4. Click OK, and the results in Table 5.10 are shown.

Mantel-Haenszel Comparison

The Mantel-Haenszel method is often used (particularly in meta-analysis) to pool the results from several 2×2 contingency tables. It is also useful for the analysis of two dichotomous variables while adjusting for a third variable to determine whether there is a relationship between the two variables, controlling for levels of the third variable.

Appropriate Applications of the Mantel-Haenszel Procedure

- *Disease Incidence*. Case control data for a disease are collected in several cities, forming a 2×2 table for each city. You could use a Mantel-Haenszel analysis to obtain a pooled estimate of the odds ratio across cities.

- *Pooling Results From Previous Studies*. Several published studies have analyzed the same categorical variables summarized in 2×2 tables. In meta-analysis, the information from the studies is pooled to provide more definitive findings than could be obtained from a single study. Mantel-Haenszel analysis can be used to pool this type of information. For more on meta-analysis, see Hunt (1997) and Lipsey and Wilson (2000).

Hypotheses Tests Used in Mantel-Haenszel Analysis

The hypotheses tested in the Mantel-Haenszel test are as follows:

H_0: There is no relationship between the two variables of interest when controlling for a third variable.

H_a: There is a relationship between the two variables of interest when controlling for a third variable.

Design Considerations for a Mantel-Haenszel Test

A Mantel-Haenszel analysis looks at several 2×2 tables from the same bivariate variables, each representing some strata or group (e.g., information from different departments at a university, etc.) or from different results of similar analyses (as in a meta-analysis). The test also assumes that the tables are independent (subjects or entities are in one and only one table).

EXAMPLE 5.5: Mantel-Haenszel Analysis

A classic data set illustrating the use of the Mantel-Haenszel test is data collected at the University of California at Berkeley concerning gender patterns in graduate admissions (Bickel & O'Connell, 1975). The crosstabulated data for acceptance (no or yes) versus gender is given in Table 5.11 for five separate departments along with row percentages, showing the percentage of each gender that was admitted within each program. From this table, it can be seen that while Department 1 seems to have higher admission rates than the other departments, the comparative acceptance rates for males and females are about the same within departments, with there being a slight tendency for females to be admitted at a higher rate.

Table 5.11   Berkeley Graduate Admissions Data

Gender * Accepted * Department Crosstabulation

Department				Accepted No	Accepted Yes	Total
1	Gender	Female	Count	8	17	25
			% within Gender	32.0%	68.0%	100.0%
		Male	Count	207	353	560
			% within Gender	37.0%	63.0%	100.0%
	Total		Count	215	370	585
			% within Gender	36.8%	63.2%	100.0%
2	Gender	Female	Count	391	202	593
			% within Gender	65.9%	34.1%	100.0%
		Male	Count	205	120	325
			% within Gender	63.1%	36.9%	100.0%
	Total		Count	596	322	918
			% within Gender	64.9%	35.1%	100.0%
3	Gender	Female	Count	244	131	375
			% within Gender	65.1%	34.9%	100.0%
		Male	Count	279	138	417
			% within Gender	66.9%	33.1%	100.0%
	Total		Count	523	269	792
			% within Gender	66.0%	34.0%	100.0%
4	Gender	Female	Count	299	94	393
			% within Gender	76.1%	23.9%	100.0%
		Male	Count	138	53	191
			% within Gender	72.3%	27.7%	100.0%
	Total		Count	437	147	584
			% within Gender	74.8%	25.2%	100.0%
5	Gender	Female	Count	317	24	341
			% within Gender	93.0%	7.0%	100.0%
		Male	Count	351	22	373
			% within Gender	94.1%	5.9%	100.0%
	Total		Count	668	46	714
			% within Gender	93.6%	6.4%	100.0%

The Mantel-Haenszel test can be used to test the following hypotheses:

H_0: Controlling for (or within departments), there is no relationship between gender and acceptance.

H_a: Controlling for (or within departments), there is a relationship between gender and acceptance.

Mantel-Haenszel results are shown in Table 5.12, where it can be seen that $p = 0.756$, indicating that controlling for departments, there is no reason to conclude that there is a difference between male versus female admission rates. As mentioned previously, the consistent pattern is that the admission rates for males and females are about the same for each department, with perhaps a slight tendency for females to have a higher rate of admission. Cochran's test is similar to the Mantel-Haenszel test but is not commonly reported. In this example, Cochran's test gives results consistent with the Mantel-Haenszel test.

Table 5.12   Mantel-Haenszel Results for Berkeley Graduate Admissions Data

Tests of Conditional Independence

	Chi-Squared	df	Asymp. Sig. (2-sided)
Cochran's	.125	1	.724
Mantel-Haenszel	.096	1	.756

Reporting Results of a Mantel-Haenszel Analysis

Narrative for the Methods Section

"Controlling for department, the relationship between gender and acceptance is examined using a Mantel-Haenszel analysis."

Narrative for the Results Section

"Adjusting or controlling for department, no significant difference was found between male and female acceptance rates, χ^2 (1, $N = 3,593$) = 0.10, $p = 0.76$."

SPSS Step-by-Step. EXAMPLE 5.5: Mantel-Haenszel Analysis

The data in Table 5.11 are contained in the file BIAS.SAV. To perform the Mantel-Haenszel analysis on the Berkeley admissions data, open the data set BIAS.SAV and follow these steps:

1. Select **Analyze/Descriptive Statistics/Crosstabs.**

2. Select *Gender* as the row(s) variable and *Accepted* as the column(s) variable. Select *Department* as the "Layer 1 of 1" variable.

3. Click the Statistics button and check the "Cochran's and Mantel-Haenszel Statistics" checkbox and Continue.

4. Click the Cells button and select Row in the Percentages section and Continue. Click OK, and the output includes the information in Tables 5.11 and 5.12.

5. To produce Table 5.13, leave off the *Department* variable in Step 2. To produce the percentages, select the Cells button and check the Row percentages option.

Tips and Caveats for Mantel-Haenszel Analysis

Simpson's Paradox

Historically, the real interest in the Berkeley admissions data set (and the reason for Bickel and O'Connell's [1975] article in *Science*) is the apparent inconsistency between the conclusions based on evidence of a possible bias against females using the combined data (see Table 5.13) and the conclusions obtained previously based on the departmental data in Table 5.11 (i.e., within departments, the acceptance rates for men and women were not significantly different). In Table 5.13, we show an overall comparison between gender and admission combined over the five departments. Interestingly, in Table 5.13, the overall admission rates for males is 37% (686/1,866), while for females, it is only 27% (468/1,727). In addition, for this 2 × 2 table, the chi-square test for independence (computer output not shown here) gives $p < 0.001$, indicating a relationship between gender and admission. On the surface, these data seem to indicate a sex bias against women.

Table 5.13   Berkeley Graduate Admissions Data
Combined Across Departments

Gender * Accepted Crosstabulation

			Accepted		
			No	Yes	Total
Gender	Female	Count	1259	468	1727
		% within Gender	72.9%	27.1%	100.0%
	Male	Count	1180	686	1866
		% within Gender	63.2%	36.8%	100.0%
Total		Count	2439	1154	3593
		% within Gender	67.9%	32.1%	100.0%

To explain the reasons for these seeming contradictions, note that admissions rates into Department 1 were substantially higher than were those for the other four majors. Further examination of the data in Table 5.11 indicates that males applied in greater numbers to Department 1, while females applied in greater numbers to departments into which admission was more difficult. The important point is that relationships between variables within subgroups can be entirely reversed when the data are combined across subgroups. This is called *Simpson's paradox*. Clearly, analysis of these data by department, as shown in Table 5.11, provides a better picture of the relationship between gender and admission than does use of the combined data in Table 5.13.

Tests of Interrater Reliability

Interrater reliability is a measure used to examine the agreement between two people (raters/observers) on the assignment of categories of a categorical variable. It is an important measure in determining how well an implementation of some coding or measurement system works.

Appropriate Applications of Interrater Reliability

- Different people read and rate the severity (from 0 to 4) of a tumor based on a magnetic resonance imaging (MRI) scan.
- Several judges score competitors at an ice-skating competition on an integer scale of 1 to 5.
- Researchers want to compare the responses to a measure of happiness (scaled 1 to 5) experienced by husbands and wives.

A statistical measure of interrater reliability is Cohen's kappa, which ranges from -1.0 to 1.0, where large numbers mean better reliability, values near zero suggest that agreement is attributable to chance, and values less than zero signify that agreement is even less than that which could be attributed to chance.

EXAMPLE 5.6: Interrater Reliability Analysis

Using an example from Fleiss (2000, p. 213), suppose you have 100 subjects whose diagnosis is rated by two raters on a scale that rates each subject's disorder as being psychological, neurological, or organic. The data are given in Table 5.14.

The results of the interrater analysis are given in Table 5.15, where kappa = 0.676 with $p < 0.001$. This measure of agreement, while statistically significant, is only marginally convincing. Most statisticians prefer kappa

Table 5.14   Data for Interrater Reliability Analysis

		Rater A		
		Psychological	Neurological	Organic
Rater B	Psychological	75	1	4
	Neurological	5	4	1
	Organic	0	0	10

SOURCE: *Statistical Methods for Rates & Proportions, Second Edition*, copyright © 2000, by Joseph L. Fleiss. Reprinted with permission of Wiley-Liss, Inc., a subsidiary of John Wiley & Sons, Inc.

values to be at least 0.6 and most often higher than 0.7 before claiming a good level of agreement. Although not displayed in the output, you can find a 95% confidence interval using the generic formula for 95% confidence intervals:

$$\text{Estimate} \pm 1.96 \; SE$$

Using this formula and the results in Table 5.15, an approximate 95% confidence interval on kappa is (0.504, 0.848). Some statisticians prefer the use of a weighted kappa, particularly if the categories are ordered. The weighted kappa allows "close" ratings to not simply be counted as "misses." However, SPSS does not calculate weighted kappas.

Reporting the Results of an Interrater Reliability Analysis

The following illustrates how you might report this interrater analysis in a publication format.

Narrative for the Methods Section

"An interrater reliability analysis using the kappa statistic was performed to determine consistency among raters."

Narrative for the Results Section

"The interrater reliability for the raters was found to be kappa = 0.68 ($p <$ .0.001), 95% CI (0.504, 0.848)."

Table 5.15 Results for Interrater Reliability Analysis

Symmetric Measures

		Value	Asymp. Std. Error[a]	Approx. T[b]	Approx. Sig.
Measure of Agreement	Kappa	.676	.088	8.879	.000
N of Valid Cases		100			

a. Not assuming the null hypothesis.
b. Using the asymptotic standard error assuming the null hypothesis.

SPSS Step-by-Step. EXAMPLE *5.6: Interrater Reliability Analysis*

The data set KAPPA.SAV contains the data in Table 5.14 in count form. You can create this data set in a manner similar to the data set CRIME.SAV used earlier in this chapter. The data set contains the following variables: *Rater_A, Rater_B,* and *Count.* Figure 5.4 shows the data file in count (summarized) form.

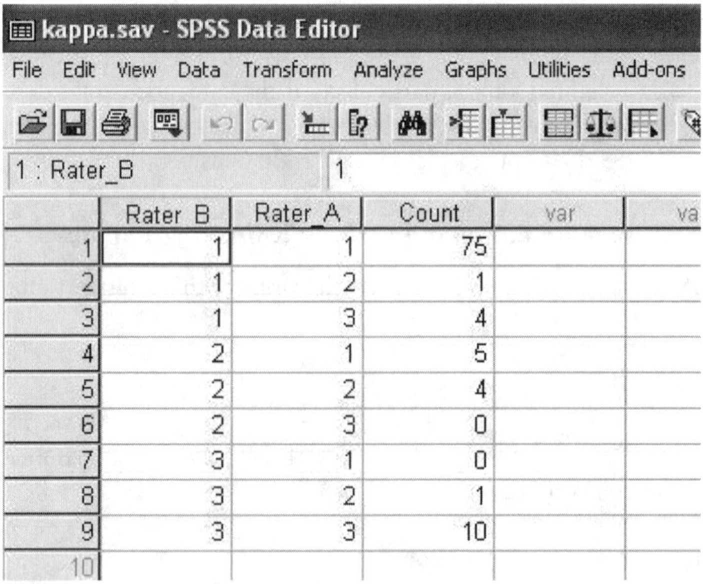

	Rater_B	Rater_A	Count	var	va
1	1	1	75		
2	1	2	1		
3	1	3	4		
4	2	1	5		
5	2	2	4		
6	2	3	0		
7	3	1	0		
8	3	2	1		
9	3	3	10		
10					

Figure 5.4 Interrater Reliability Data in SPSS

To analyze these data, follow these steps:

1. Open the file KAPPA.SAV. Before performing the analysis on these summarized data, you must tell SPSS that the *Count* variable is a "weighted" variable. Select **Data/Weight Cases . . .** and select the "weight cases by" option with *Count* as the Frequency variable.

2. Select **Analyze/Descriptive Statistics/Crosstabs.**

3. Select *Rater A* as the row and *Rater B* as the column.

4. Click on the Statistics button and select Kappa and Continue.

5. Click OK to display the results for the kappa test in Table 5.15.

Goodness-of-Fit Test

A goodness-of-fit test is used to ascertain whether the distribution of observed counts in the various categories of a categorical variable matches the expected distribution of counts under a hypothetical model for the data.

Appropriate Applications of the Goodness-of-Fit Test

The following are examples of situations in which a chi-square goodness-of-fit test would be appropriate.

- Genetic theory indicates that the result of crossing two flowering plants to create a number of progeny should result in flowers that are 50% red, 25% yellow, and 25% white. When the cross-bred flowers bloom, the observed number of each color is compared with the numbers expected under the theory to see whether the genetic theory seems to apply in this case.
- A zoologist wants to know whether there is a directional preference in the positioning of nests for a particular species of birds. A sample of 300 nests is observed, and each nest is categorized as facing north, northeast, and so on. The counts for each of the eight directions are compared with the counts expected if there is no directional preference.
- The U.S. Bureau of Labor Statistics provides the percentages of U.S. full-time workers in 1996 who fell into the following five categories: less than high school, high school degree—no college, some college, bachelor's degree, and advanced degree. A sample of 1,000 full-time workers is selected this year to determine whether the distribution of educational attainment has changed since 1996.

Design Considerations for a Goodness-of-Fit Test

1. The test assumes that a random sample of observations is taken from the population of interest.

2. The appropriate use of the chi-square to approximate the distribution of the goodness-of-fit test statistic depends on both the sample size and the number of cells. A widely used rule of thumb suggested by Cochran (1954) is that the approximation is adequate if no expected cell frequencies are less than 1 and no more than 20% are less than 5.

Hypotheses for a Goodness-of-Fit Test

The hypotheses being tested in this setting are as follows:

H_0: The population (from which the sample is selected) follows the hypothesized distribution.

H_a: The population does not follow the hypothesized distribution.

To test these hypotheses, a chi-squared test statistic is used that compares the observed frequencies with what is expected if the hypothesized model under the null is correct. Large values of the test statistic suggest that the alternative is true, while small values are supportive of the null. A low p-value suggests rejection of the null hypothesis and leads to the conclusion that the data do not follow the hypothesized, or theoretical, distribution.

Tips and Caveats for a Goodness-of-Fit Test

No One-Sided Tests

There are no one-sided/two-sided decisions to be made regarding these tests. The tests are inherently nondirectional ("sort of two-sided") in the sense that the chi-square test is simply testing whether the observed frequencies and expected frequencies agree without regard to whether particular observed frequencies are above or below the corresponding expected frequencies. If the null hypothesis is rejected, then a good interpretation of the results will involve a discussion of differences that were found.

EXAMPLE 5.7: Goodness-of-Fit Test

As an illustration of the goodness-of-fit test, we consider a classic experiment in genetics. Gregor Mendel, a Czechoslovakian monk in the 19th century, identified some basic principles that control heredity. For example, Mendel's theory suggests that the phenotypic frequencies resulting from a dihybrid cross of two independent genes, where each gene shows simple dominant/recessive inheritance, will be expected to be in a 9:3:3:1 ratio. In Mendel's classic experiment using the garden pea, he predicted that the frequencies of smooth yellow peas, smooth green peas, wrinkled yellow peas, and wrinkled green peas would be in a 9:3:3:1 ratio. The hypotheses being tested in this setting are the following:

H_0: The population frequencies of smooth yellow, smooth green, wrinkled yellow, and wrinkled green peas will be in a 9:3:3:1 ratio.

H_a: The population frequencies will not follow this pattern.

Mendel's experiment yielded 556 offspring, so the expected frequencies would be $(9/16)556 = 312.75$, $(3/16)556 = 104.25$, $(3/16)556 = 104.25$, and $(1/16)556 = 34.75$ for smooth yellow, smooth green, wrinkled yellow, and wrinkled green peas, respectively. The frequencies that Mendel actually

Table 5.16   Goodness-of-Fit Analysis for Mendel's Data

Phenotype

	Observed N	Expected N	Residual
Smooth Yellow	315	312.8	2.3
Smooth Green	108	104.3	3.8
Wrinkled Yellow	101	104.3	-3.3
Wrinkled Green	32	34.8	-2.8
Total	556		

Test Statistics

	Phenotype
Chi-Square[a]	.470
df	3
Asymp. Sig.	.925

a. 0 cells (.0%) have expected frequencies less than 5. The minimum expected cell frequency is 34.8.

observed were 315, 108, 101, and 32, respectively (i.e., quite close to those expected).

In Table 5.16, we show the results for this analysis where you can see the observed and expected frequencies. The chi-square statistic is .470 with 3 degrees of freedom and $p = .925$. That is, the observed phenotypic ratios followed the expected pattern quite well, and you would not reject the null hypothesis. There is no evidence to suggest that the theory is not correct. In general, if the p-value for this test is significant, it means that there is evidence that the observed data do not fit the theorized ratios.

Reporting the Results of a Chi-Square Goodness-of-Fit Analysis

The following examples illustrate how you might report this goodness-of-fit test in a publication format.

Narrative for the Methods Section

"A chi-square goodness-of-fit test was performed to test the null hypothesis that the population frequencies of smooth yellow, smooth green, wrinkled yellow, and wrinkled green peas will be in a 9:3:3:1 ratio."

Narrative for the Results Section

"The results were not statistically significant, and there is no reason to reject the claim that Mendel's theory applies to this dihybrid cross, χ^2 (3, N = 556) = 0.470, $p = 0.925$."

SPSS Step-by-Step. EXAMPLE 5.7: Goodness-of-Fit Test

To perform a goodness-of-fit test in SPSS, you must have a data set consisting of counts. This data set can be set up in two ways. If you know the counts in each category, you can set up a data set consisting specifically of these counts. If you have a standard casewise data set, then you can also run a goodness-of-fit test using that file directly.

The file MENDELCNT.SAV contains the actual counts Mendel obtained. To create a data set consisting of the counts and perform the goodness-of-fit test in SPSS, follow these steps:

1. Select **File/New/Data. . . .**

2. This new data set will have two numeric variables: *Phenotype* and *Count*. In the first column (i.e., for the *Phenotype* variable), enter the numbers 1 for

smooth yellow, 2 for smooth green, 3 for wrinkled yellow, and 4 for wrinkled green, and in the second column, enter the corresponding counts (i.e., 315, 108, 101, and 32). Click on the variable View and enter the variable names *Phenotype* and *Count*. In the values column, specify value labels associated with the phenotype codes (i.e., 1 = smooth yellow, etc.). (See Appendix A: A Brief Tutorial for Using SPSS for Windows if you do not know how to do this.)

3. Select **Data/Weight Cases . . .** and select the "weight case by" option with *Count* as the Frequency variable.

4. Select **Analyze/Nonparametric Tests/Chi Square . . .** and select *Phenotype* as the test variable.

5. In Expected Values, click on the Values radio button. Enter the theorized proportions in the order you entered the data. Thus, enter a 9 and click Add, enter 3 and click Add, enter another 3 and click Add, and finally add 1 and click Add. This specifies the theoretical 9:3:3:1 ratio.

6. Click OK to display the output shown in Table 5.16.

Program Comments

- In this example, notice that we entered 9, 3, 3, and 1 as the expected frequencies. You can enter any set of frequencies as long as they are multiples of the expected proportions—in this case, 9/16, 3/16, 3/16, and 1/16. So, for example, you could enter 18, 6, 6, and 2 and still obtain the same results. A natural set of expected frequencies to use is 312.75, 104.25, 104.25, and 34.75, which are the expected frequencies out of 556. However, SPSS does not allow an entry as long as 312.75. SPSS will accept 312.8 and so forth, and use of these rounded expected frequencies results in very minor differences from the results in Table 5.16.
- If you have a data set (such as the example described earlier involving the directional preference in the positioning of nests for a certain species of bird), you would select "All categories equal" in the "Expected Values" section.
- The chi-square procedure in SPSS does not recognize string (text) variables. This is the reason we assigned *Phenotype* to be a numeric variable and assigned the associated value labels rather than simply specifying *Phenotype* as a string variable and using the four phenotypes as observed values.

Other Measures of Association for Categorical Data

Several other statistical tests can be performed on categorical data. The test performed depends on the type of categorical variables and the intent of the analysis. The following list describes several of these briefly.

Correlation. If both the rows and columns of your table contain ordered numeric values, you can produce a Spearman's rho or other nonparametric correlations. See Chapter 7: Nonparametric Analysis Procedures for a discussion of nonparametric procedures.

Nominal Measures. A number of other specialty measures can be calculated for crosstabulation tables in which both variables are nominal. These include the following:

- *Contingency Coefficient.* This is a measure designed for larger tables. Some statisticians recommend that the table be at least 5 by 5. The values of the contingency coefficient range from 0 to 1, with 1 indicating high association. For smaller tables, this statistic is not recommended.
- *Phi.* The phi coefficient is a measure of association that is adjusted according to sample size. Specifically, it is the square root of chi-square divided by n, the sample size. Phi ranges from –1 to 1 for 2×2 tables and, for larger tables, from 0 to the square root of the minimum of $r - 1$ or $c - 1$, where r and c denote the number of rows and columns, respectively. Phi is most often used in a 2×2 table where the variable forms true dichotomies. In the case of 2×2 tables, the phi coefficient is equal to Pearson's correlation coefficient.
- *Cramer's* V. This is a measure of association based on chi-square, where the upper limit is always 1. In a 2×2 table, Cramer's V is equal to the absolute value of the phi coefficient.
- *Lambda.* Also called the Goodman-Kruskal index, lambda is a measure of association where a high value of lambda (up to 1) indicates that the independent variable perfectly predicts the dependent variable and where a low value of lambda (down to 0) indicates that it is of no help in predicting the dependent variable.
- *Uncertainty Coefficient.* Sometimes called the entropy coefficient, this is a measure of association that indicates the proportional reduction in error (or uncertainty) when predicting the dependent variable. SPSS calculates symmetric and asymmetric versions of the uncertainty coefficient.

Ordinal Measures. Ordinal measures of association are appropriate when the two variables in the contingency table both have order.

- *Gamma.* This statistic ranges between –1 and 1 and is interpreted similarly to a Pearson's correlation. For two-way tables, zero-order gammas are displayed. For three-way to *n*-way tables, conditional gammas are displayed.
- *Somer's* d. This measure of association ranges between –1 and 1. It is an asymmetric extension of gamma. Asymmetric values are generated according to which variable is considered to be the dependent variable.

- *Kendall's tau-b*. A measure of correlation for ordinal or ranked measures where ties are taken into account. It is most appropriate when the number of columns and rows is equal. Values range from −1 to 1.
- *Kendall's tau-c*. This is similar to tau-b, except this measure ignores ties.

Eta. This is a measure of association that is appropriate when the dependent variable is a quantitative measure (such as age or income) and the independent variable is categorical (nominal or ordinal). Eta ranges from 0 to 1, with low values indicating less association and high values indicating a high degree of association. SPSS calculates two eta values, one that treats the row variable as the quantitative variable and one that treats the column variable as the quantitative variable.

Summary

This chapter explains how to analyze categorical data using a variety of techniques for measuring association and goodness-of-fit. The following chapter examines a comparison of three or more means.

References

Bickel, P. J., & O'Connell, J. W. (1975). Is there a sex bias in graduate admissions? *Science, 187*, 398–404.

Cochran, W. G. (1954). Some methods for strengthening the common chi-square test. *Biometrics, 10*, 417–451.

Fleiss, J. L. (2000). *Statistical methods for rates & proportions* (2nd ed.). New York: John Wiley.

Hunt, M. (1997). *How science takes stock: The story of meta-analysis.* New York: Russell Sage Foundation.

Lipsey, M. W., & Wilson, D. (2000). *Practical meta-analysis.* Thousand Oaks, CA: Sage.

6

Analysis of Variance
and Covariance

Sometimes, that "keep it simple" principle just doesn't meet your needs. Occasionally, you've got to make the leap from simple models to the more complex. This chapter takes the leap from the *t*-test to a series of tests designed to compare three or more means at a time or to compare means that are adjusted by some covariate. And even though it's a bit more involved than the *t*-test chapter, we'll try to keep it as simple and straightforward as possible. Specifically, this chapter discusses the following analyses:

- *One-Way Analysis of Variance (ANOVA):* an extension of the two-sample *t*-test used to determine whether there are differences among more than two group means
- *One-Way Analysis of Variance With a Test for Trend:* used to test for a polynomial trend in the group means
- *Two-Way Analysis of Variance:* used to evaluate the combined effect of two experimental factors
- *Repeated-Measures Analysis of Variance:* an extension of the paired *t*-test for comparing means of the same or related subjects or objects over time or in differing circumstances
- *Analysis of Covariance:* a one-way ANOVA in which the group means are adjusted by a covariate

These sections include discussion of multiple comparisons and graphs where appropriate. Although this chapter covers the most commonly used analysis of variance models, there are in fact a smorgasbord of analyses that can be classified under this umbrella. However, if you find that your experimental design goes beyond what is covered here, or if you do not understand how these models work, we suggest that you check out the references at the end of the chapter. Even better advice is to consult a statistician.

One-Way ANOVA

The one-way ANOVA (also called a one-factor ANOVA or completely randomized design) is a staple of almost every research discipline. It is widely used and, as you will see, relatively easy to perform and interpret. This model is a direct extension of the two-sample (independent group) *t*-test covered in Chapter 3: Comparing One or Two Means Using the *t*-Test. It is used to determine whether there are differences among the group means.

Appropriate Applications for a One-Way ANOVA

Examples of research that might use this design include the following:

- *Length of Hospital Stay.* Anorexic patients in a psychiatric ward are randomly grouped into a control treatment group (standard treatment) and two experimental treatment groups to determine whether either of the two experimental treatments reduces the average length of stay.
- *Is Acme the Best Brand?* The shear strengths of bolts manufactured by four different companies are compared to establish whether there are differences in the average shear strength.
- *What Is Best Package Color?* A marketing study attempts to find out whether average sales are different for three choices of packaging color.

Design Considerations for a One-Way ANOVA

The design of a one-way ANOVA is similar to that for a two-sample (independent group) *t*-test, except that there are more than two groups. The key factors in designing such an analysis include the following.

The One-Way ANOVA Assumptions

1. *Independent Samples.* The groups contain observed subjects (or objects) that are split into groups but are not paired or matched in any way. The groups are typically obtained in one of two ways:

a. *Random Split.* Subjects (or items) all come from the same population and are *randomly* split into groups. Each group is exposed to identical conditions, except for a "treatment" that may be a medical treatment, a marketing design factor, exposure to a stimulus, and so on.

b. *Random Selection.* Subjects are randomly selected from separate populations (i.e., by race, stores by region, machine by manufacturer, etc.).

2. *Normality.* A standard assumption for the one-way ANOVA to be valid is that the measurement variable is normally distributed within each group. That is, when graphed as a histogram, the shape approximates a bell curve (see Chapter 2: Describing and Examining Data).

3. *Equal Variances.* Another assumption is that the within-group variances are the same for each of the groups.

- *How Stringent Are These Assumptions?* As in the case of the *t*-test discussed in Chapter 3, studies have shown the one-way ANOVA to be robust against some departures from assumptions. Generally, nonnormality of the data is not a concern unless you have small sample sizes or your data are highly nonnormal. If you have equal or near-equal sample sizes in each group, the equal variance assumption becomes less important. However, the assumption of independence of the subjects is critical (Glass, Peckham, & Sanders, 1972).
- *An ANOVA Compares Means.* Your outcome variable must be a quantitative variable such as height, weight, amount spent, or grade.
- *Control Group.* The groups to be compared may or may not include a control group. That is, one "control" group may receive a standard treatment or no treatment, while the others receive experimental treatments. If the experimental treatments are better than the control, then this may add more credibility to their use than if they are simply compared to other experimental groups.
- *Predefined Comparisons.* The experimenter may have a special interest in certain comparisons among group means. These can be tested using contrasts. This topic is discussed later in this chapter.
- *Are Group Sample Sizes Equal?* The sample sizes in each group need not be equal, but if they are not equal, then care must often be taken when performing the post hoc analysis, as will be demonstrated in EXAMPLE 6.1. In general, it is usually best to design your experiment so there are an equal (or almost equal) number of subjects in each group.
- *Are the Groups Ordered?* If groups have an inherent ordering such as age groups (0–15, 16–30, 31–50, 51 and above), torque pressure (mild, medium, strong), or dose (four increasingly strong levels), then your analysis could include an analysis of trend. The analysis in EXAMPLE 6.2 includes a trend analysis.

Hypotheses for a One-Way ANOVA

The hypotheses for the comparison of the means in a one-way ANOVA are as follows:

H_0: $\mu_1 = \mu_2 = \ldots = \mu_k$ (the population means of the all groups are the same).

H_a: $\mu_i \neq \mu_j$ for some $i \neq j$ (the population means of at least two groups are different).

Tips and Caveats for a One-Way ANOVA

• *Sample Size Considerations.* Inadequate sample sizes can result in a test without adequate power and can result in a nonsignificant finding, even if there are real differences in the group population means. Also, small sample sizes cause the normality assumption to be more important and more difficult to assess.

• *Why Not Simply Do Several t-Tests?* Since a one-way ANOVA usually involves examining pairwise comparisons, you may wonder why you would not simply perform the *t*-tests in the first place and make the analysis simpler. These comparisons are done within the context of an ANOVA to control the level of significance. For example, if you took four independent samples from the same population (i.e., the null hypothesis is true) and made all possible comparisons using *t*-tests, then there would be six total comparisons, each performed at the 0.05 level of significance. However, using this procedure, it can be shown that there is a $1 - (0.95)^6 = 0.26$ probability that at least one of the six comparisons will result in a finding of a significant difference. That is, there is a 0.26 probability of rejecting the null hypothesis (which in this case is true). That is, the overall significance level is no longer 0.05. By using the controlled environment of the one-way ANOVA, you preserve the error rate for the experiment. No knowledgeable reviewer would let a paper or article pass in which multiple *t*-tests are used in lieu of an appropriate ANOVA. See Chapter 1: Introduction for more discussion of these issues.

EXAMPLE 6.1: One-Way ANOVA

Describing the Problem

A university is experimenting with teaching a statistics course using three different methods, including the classical 3-day-a-week lecture, 1-day-a-week lecture plus CD lessons (including taped lectures), and 1-day–a-week lecture plus online (Internet) tutorials. Students are randomly placed into one of the three methods, and all three methods are taught by the same instructor. Identical 100-point final exams are given to each section of the course. We will use the one-way ANOVA to compare the average learning (as measured by the final exam) for these three types of classes. Although it is highly desirable to have the same sample size in each group, it often doesn't work out that way in practice. In this example, 98 students signed up for the course, which means that the three groups will not have equal sample sizes if we use all of the students.

Before performing the analysis, you should check out the assumptions listed earlier. Because there are at least 32 subjects in each group, the question of normality for each group is not a major concern. The students in each section are independent and randomly assigned. To consider the question of equal variances, you could examine the descriptive statistics for each group. For these data, the following descriptive statistics were produced, as shown in Table 6.1

Table 6.1   Descriptive Statistics for a One-Way ANOVA

Descriptives

GRADE

	N	Mean	Std. Deviation	Std. Error	95% Confidence Interval for Mean		Minimum	Maximum
					Lower Bound	Upper Bound		
Standard	33	83.5455	10.16148	1.76889	79.9424	87.1486	58.00	100.00
Internet	32	74.4688	12.70251	2.24551	69.8890	79.0485	45.00	94.00
CD Lessons	33	78.7879	12.60644	2.19450	74.3178	83.2579	49.00	100.00
Total	98	78.9796	12.32379	1.24489	76.5088	81.4504	45.00	100.00

Notice that the standard deviations are 10.16, 12.70, and 12.61, which lend credence to the assumption of equal variances (remember that the variance is the square of the standard deviation). For further confirmation, a statistical test such as Levene's test for homogeneity of variances may be used. In this case, Levene's test yields a nonsignificant $p = 0.23$ for the comparison of these three variances.

Good advice is to examine a graph of your results, even if you do not intend to include a graph with your final report. Side-by-side boxplots (Figure 6.1) and a graph of means can be used to give a visual comparison of the groups. In Figure 6.1, we see that there is no evidence of any sizable outliers and that there is no obvious difference in variability for the three groups. The graph also shows that the final exam scores for the standard course were somewhat higher in general than for the two newer teaching methods but that there was considerable overlap between the distributions.

Until further analysis, we cannot draw conclusions about significance of the differences in the mean final exam scores for the three methods.

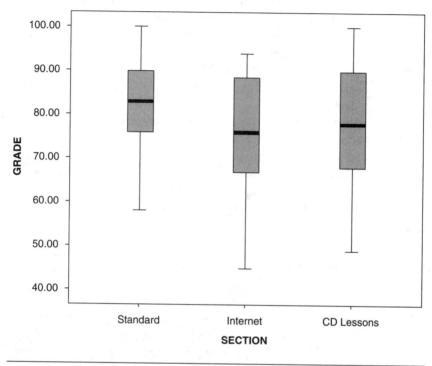

Figure 6.1   Boxplots for Course Data

Since there are no apparent violations of the assumptions, we next examine the ANOVA table in Table 6.2. This table provides an omnibus test of equality of means (labeled the "between-group" test). In this case, the ANOVA table reports an F-statistic of 4.754 with 2 and 95 degrees of freedom and $p = 0.011$. Because this p-value is less than 0.05, we reject the null hypothesis that all means are equal and conclude that there are some differences among the means. If the p-value had been nonsignificant, we would not conclude that there are differences in the means. No further multiple comparisons would be performed.

Failing to reject the null hypothesis does not indicate a finding that there are no differences among the means. It simply indicates that we have been unable to detect differences. See the section in Chapter 1 titled "Understanding Hypothesis Testing, Power, and Sample Size."

Table 6.2   ANOVA Table for COURSE.SAV Data

ANOVA

GRADE

	Sum of Squares	df	Mean Square	F	Sig.
Between Groups	1340.293	2	670.147	4.754	.011
Within Groups	13391.666	95	140.965		
Total	14731.959	97			

Since this ANOVA table indicates an overall significant difference among means, we now further investigate these differences using multiple comparisons. In this case, with three groups, there are three possible comparisons: standard versus Internet, standard versus CD, and Internet versus CD.

There is an alphabet soup of multiple comparison tests available (most named after the statistician who came up with the technique). These include tests by the names of Tukey, Bonferroni, Duncan, Scheffé, R-E-G-W-F, and others. These tests each have their own characteristics (e.g., Bonferroni's test is quite conservative), and there are many opinions about which test to use and when. In this example, we limit our discussion to the use of Tukey's procedure to exemplify the technique. In practice, you may want to consider others. You may want to familiarize yourself with your discipline's literature to find out which techniques are commonly used.

Most common of all post hoc tests are a comparison of all possible pairs of means. These are called multiple comparison tests. The multiple comparison results, based on the Tukey procedure, are reported in Tables 6.3 and 6.4. Using this procedure, two means are considered to be significantly different if the absolute difference in their corresponding sample means is greater than a specific threshold value. When sample sizes are equal, the formula for this threshold value involves this common sample size. When the sample sizes are not equal, the harmonic mean of the corresponding sample sizes is typically used. Note that the harmonic mean is reported in Table 6.4. For a discussion of potential concerns associated with unequal cell sizes in two-way ANOVA, refer to Elliott and Woodward (1986).

The sample means, in ascending order, are given in Table 6.4. There it can be seen that based on this criterion, the standard classes and Internet classes are significantly different while the other two comparisons (i.e., standard vs. CD and CD vs. Internet) are not significant. The results are displayed in Table 6.3 in a format that is often used for reporting the differences and can be quickly understood at a glance. Specifically, any two means that are underscored by the same line are not significantly different from each other.

In Table 6.4, we show the SPSS output for this analysis. This output refers to the groups that are not significantly different from each other as subsets. Thus, Internet and CD formed one subset, while CD and standard formed the other subset. Since Internet and standard do not both appear in the same subset, they are significantly different from each other. Spend a moment to see how Table 6.3 and Table 6.4 are reporting the same results. Notice that SPSS warns that unequal sample sizes may compromise the results. In this case, with the sample sizes nearly equal, this is not an important concern.

Table 6.3   Tukey Multiple Comparison Results

Standard	CD	Internet
83.5455	78.7879	74.4688

Table 6.4   Tukey Multiple Comparison Results as Reported by SPSS

GRADE

Tukey HSD[a,b]

SECTION	N	Subset for alpha = .05	
		1	2
Internet	32	74.4688	
CD Lessons	33	78.7879	78.7879
Standard	33		83.5455
Sig.		.310	.243

Means for groups in homogeneous subsets are displayed.
a. Uses Harmonic Mean Sample Size = 32.660.
b. The group sizes are unequal. The harmonic mean of the group sizes is used. Type I error levels are not guaranteed.

To summarize, the overall ANOVA table results reported that at the $p = 0.011$ level of significance, there was at least one mean that was different from the rest. The post hoc Tukey test (performed at the 0.05 level of significance) examined all possible pairwise comparisons and determined that there was a statistically significant difference in the mean scores of the standard and Internet groups. Specifically, the standard teaching method seems to have better average final exam performance than use of the Internet. The standard method also has a higher mean score than the CD method, although the difference is not significant.

Reporting Results of a One-Way ANOVA

The following illustrates how you might report these one-way ANOVA results in a publication format.

Narrative for the Methods Section

"A one-way ANOVA was performed to test the hypothesis that the average final grades for the three course sections were equal. Multiple comparisons were performed using the Tukey procedure."

Narrative for the Results Section

"The average grades were found to be different across sections, $F(2, 95) = 4.95$, $p = 0.011$. Tukey multiple comparisons performed at a 0.05 significance level found that the average grade for the standard section is significantly higher than that for the Internet section."

Or, to be more complete,

"The average grades were found to be different across sections, $F(2, 95) = 4.95$, $p = 0.011$. The Tukey multiple comparisons performed at the 0.05 significance level found that the mean final exam grade for the standard course section ($M = 83.5$, $SD = 10.16$, $N = 33$) was significantly higher than that for the Internet section ($M = 74.5$, $SD = 12.7$, $N = 32$) but not significantly higher than the CD section ($M = 78.8$, $SD = 12.6$, $N = 33$). Mean exam grades for the CD and Internet sections were not found to be significantly different from each other."

Other Comparison Tests for a One-Way ANOVA

There are times when the standard "all-possible multiple comparisons" tests for a one-way ANOVA are not really what you want. Three alternatives to the all-possible comparisons are briefly discussed here:

- Dunnett's test
- Specified contrasts
- Trend analysis

Dunnett's Test. Dunnett's test is appropriate when the purpose of your analysis is to compare one group (usually the standard or control) against all other groups. For instance, in the previous example, we were interested in comparing all courses with each other. However, the real interest may be only the comparison between the standard course and the new methods. Thus, the standard method would be the control group to which the other two methods are compared. The preliminary analysis of variance would be performed exactly as above, and Dunnett's test is a post hoc test designed specifically for comparing treatment groups to a control group. It should be noted that for Dunnett's test, you can use two-sided or one-sided tests. In this example, we will use a two-sided test if there is a question concerning whether to expect the new sections to do better or worse. The Dunnett's test results are shown in Table 6.5.

Table 6.5   Dunnett's Test Results

Multiple Comparisons

Dependent Variable: GRADE
Dunnett t (2-sided)[a]

(I) SECTION	(J) SECTION	Mean Difference (I-J)	Std. Error	Sig.	95% Confidence Interval	
					Lower Bound	Upper Bound
Internet	Standard	-9.07670*	2.94564	.005	-15.6923	-2.4611
CD Lessons	Standard	-4.75758	2.92290	.187	-11.3221	1.8069

*. The mean difference is significant at the .05 level.
a. Dunnett t-tests treat one group as a control, and compare all other groups against it.

The results reported in Table 6.5 are specifically for the comparison of the Internet and CD sections against the standard section. The "Sig." column shows that there is a significant difference between the Internet section and the standard section ($p = 0.005$) but no difference between the CD section and the standard ($p = 0.187$). These findings are consistent with those obtained using Tukey multiple comparisons previously.

Contrasts for a One-Way ANOVA. In some cases, you may simply want to examine certain specific group comparisons. Customized comparisons (planned contrasts) can be built around specific comparisons rather than simply investigating all-pairwise comparisons that are typical of the post hoc multiple comparison procedures. For example, suppose in the "course data" experiment, our alternative hypothesis is that the standard teaching method results in a higher mean final exam grade than the other two methods. That is, we want to compare the standard group with the two experimental groups in one comparison. To do that, we would need to combine, in some sense, the experimental groups. Thus, our comparison becomes the standard group versus the average of the experimental groups, and the null hypothesis of interest is H_0: $\mu_S = (\mu_I + \mu_C)/2$; that is, H_0: $\mu_S - (\mu_I + \mu_C)/2 = 0$, where μ_S, μ_I, and μ_C denote the population means for the standard, Internet, and CD sections, respectively.

A contrast is a weighted sum of means. The tricky part in designing a contrast is to assign weights (called contrast codes) to each group. These weights specify how the comparison will be made. In general, you assign a positive weight to one group or groups and negative weights to the remaining groups so that the weights add to zero. Based on the second form of the null hypothesis in the preceding paragraph, it makes sense to assign a weight (i.e., contrast code) of 1 to the standard group and a –0.5 to each of the other teaching methods. Multiplying a set of contrast codes by a constant gives another set of contrast codes that will also be appropriate. For example, you could also use 2 for the standard group and a –1 to each of the other teaching methods. Results based on the contrast codes 1, –0.5, –0.5 are shown in Table 6.6.

Table 6.6   Contrasts for Course Data

Contrast Tests

		Contrast	Value of Contrast	Std. Error	t	df	Sig. (2-tailed)
GRADE	Assume equal variances	1	6.9171	2.53789	2.726	95	.008
	Does not assume equal	1	6.9171	2.36506	2.925	77.731	.005

Two versions of the contrast are given, one that assumes equal variances and one that does not. Since we have already examined the variances and found them similar, the equal variances test is sufficient. In this case, $p = 0.008$ so we conclude that the mean grade of the standard course is different (higher) than the mean grades of the other two methods combined. If there is any question about the equality of variances, you should use the unequal variance option, which in this case gives a smaller p-value ($p = 0.005$) but leads to the same conclusion.

SPSS Step-by-Step. EXAMPLE 6.1: One-Way ANOVA

To perform a one-way ANOVA on the teaching method data, follow these instructions in SPSS:

1. Open the data set COURSES.SAV and select **Analyze/Compare Means/one-way ANOVA.**

2. Select *Section* as the factor and *Grade* as the dependent variable.

3. Click Options to select the means plot and descriptive statistics and click Continue.

4. Click Post Hoc to select the Tukey multiple comparison test (or whichever you choose) or the Dunnett's test. If you select the Dunnett's test, also select First as the Control category. Click Continue.

5. Click Contrasts to specify the contrast in the example above. Enter the coefficients (1, –0.5, –0.5) in the order of the sections. That is, enter 1 in the Coefficients text box and click Add, then enter –0.5 and Add, and –0.5 and Add to specify the complete contrast. Click Continue.

To create the side-by-side boxplots in Figure 6.1, use the following steps:

6. Using the COURSES.SAV data set, select **Graph/Boxplot/ Simple. . . .**

7. Select *Grade* as the variable and *Section* for the category axis.

8. Click OK, and the plot shown in Figure 6.1 will be displayed.

EXAMPLE 6.2: One-Way ANOVA With Trend Analysis

Describing the Problem

A wholesale nursery is experimenting with a plant supplement that is designed to increase the number of flowers produced on a plant. To determine whether the supplement works and what strength to use, the nursery randomly selects 12 plants for five different commercially available strengths (1 to 5) of the supplement. After 2 weeks, the number of opened flowers per plant is counted. Table 6.7 gives the number of flowers counted for the 60 plants. It should be noted that there is no pairing in the data in this table. For example, the first entry under Strength 1 is not related in any way to the first entry under Strength 2.

We present this table here to make a point that will be clearer in the next section. For this example, notice that the way the data are presented in Table 6.7 is not the format in which it should be entered into the computer program. Rule 2 in "Guidelines for Creating Data Sets" given in Chapter 1 states that (usually) each line (row) of your data should contain the observations from a single subject. Each row in Table 6.7 contains observations from 5 separate plants that are not related to each other in any way. In general, the 60 observations in that table represent 60 randomly selected plants. The computer data file structure for a one-way ANOVA should take the form shown in Figure 6.2, which contains one subject (plant) per row and contains a "grouping" variable called *Strength* to indicate the concentration

Table 6.7   One-Way ANOVA Data for EXAMPLE 6.2

		Strength		
1	2	3	4	5
25	45	51	45	56
36	36	38	54	43
41	40	38	45	49
39	32	48	44	40
28	37	45	47	53
44	28	50	52	57
36	32	46	59	56
33	38	45	59	38
40	44	42	54	45
26	40	48	59	57
42	45	49	51	42
41	39	36	54	55

of the supplement that was used for that plant. For this data set, there are 60 rows, one for each plant.

What makes this analysis different from a typical one-way ANOVA is that the groups have an order (i.e., the strength 1 to 5). For this case, you may want to perform a trend analysis rather than use nonordered pairwise comparisons. A trend analysis tests the hypothesis that the means of the ordered groups change in a linear or higher order (e.g., quadratic or cubic) fashion. Figure 6.3 shows a plot of the mean number of flowers for each supplement strength.

It appears that the number of flowers increases as the strength of the supplement increases (up to a point). A test for a linear, quadratic, and cubic trend is shown in Table 6.8. A quadratic trend is one that has a consistent curving pattern either upward or downward, while a cubic trend is characterized by a shift in curvature from upward to downward or vice versa.

In this analysis, the "Between (Combined)" test is the same as the standard ANOVA test, and it shows that there is a difference among means across levels of strength ($p = 0.000$). The "Linear Term Contrast" test is a test that there is a linear trend ($p = 0.000$). "Deviation" ($p = 0.038$) tests for the existence of a more complex trend. In this case, the results indicate

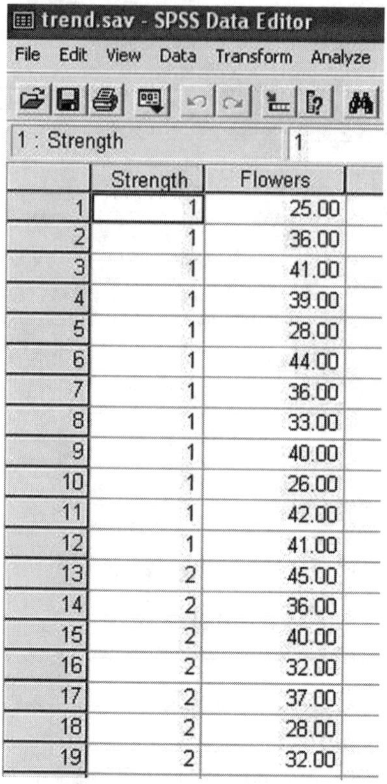

trend.sav - SPSS Data Editor

File   Edit   View   Data   Transform   Analyze

1 : Strength   1

	Strength	Flowers
1	1	25.00
2	1	36.00
3	1	41.00
4	1	39.00
5	1	28.00
6	1	44.00
7	1	36.00
8	1	33.00
9	1	40.00
10	1	26.00
11	1	42.00
12	1	41.00
13	2	45.00
14	2	36.00
15	2	40.00
16	2	32.00
17	2	37.00
18	2	28.00
19	2	32.00

Figure 6.2   Data Entered for a One-Way ANOVA

that there is a more complex trend than linear. Therefore, we go to the quadratic trend and find that there is not a significant quadratic (single-curve) trend ($p = 0.176$), but there is still a more complex trend ($p = 0.035$). That more complex trend is the cubic term ($p = 0.011$) and nothing more complex ($p = .657$). The results of this analysis suggest that there is a somewhat linear increase in mean flower production as the level of the supplement increases. The cubic term suggests (from examination of the plot) that there is a faster increase as the strength is increased from 2 to 3 and a downturn in flower production when the strength reaches 5.

SPSS Step-by-Step. EXAMPLE 6.2: One-Way ANOVA With Trend Analysis

To perform the example on the TREND.SAV data set, follow these instructions:

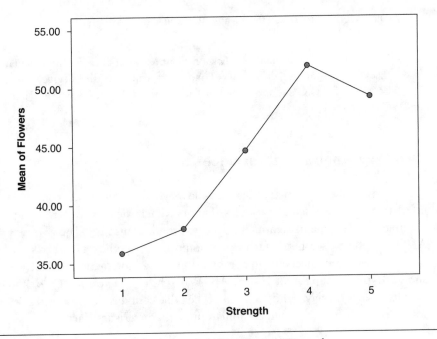

Figure 6.3   Mean Number of Flowers by Supplement Strength

Table 6.8   Test for Trend

ANOVA

Flowers

			Sum of Squares	df	Mean Square	F	Sig.
Between Groups	(Combined)		2304.100	4	576.025	15.851	.000
	Linear Term	Contrast	1976.408	1	1976.408	54.385	.000
		Deviation	327.692	3	109.231	3.006	.038
	Quadratic Term	Contrast	68.149	1	68.149	1.875	.176
		Deviation	259.543	2	129.771	3.571	.035
	Cubic Term	Contrast	252.300	1	252.300	6.943	.011
		Deviation	7.243	1	7.243	.199	.657
Within Groups			1998.750	55	36.341		
Total			4302.850	59			

1. Open the data set TREND.SAV and select **Analyze/Compare Means/one-way ANOVA.** (Notice how the data set is set up with one flower per row and with *Strength* as a grouping [factor] variable.)

2. Select *Strength* for factor and *Flowers* for the dependent variable.

3. Click Options to select the means plot and descriptive statistics and click Continue.

4. To specify the trend analysis, click on Contrasts and click the Polynomial checkbox. From the drop-down box, select Cubic as the degree. Click Continue and OK, and the output in Table 6.8 and the means plot in Figure 6.3 appear.

Two-Way Analysis of Variance

A two-way ANOVA is an analysis that allows you to evaluate the combined effect of two experimental variables (factors). Each factor is a "grouping" variable such as type of treatment, gender, brand, and so on. The two-way ANOVA tests to see if the factors are important (significant) either separately (called main effects) or in combination (via an interaction). Table 6.9 shows a typical setup for a two-way ANOVA. The two factors are *Color* and *Height* of sales displays, and each cell of the table contains the observed sales for a display containing each combination of characteristics (factors.)

Table 6.9   Two-Way ANOVA Data

Height/Color	Blue	Red	Black
Short	24	31	35
	25	28	32
	30	33	31
	28	35	38
	25	32	35
Tall	31	36	41
	32	32	36
	33	33	34
	36	41	32
	32	34	39

It is important to point out that this design, like the one-way ANOVA above, is based on the assumption that the observations in the cells are independent within and between cells. There are no repeated objects or subjects in any factor combination. Sometimes a two-way ANOVA is referred to as a $p \times q$ factorial design, where there are p levels of one factor and q levels of the other.

Appropriate Applications for a Two-Way ANOVA

- *Discrimination?* How do age and gender affect the salaries of 10-year employees at a national department store?
- *Product Display Strategies.* A manufacturer who displays products for sale wants to understand how the height of a display and the color of the display (or the combined effects of both height and color) affect sales.
- *Effectiveness of Cholesterol-Lowering Drug.* Investigators want to know the effects of dosage and gender on the effectiveness of a cholesterol-lowering drug.

Design Considerations for a Two-Way ANOVA

When conducting a two-way ANOVA, there are several design considerations you should keep in mind. Most of these are extensions of those mentioned previously for the one-way ANOVA. These include the following:

Two-Way ANOVA Assumptions

1. *Independent Samples.* Subjects should be randomly assigned to treatment combinations, that is, to the $p \times q$ possible combinations of factors (cells). Observations are independent in that there are no repeated objects or subjects in any factor combination.

2. *Normality.* Data within each cell of the design are assumed to be normally distributed.

3. *Equal Variances.* The population variances within each combination of factors should be equal.

- *How Stringent Are the Assumptions?* As in the previous discussion for the one-way ANOVA, studies have shown that ANOVA models are robust against moderate departures from the assumptions of normality and equal variances. In particular, the ANOVA is quite robust to the equal variance assumption if the cell sizes are equal or nearly equal (Glass et al., 1972). As with the *t*-test and one-way ANOVA, the assumption of independence of the subjects is critically important.
- *Comparing Means.* Your outcome variable must be a quantitative variable such as height, weight, amount spent, or grade.
- *Are Sample Sizes Equal for Each Cell?* The sample sizes in each group do not have to be equal, but if they are not, then care must often be taken in performing the analysis.
- *Are Factor Categories Random or Fixed?* In this guidebook, we discuss only a fixed factor analysis. That is, the factor levels are selected by the experimenter, such as a selection of specific doses of an experimental drug. In some

cases, factor categories are randomly selected from a larger list of possible categories (a random selection of cities, for example). Random effects models and mixed models, i.e., with fixed and random effects, are not discussed here. For a discussion of random effects or mixed models, we recommend Winer (1991); Neter, Wasserman, and Kutner (1990); and Keppel and Wickens (2004).

Hypotheses for a Two-Way ANOVA

The statistical model for the two-way ANOVA includes the main effects (i.e., the additive effects of each factor) along with an interaction effect. Interaction measures the extent to which the combined effects of the factors are *not* additive. To illustrate the effect of interaction, suppose your outcome variable is annual income (in $1,000) and your two factors are gender and job category, as shown in Figure 6.4, where the four means (hourly-male, hourly-female, salaried-male, salaried-female) are plotted for two hypothetical scenarios.

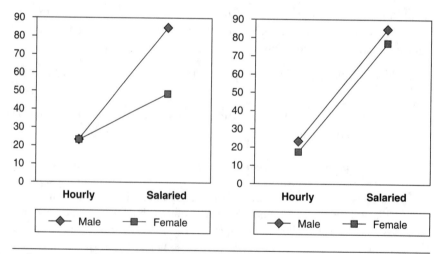

Figure 6.4   Interaction Plots

The right-hand graph illustrates a situation in which the combined effects of the two factors are additive and there is no interaction effect. In this case, the salaried employees (both male and female) make about $55,000 to $60,000 per year more than the corresponding hourly employees of the same sex. Also, for each job category, the males make $5,000 to $10,000 more per year than the female employees on average. The result of this additive behavior is that the lines are almost parallel.

The left-hand graph shows an interaction effect. Specifically, for hourly employees, males and females have approximately the same average salaries. However, for salaried employees, males make about $35,000 more per year on average. This behavior is known as an interaction, and in the presence of such an interaction, you cannot make a blanket statement comparing the effect of gender on salary that applies to both job types. Instead, if you want to discuss the effect of gender on salary, you will need to consider each job category separately. Similarly, the effect that employee type (hourly vs. salaried) has on salary is only really understood when it is considered separately for males and females.

If you do not have a significant interaction (such as the right-hand graph), you can meaningfully test the main effects of job type and gender. However, if you have a significant interaction, such blanket statements may be meaningless since these two factors are interrelated (i.e., they "interact").

The testing procedure in a two-way ANOVA is as follows:

1. First Test for Interaction

The interaction hypotheses are as follows:

H_0: There is no interaction effect.

H_a: There is an interaction effect.

2. Test for Main Effects

If there is not a significant interaction, then test the following hypotheses regarding main effects:

The "main effects" hypotheses are

a. For Factor A:

   H_0: Population means are equal across levels of Factor A.

   H_a: Population means are not equal across levels of Factor A.

b. For Factor B:

   H_0: Population means are equal across levels of Factor B.

   H_a: Population means are not equal across levels of Factor B.

These three tests (interaction and two main effects tests) are performed in an analysis of variance table as F-tests. A low p-value (usually less than 0.05) for a test indicates evidence to reject the null hypothesis in favor of the alternative. It may be useful to refer to a standard textbook on the subject (e.g., Neter et al., 1990; Winer, 1991) for more discussion of the actual statistical model.

Tips and Caveats for a Two-Way ANOVA

Unequal Sample Sizes Within Cells

A number of calculation and interpretation problems arise when you have an unequal number of observations in the cells of a two-way ANOVA. In SPSS, for example, if cell sizes are unequal, then it is important that the calculations be performed using the Type III ANOVA sum of squares (the default in SPSS). Small departures from equal cell sizes are not a serious concern, but you should examine why such unequal sizes exist. For example, if your sampling procedure has caused some values in some cells to be systematically eliminated, then you may be introducing bias into the model (see Elliott & Woodward, 1986).

Significant Interactions

If an interaction exists, the effects of the factors should not be interpreted in isolation from each other, and tests for main effects will often not be meaningful. It will usually be more appropriate, for example, to compare effects of the first factor within levels of the second factor and vice versa. That is, compare cell means rather than marginal means. A variety of methods could be used, including some that make use of the mean square error from the ANOVA table and others that involve considering each cell as a sample for use with an independent sample t-test. Bonferroni or some other adjustment is advisable. For more details, see Neter et al. (1990, p. 739) and Keppel and Wickens (2004).

If an interaction exists, the effects of the factors should not be interpreted in isolation from each other, and tests for main effects will often not be meaningful. It will usually be more appropriate, for example, to compare effects of the first factor within levels of the second factor and vice versa. That is, compare cell means rather than marginal means.

EXAMPLE 6.3: Two-Way ANOVA

Describing the Problem

A manufacturer of a consumer retail product wants to examine the effectiveness of display strategies on sales. Six different displays are designed, which include three different highlight colors (red, blue, and black) and two different heights: short (45 inches) and tall (60 inches). To compare sales for each combination of height and color, one of the six display combinations is randomly placed at each of five discount department stores, a total of 30 different locations. After 2 months, the sales from each combination are compared. The data for this analysis are given in Table 6.9, and we assume the data in each cell are normally distributed.

Descriptive statistics for the data are shown in Table 6.10. A test for homogeneity of variance within cells (Levene's test) gives $p = 0.654$, suggesting that the assumption of equal variances within cells is not a problem. You may also examine side-by-side boxplots of data within each color-height combination for a visual check of the homogeneity of variance assumption. The ANOVA table for this analysis is shown in Table 6.11.

Table 6.10   Descriptive Statistics for Two-Way ANOVA

Descriptive Statistics

Dependent Variable: Sales

Display Height	Display Color	Mean	Std. Deviation	N
Short	Blue	26.40	2.510	5
	Red	31.80	2.588	5
	Black	34.20	2.775	5
	Total	30.80	4.161	15
Tall	Blue	32.80	1.924	5
	Red	35.20	3.564	5
	Black	36.40	3.647	5
	Total	34.80	3.299	15
Total	Blue	29.60	3.978	10
	Red	33.50	3.440	10
	Black	35.30	3.268	10
	Total	32.80	4.213	30

To interpret the ANOVA table, you should first look at the interaction term (*Height* * *Color*). The nonsignificant $p = 0.268$ means that the interaction term is not significant. A graph to visually examine the possibility of an interaction effect is shown in Figure 6.5.

Table 6.11   Table for Two-Way ANOVA

Tests of Between-Subjects Effects

Dependent Variable: Sales

Source	Type III Sum of Squares	df	Mean Square	F	Sig.
Corrected Model	313.200[a]	5	62.640	7.457	.000
Intercept	32275.200	1	32275.200	3842.286	.000
HEIGHT	120.000	1	120.000	14.286	.001
COLOR	169.800	2	84.900	10.107	.001
HEIGHT * COLOR	23.400	2	11.700	1.393	.268
Error	201.600	24	8.400		
Total	32790.000	30			
Corrected Total	514.800	29			

a. R Squared = .608 (Adjusted R Squared = .527)

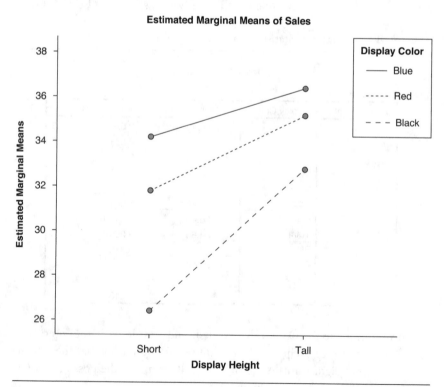

Estimated Marginal Means of Sales

Figure 6.5   Graph of Two-Way Interactions

The lines showing the means for sales by height and color are fairly close to parallel (as measured by the interaction p-value [$p = 0.268$]), so the assumption of no interaction (i.e., that the effects are additive) seems plausible. Thus, it is appropriate to test for main effects, that is, to compare sales by color and sales by height. This graph helps explain the main effects tests. Before examining the statistical results, note that from the table, it can be seen that tall displays tend to have higher sales (at all colors) and that at each height, black displays yield the highest average sale followed by red and blue, in that order. The significance of these differences will be examined below.

The main effect for height is significant ($F = 14.286$ with 1 and 24 degrees of freedom, $p = 0.001$). This indicates that there is a statistically significant difference in sales by height. Thus, taller displays produced significantly greater sales. It should be noted that post hoc tests are not needed since there are only two levels of height.

The main effect for color is also significant ($F = 10.107$ with 2 and 24 degrees of freedom, $p = 0.001$). This indicates that there is a statistically significant difference in sales by color. However, post hoc tests are needed to determine which differences are significant, although it is a safe conjecture that black displays (top line in Figure 6.5) are significantly higher than blue displays (bottom line). Table 6.12 shows the results of Tukey's test to identify specific differences. In the table, it can be seen that sales for red and black displays were not significantly different from each other, but both were significantly higher than sales for the blue display. A graphical display of the comparison results is shown in Table 6.13.

Table 6.12   Tukey Comparisons for Sales by Display Color in a Two-Way ANOVA

Sales

Tukey HSD[a,b]

Display Color	N	Subset	
		1	2
Blue	10	29.60	
Red	10		33.50
Black	10		35.30
Sig.		1.000	.362

Means for groups in homogeneous subsets are displayed.
Based on Type III Sum of Squares
The error term is Mean Square (Error) = 8.400
  a. Uses Harmonic Mean Sample Size = 10.000.
  b. Alpha = .05.

In summary, the conclusion from this analysis is that taller displays are better and that red and black displays are better than blue displays.

Table 6.13 Tukey Comparison Results in Graphical Form

Blue	Red	Black
29.6	33.5	35.3

Reporting the Results of a Two-Way ANOVA

The following illustrates how you might report these two-way ANOVA results in a publication format.

Narrative for the Methods Section

"A two-way ANOVA was performed to determine if there is a difference in average sales for displays with different heights or highlight colors. In the presence of a significant difference, multiple comparisons were performed using the Tukey procedure at the $\alpha = 0.05$ significance level."

Narrative for the Results Section

"The test for interaction was not significant, $F(2, 24) = 1.393, p = 0.268$. Since there was no significant interaction, we tested main effects. The main effect for height was significant, $F(1, 24) = 14.286, p = 0.001$, where it is seen that taller displays have higher average sales. The main effect for color was also significant, $F(2, 24) = 10.107, p = 0.001$. Multiple comparisons using Tukey's test indicate that black and red displays have higher average sales than blue displays. Statistics are displayed in Table 6.14."

Table 6.14 Example Table Showing Descriptive Statistics for a Two-Way ANOVA

Height/Color	Blue		Red		Black		Marginal	
	Mean	SD	Mean	SD	Mean	SD	Mean	SD
Short	26.4	2.51	31.8	2.59	34.2	2.78	30.8	4.17
Tall	32.8	1.92	35.2	3.56	36.4	3.65	34.8	3.30
Marginal	29.6	3.98	33.5	3.44	35.3	3.27	32.8	4.21

NOTE: N for each cell is 5.

SPSS Step-by-Step. EXAMPLE *6.3: Two-Way ANOVA*

The output for the analysis can be obtained by following these instructions in SPSS:

1. Open the data set named DISPLAY.SAV and select **Analyze/General Linear Models/Univariate.** . . .

2. Select *Sales* as the dependent variable and *Height* and *Color* as fixed factors.

3. Click on Plots and select *Height* for the horizontal axis and *Color* for separate lines and click Add. Next select *Color* for the horizontal axis and *Height* for separate lines and click Add. Click Continue.

4. Click Post Hoc test and select *Color* for post hoc tests. Select the Tukey (or your favorite test under the equal variances assumed list). We won't need a post hoc comparison for *Height* since there are only two heights. Click Continue.

5. Click Options and select means for *Height, Color,* and *Height*Color.* Select Descriptive Statistics and whatever other statistics you desire. Click Continue. Click OK to produce the output (and more) that was used in the Display Example.

Table 6.14, which contains summary statistics, was created using a word processor. If you have a version of SPSS that contains the Tables add-in, you can create a similar table using that procedure.

Repeated-Measures Analysis of Variance

A repeated-measures ANOVA (and its close cousin, the randomized complete block design, or sometimes called the randomized block design) is an extension of the paired *t*-test in the sense that observations are paired or linked together. The one-way and two-way ANOVA models discussed previously are sometimes referred to as "independent group" ANOVAs since there is no such pairing. In a repeated-measures ANOVA, observations are taken from the same or related subjects or objects over time or in differing circumstances. (In the randomized complete block design, we consider several "blocks" of subjects or objects that are similar in some respect. Then within a block, investigators randomly assign each treatment so that a different treatment is applied to each subject or object within the block.)

Appropriate Applications for a Repeated-Measures ANOVA

- *Which Drug Is Best?* Four drugs to control high blood pressure are given to a group of individuals. Each subject receives the drugs in a random order with a washout period between doses.

- *What Type of Music Increases Sales?* A study is designed to study the effects of playing background music in grocery stores. Ten stores participate in the study, and three music genres are tested (country, hip-hop, and oldies). Each store cycles through the three genres in a randomly assigned order, using each genre for a 1-month period. The researcher wants to know if the music selection influences sales.
- *Effectiveness of Gasoline Additive.* Five different gasoline additives are compared regarding their ability to improve gas mileage. Four cars are chosen for testing, and each additive is used once for each car.

Design Considerations for a Repeated-Measures ANOVA

Repeated Measurements May Increase the Ability to Detect Differences

An advantage of a repeated-measures design is that each subject acts as his or her own control, and this can increase the ability to detect differences. That is, suppose a measurement is to be made on the cholesterol level at four time points (1 month, 3 months, 6 months, 1 year) after receiving a particular statin drug. Suppose we want 10 cholesterol readings at each of the four times. One method for doing this would be to use one-way ANOVA and select 40 patients on the medication and randomly select 10 to have their cholesterol readings taken at the end of 1 month, select 10 other patients to have cholesterol readings at the end of 3 months, and so on. This is clearly a poor design since any time differences in cholesterol readings may be obscured by the patient-to-patient variability in cholesterol levels. It makes more sense to take, say, 10 patients and measure each patient at the four times (repeated-measures design). Using this method, we more directly measure the effect of the medication over time.

Two Steps in the Analysis

As in the one-way ANOVA, the analysis has two steps. First, an *F*-test is used to test for a significant difference among the means across the repeated measure. If a difference is detected, then post hoc tests are used to determine where the differences lie.

Normality and Equal Variance Assumptions

The repeated-measures ANOVA assumes that the outcome measure is a normal variable and that the variances across repeated measures are equal. As with other versions of the ANOVA, the test is robust against moderate departures from the assumptions of normality and equality of variances. An additional assumption is that of sphericity, which assumes that the pairwise differences between treatment levels all have equal population variances. Mauchly's test for sphericity is commonly used to test this assumption (see Keppel & Wickens, 2004).

Randomization

This model also assumes that the participants are randomly selected from the population of interest.

Hypotheses for a Repeated-Measures ANOVA

The primary hypotheses for a repeated-measures ANOVA are written as follows:

H_0: There is no difference among means of the repeated measures.

H_a: At least one pair of repeated means are different.

Tips and Caveats for a Repeated-Measures ANOVA

- *Don't Confuse One-Way ANOVA Types.* Be careful not to confuse an independent group (i.e., one-way and two-way) ANOVA with a repeated-measures ANOVA. Use of an independent group ANOVA procedure to analyze data that should be analyzed as a repeated measure is incorrect—don't do it.
- *Sample Size.* As with other analyses, small sample sizes can lead to nonsignificant results even when a difference exists (see Moher, Dulberg, & Wells, 1994).

EXAMPLE 6.4: Repeated-Measures ANOVA

Description of Problem

A researcher is interested in comparing four different drugs that are believed to temporarily reduce the amount of snoring. Eight patients are given the drugs in a random order for 1 week. The number of minutes snoring was compared to the results of each individual's previous sleep test (baseline), and a snoring index was calculated where 100 means no reduction from baseline, less than 100 is a decrease, and more than 100 is an increase. Between each episode of drug therapy, there is a 1-week period of washout with no drug. Figure 6.6 shows the SPSS data file, and Figure 6.7 shows a graph of the mean results for each of the four drugs. It should be noted that, for example, the first entries under each drug are linked together since they all are measurements on the same person. This should be contrasted with the one-way ANOVA data in Table 6.7, in which the first entries under each treatment (strength) are unrelated to each other. In the current repeated-measures example, each subject has four observations—thus four "drug" entries per row in the data file—whereas in the data file for one-way ANOVA shown in Figure 6.2, each subject (plant) has only a single observation (number of flowers), and there is only one observation per row (plus a grouping value).

	Subject	DRUG1	DRUG2	DRUG3	DRUG4	var	var
1	1	89	78	79	98		
2	2	88	74	75	89		
3	3	80	75	76	94		
4	4	79	71	77	95		
5	5	91	68	83	91		
6	6	85	81	77	86		
7	7	87	73	73	104		
8	8	86	76	76	93		
9							

Figure 6.6   Data for Repeated-Measures ANOVA

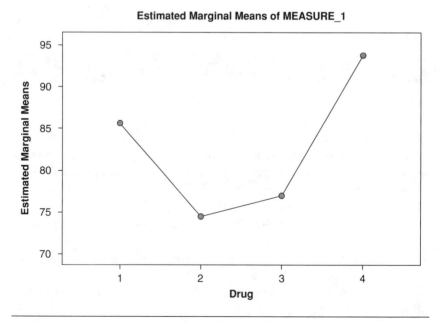

Figure 6.7   Plot of Means for Snoring Data

The purpose of this experiment is to determine whether there are any differences among the drugs in their effect on snoring. Before examining the results of the repeated-measures ANOVA, you should check the assumptions. To test for sphericity, you can perform Mauchly's test. For these data, Mauchly's test yields $p = 0.786$, which indicates that we can safely assume sphericity. The ANOVA results given in Table 6.15 are presented in four versions. With sphericity as a plausible assumption, the standard F-test on the top row of Table 6.15 can be used to test for a drug effect, and this gives $F = 30.238$ with 3 and 21 degrees of freedom and $p = 0.000$. Because of the low p-value for the F-test on the drug effect, we reject the null hypothesis that the drugs are equivalent and conclude that there is a difference in means for the drugs. The other three tests in Table 6.15 are adjustments for the standard F-test and are used if the assumption of sphericity is not acceptable. Note that these alternative versions of the test give results consistent with the standard F-test in this case.

Table 6.15   ANOVA Results for Repeated-Measures Analysis

Tests of Within-Subjects Effects

Measure: MEASURE_1

Source		Type III Sum of Squares	df	Mean Square	F	Sig.
drug	Sphericity Assumed	1843.094	3	614.365	30.239	.000
	Greenhouse-Geisser	1843.094	2.437	756.269	30.239	.000
	Huynh-Feldt	1843.094	3.000	614.365	30.239	.000
	Lower-bound	1843.094	1.000	1843.094	30.239	.001
Error(drug)	Sphericity Assumed	426.656	21	20.317		
	Greenhouse-Geisser	426.656	17.060	25.010		
	Huynh-Feldt	426.656	21.000	20.317		
	Lower-bound	426.656	7.000	60.951		

Part two of this ANOVA analysis is to determine where these differences lie. As in other ANOVA models, these differences can be examined using pairwise comparisons. Table 6.16 shows SPSS output of pairwise comparisons using the Bonferroni method.

This table compares each pair of means for each drug. For example, the comparison of *Drug1* to *Drug2* gives a mean difference of 11.125 and a p-value of 0.008. The overall conclusion of the pairwise comparisons is that there is no significant difference between *Drug2* and *Drug3* ($p = 1.0$), but all other drug differences are significantly different (at the 0.05 level). Since *Drug2* and *Drug3* have the lowest means, our conclusion is that both *Drug2* and *Drug3* are better at decreasing snoring than *Drug1* and *Drug4*, but we don't have sufficient evidence to choose between *Drug2* and *Drug3*.

Table 6.16   Bonferroni Comparisons for Repeated-Measures ANOVA

Pairwise Comparisons

Measure: MEASURE_1

(I) drug	(J) drug	Mean Difference (I-J)	Std. Error	Sig.[a]	95% Confidence Interval for Difference[a]	
					Lower Bound	Upper Bound
1	2	11.125*	2.142	.008	3.338	18.912
	3	8.625*	1.451	.003	3.350	13.900
	4	-8.125	2.482	.082	-17.148	.898
2	1	-11.125*	2.142	.008	-18.912	-3.338
	3	-2.500	2.027	1.000	-9.868	4.868
	4	-19.250*	2.678	.001	-28.985	-9.515
3	1	-8.625*	1.451	.003	-13.900	-3.350
	2	2.500	2.027	1.000	-4.868	9.868
	4	-16.750*	2.520	.002	-25.911	-7.589
4	1	8.125	2.482	.082	-.898	17.148
	2	19.250*	2.678	.001	9.515	28.985
	3	16.750*	2.520	.002	7.589	25.911

Based on estimated marginal means
 *. The mean difference is significant at the .05 level.
 a. Adjustment for multiple comparisons: Bonferroni.

Reporting Results of a Repeated-Measures ANOVA

The following illustrates how you might report this repeated-measures ANOVA in a publication format.

Narrative for the Methods Section

"A repeated-measures analysis of variance was performed to compare the ability of each of the four drugs to reduce snoring (decrease the snoring index). The assumption of sphericity was checked using Mauchly's test, and the Bonferroni method was used to perform pairwise comparisons following a significant overall test result."

Narrative for the Results Section

"Mauchly's test found that an assumption of sphericity is plausible ($p = 0.79$). The overall test for differences in means in the repeated-measures ANOVA was significant, $F(3, 21) = 30.2$, $p < 0.001$. Pairwise comparisons indicate at the overall 0.05 level that *Drug2* ($M = 74.5$, $SD = 4.04$) and *Drug3* ($M = 77.0$, $SD = 3.0$) were better at reducing snoring than *Drug1* ($M = 85.6$, $SD = 4.21$)

or *Drug4* (M = 93.8, SD = 5.55). However, no significant difference was found between *Drug2* and *Drug3*."

You might choose to include the comparison results in a table or include the simple graphical display in Table 6.17 to summarize the pairwise comparisons.

Table 6.17   Results of Bonferroni Comparison

Drug2	Drug3	Drug1	Drug4
74.5	77.0	85.6	93.8

The interpretation of Table 6.17 is that any two drugs that are underscored by the same line are not significantly different. This display quickly and succinctly illustrates that *Drug2* and *Drug3* are not significantly different from each other and that *Drug1* and *Drug4* are not significantly different. However, the means for *Drug2* and *Drug3* are both significantly lower than the means for *Drug1* and *Drug4*.

SPSS Step-by-Step. EXAMPLE 6.4: Repeated-Measures ANOVA

To perform the previous example in SPSS, follow these instructions:

1. Open the data set SNORING.SAV and select **Analyze/General Linear Model/Repeated Measures. . . .**

2. For the "Within-Factor" name, enter *DRUG* and 4 for number of levels. Click Add and Define.

3. For the "Within-Subjects Variables," select (in order) *Drug1* (click on right arrow), *Drug2* (click), *Drug3* (click), and *Drug4* (click).

4. Click on Options and place the *drug* factor in the "Display Means for" box. Select the "Descriptive Statistics" checkbox and any other measures you want to observe. Click on the "Compare main effects" checkbox and select Bonferroni confidence interval adjustment. (This produces the pairwise comparisons.) Click Continue.

5. To produce the means plot, click on the Plots button and place the *drug* factor in the horizontal axis list and click Add and Continue.

6. Click OK to produce all of the output used in the example.

Analysis of Covariance

The final topic for this chapter is really a combination of analysis of variance and regression. We consider a one-way analysis of covariance (ANCOVA), which is essentially a one-way ANOVA with a twist. That twist is that the means across groups are not compared directly. Instead, the means are adjusted by some other quantitative variable called a covariate. Notice that the covariate variable is not a value controlled by the researcher but is instead a value that is intrinsic to the subject (or entity) observed. When an appropriate covariate is used, an ANCOVA is an improvement over the corresponding ANOVA model since it explains additional variability and thus results in a more precise analysis.

Appropriate Applications for Analysis of Covariance

- *Which Promotion Is Most Effective?* A car dealership wants to know if placing trucks, SUVs, or sports cars in his outside display area affects the number of customers who enter the showroom. However, he is also aware that outside temperature may affect the number of customers. His study compares customer traffic for the three different display options with daily high temperature as a covariate.
- *Which Drug Is Best?* A researcher is comparing three drugs for decreasing triglyceride levels and suspects that the effectiveness of the drugs is related to the subject's age. Therefore, she uses age as a covariate in the comparison.
- *Which Teaching Method Is Better?* A school system is trying to decide among three proposed methods for teaching math. The teaching methods are allocated to randomly selected sections, and performance is evaluated using the final exam. To standardize the comparisons, a pretest (covariate) is given to each student at the beginning of the year.

Design Considerations for an Analysis of Covariance

Because an analysis of covariance is a combination of one-way ANOVA and regression, considerations from both perspectives should be made when performing this type of analysis:

1. *Normality.* A standard assumption for the ANOVA model to be valid is that the measurement variable is normally distributed within each group. See Chapter 2: Describing and Examining Data concerning how to assess these characteristics for a variable.

2. *The Groups Must Be Independent.* Each subject (or entity) in each group should be different. Subjects should be randomly assigned to each group.

3. *The Covariate Must Be Quantitative and Should Be Linearly Related to the Outcome Measure in Each Group or Treatment Level.* If the covariate is not correlated with the outcome measure, it will be of little use in the analysis. This assumption implies that for each treatment level, there is a regression line relating the covariate with the response variable.

4. *Homogeneity of Regressions.* A key assumption in ANCOVA is that the slopes of the regression lines discussed in Item 3 above are equal. That is, this assumption specifies that these regression lines are parallel.

5. *Other Considerations.* As in all analysis of variance models, it is assumed that the variances across groups are equal and error terms are uncorrelated. It is also assumed that the treatments do not affect the covariates.

The covariate (also called a concomitant variable) should be something that is observed prior to the study, or it should be a variable that is not influenced by the study. Typical covariates include age, pretest scores, IQ, and so on. As with the analysis of variance and *t*-test, the procedure is robust against moderate departures from normality and variance assumptions, particularly if the sample size per group is moderately large. The independent group assumption should not be violated.

Hypotheses for an Analysis of Covariance

An analysis of covariance model consists of two components: (1) the component specifying the group effect as in an ANOVA model and (2) a component indicating the linear relationship between the dependent variable and the covariate. Typically, analysis of covariance testing proceeds in two steps:

1. *Homogeneity of Regressions.* The null hypothesis is tested that the regression lines relating the dependent variable and the covariate have the same slopes in all groups.

2. *Group Effects.* If the null hypothesis in (1) is not rejected, then we test the group effect by testing the null hypothesis that the group regression lines are not only parallel but also are actually equal to each other. If they are determined to be separate lines, then this is an indication of a group effect after adjusting for the covariate.

The hypotheses related to the homogeneity of regressions assumption are given as follows:

H_0: The regression lines for each group are parallel.

H_a: At least two of the regression lines for groups are not parallel.

If the F-test for testing these hypotheses is not rejected, then we move on to test for a group effect. These hypotheses can be stated very informally as follows:

H_0: All group means (adjusted by the covariate) are equal.

H_a: At least two means (adjusted by the covariate) are not equal.

An F-test is used to test for differences in adjusted group means. As with a one-way ANOVA, if differences are found and there are more than two groups, you may want to use a multiple comparison procedure to identify the differences. For more discussion of ANCOVA models, see Keppel and Wickens (2004).

EXAMPLE 6.5: Analysis of Covariance

Description of Problem

A school system is trying to choose among three proposed methods of teaching math in the fifth grade. Nine classes are randomized to the three methods and are taught for 3 months. Pretest and posttest scores are compared. Using the pretest score as a covariate, an analysis is performed to determine if there are any differences and, if so, which method or methods are best.

To visually examine the data, a scatterplot of the pretest and posttest scores is shown in Figure 6.8 along with the fitted within-group regression lines.

It is always a good idea to study a plot of your data before performing your analysis. In this case, you are interested in determining if the lines are parallel and, if so, whether some are different from others (i.e., that some teaching methods produce higher scores adjusted for a pretest). In the graph, you can see three lines, each representing one of the methods. The top line represents Method 3, and the other two lines represent Methods 1 and 2. Visually, we see that these lines are not perfectly parallel but that the slopes are quite similar. In addition, we see that two of the lines (for Methods 1 and 2) are quite similar, while the line for Method 3 seems to be distinct and stays above the other two lines. This suggests that Method 3 is preferable to the other two methods and that Methods 1 and 2 are very similar to each other. Analysis of covariance is a formalized method for checking these observations. The following procedure is used to perform the analysis of covariance:

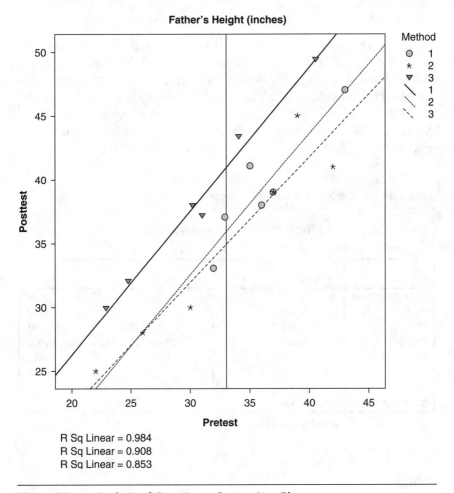

Figure 6.8   Analysis of Covariance Comparison Plot
With Reference Line for Pretest

1. An *F*-test is used to determine if the regression lines are parallel. This is similar to an interaction test in a two-way analysis. The model required to create this output is one that contains the fixed factor (*Method*), the covariate (*Pretest*), and an interaction term (*Method*Pretest*).

2. If the assumption of parallel regression lines is not rejected, then another *F*-test is used to compare the adjusted means to determine if any are different.

3. If there are significant differences among the adjusted means, then a pairwise comparison is performed to determine which methods are different.

Step 1

Table 6.18 shows SPSS output related to this step. The table provides output for the ANOVA model containing the terms *Method, Pretest,* and *Method*Pretest.* The test for the significance of the interaction term (i.e., *Method*Pretest*) is the only test to consider at this stage to test the assumption of parallel slopes (lines). Since $p = 0.683$ for this F-test, we conclude that the assumption of parallel slopes for the lines is reasonable, and we can proceed to Step 2, the test for differences in the adjusted means.

Table 6.18   ANCOVA Analysis Containing Test for Equal Slopes

Tests of Between-Subjects Effects

Dependent Variable: Posttest

Source	Type III Sum of Squares	df	Mean Square	F	Sig.
Corrected Model	698.179[a]	5	139.636	33.633	.000
Intercept	1.326	1	1.326	.319	.582
Method	.820	2	.410	.099	.907
Pretest	476.450	1	476.450	114.759	.000
Method * Pretest	3.262	2	1.631	.393	.683
Error	49.821	12	4.152		
Total	25836.000	18			
Corrected Total	748.000	17			

a. R Squared = .933 (Adjusted R Squared = .906)

Step 2

The F-test designed to test for differences among adjusted means (assuming parallelism) is given in Table 6.19, which is similar to Table 6.18 but does not have an interaction term. In this case, we are interested in the term labeled *Method* since that is the term that compares the three teaching methods. Since $p < 0.001$ for this test, we reject the null hypothesis that the adjusted means are equal and conclude that there is at least one pair of adjusted means that are different.

Step 3

Since we found a difference among adjusted means, pairwise comparisons (Table 6.20) can be used to identify which adjusted means are different. In this case, the Bonferroni procedure is used to make the comparisons in the

Table 6.19   Analysis of Covariance Test for Group Effects (on Method)

Tests of Between-Subjects Effects

Dependent Variable: Posttest

Source	Type III Sum of Squares	df	Mean Square	F	Sig.
Corrected Model	694.917[a]	3	231.639	61.092	.000
Intercept	4.152	1	4.152	1.095	.313
Method	105.981	2	52.990	13.976	.000
Pretest	627.917	1	627.917	165.605	.000
Error	53.083	14	3.792		
Total	25836.000	18			
Corrected Total	748.000	17			

a. R Squared = .929 (Adjusted R Squared = .914)

format of Table 6.16. It can be seen that at the overall 0.05 level of significance, Method 3 is significantly different from Method 1 and Method 2 (Bonferroni-adjusted p-values are $p = 0.005$ and $p = 0.001$, respectively), but Methods 1 and 2 are not significantly different (Bonferroni-adjusted $p = 1.0$). It is clear from this analysis that Method 3 has a higher overall adjusted mean on the standardized math test than either Method 1 or 2, which is consistent with our initial visual observations.

Table 6.20   Analysis of Covariance Pairwise Comparisons

Pairwise Comparisons

Dependent Variable: Posttest

(I) Method	(J) Method	Mean Difference (I-J)	Std. Error	Sig.[a]	95% Confidence Interval for Difference[a] Lower Bound	Upper Bound
1	2	1.022	1.156	1.000	-2.120	4.165
	3	-4.738*	1.209	.005	-8.025	-1.451
2	1	-1.022	1.156	1.000	-4.165	2.120
	3	-5.761*	1.138	.001	-8.853	-2.668
3	1	4.738*	1.209	.005	1.451	8.025
	2	5.761*	1.138	.001	2.668	8.853

Based on estimated marginal means

*. The mean difference is significant at the .05 level.

a. Adjustment for multiple comparisons: Bonferroni.

For illustrative purposes, Figure 6.8 includes a vertical reference line that represents the mean of *Pretest* (33.06). The adjusted means, which are used to compare the groups under the ANCOVA model, are the values on the vertical scale at which the reference line intersects the three regression lines. These adjusted posttest means are given in Table 6.21.

The covariate has an important effect on the comparison among methods for these data. Without the covariate model, the (unadjusted) means for the *Posttest* scores are 39.17, 34.67, and 38.17 for teaching Methods 1, 2, and 3, respectively. It should be noted that if a one-way analysis of variance were performed on the *Posttest* variable without using *Pretest* as a covariate, the (unadjusted) means would not be significantly different ($p = 0.50$). These results are in contrast to the results in Figure 6.8, in which it can be seen that the adjusted means are 40.8 for Method 3 and 36.1 and 35.1 for Methods 1 and 2, respectively. That is, Method 3 yields a significantly higher adjusted mean score, even though its associated raw mean score was slightly lower than the mean for Method 1. Thus, the covariate model reveals a difference that would not have been evident otherwise.

Table 6.21   Adjusted Means for Analysis of Covariance

Estimates

Dependent Variable: Posttest

Method	Mean	Std. Error	95% Confidence Interval	
			Lower Bound	Upper Bound
1	36.095(a)	.830	34.314	37.875
2	35.072(a)	.796	33.366	36.779
3	40.833(a)	.822	39.071	42.595

a. Covariates appearing in the model are evaluated at the following values: Pretest = 33.06.

Reporting Results for an Analysis of Covariance

The following examples illustrate how you might report this analysis of covariance in a publication format.

Narrative for the Methods Section

"An analysis of covariance (ANCOVA) was used to compare final math scores by teaching method using a pretest as a covariate. Bonferroni pairwise comparisons were used to determine significant differences in the groups."

Narrative for the Results Section

"The ANCOVA test for parallel within-group regression lines was not significant ($F = 0.39$ with 2 and 12 df, $p = 0.68$). The resulting test for equality of adjusted means found a significant difference ($F = 13.98$ with 2 and 14 df, $p = < .001$). The Bonferroni pairwise comparisons found that at the overall 0.05 level, the adjusted mean posttest under Method 3 ($M_{adj} = 40.8$, $SE = 0.82$) is significantly different from Method 1 ($M_{adj} = 36.1$, $SE = 0.83$) and Method 2 ($M_{adj} = 35.1$, $SE = 0.80$), but Methods 1 and 2 are not different from each other. It is clear from this analysis that Method 3 produced a higher overall improvement in score on the standardized math test than either Method 1 or 2 when adjusted for pretest scores."

SPSS Step-by-Step. EXAMPLE 6.5: Analysis of Covariance

To produce the output used in the example above, follow these steps:

1. Open the data set MATH.SAV and select **Graphs/Scatterplot/Dot/Simple Scatter** and Define to create a graphical comparison for these data.

2. Designate *Posttest* for the "*y*-axis," *Pretest* for the "*x*-axis," and *Method* for "Set Markers." Click OK to display the preliminary graph.

3. Double-click on the graph to enter the Chart Editor. From the Elements menu, select "Fit Line at Subgroups." Close the Properties dialog box and exit the Chart Editor. The comparison graph will be displayed in the output.

4. To perform the analysis, select **Analyze/General Linear Model/Univariate . . .** and then select Posttest as the dependent variable (this is your outcome variable), Method as a fixed factor, and Pretest as a covariate.

5. To calculate the model containing the interaction term, click on the Model button and select the Custom radio button. Click on *Method* and the right arrow and *Pretest* and the right arrow. Make sure the "Build Terms" option in the middle of the dialog box is set at "Interaction." While holding down the CTRL key, select both *Method* and *Pretest* and then click on the right arrow. In the Model box, you should have three terms—*Method, Pretest,* and *Method*Pretest*. Click Continue.

6. Click OK to display the preliminary *F*-test to test for parallelism. In this case, this test yields a *p*-value of 0.683, which means that you can proceed to create a table of comparisons for means.

7. Go back to the analysis setup (**Analyze/General Linear Model/Univariate**) and click on the Model button. Click on the *Method*Pretest* term and the left arrow to remove this term from the model. Click Continue and OK.

8. To create the pairwise comparisons, click the Options button. Place Method in the "Display Means for" box. Select the "Compare Main Effects" checkbox and select the Bonferroni (or your choice) multiple comparison procedure. Check the "Descriptive Statistics" checkbox and any others that you want displayed. Click Continue and OK to produce the results in Table 6.20.

Summary

This chapter explains the most common types of analysis of variance. For more information on topics, including power and sample size for these types of analyses, see Keppel and Wickens (2004).

References

Elliott, A. C., & Woodward, W. A. (1986). Analysis of an unbalanced two-way ANOVA on the microcomputer. *Communications in Statistics, B15*(1), 215–225.

Glass, G. V., Peckham, P. D., & Sanders, J. R. (1972). Consequences of failure to meet assumptions underlying the fixed effects analysis of variance and covariance. *Review of Educational Research, 42*, 239–323.

Keppel, G., & Wickens, T. D. (2004). *Design and analysis: A researcher's handbook* (4th ed.). Upper Saddle River, NJ: Pearson Prentice Hall.

Moher, D., Dulberg, C. S., & Wells, G. A. (1994). Statistical power, sample size, and their reporting in randomized controlled trials. *Journal of the American Medical Association, 272*, 122–124.

Neter, J., Wasserman, W., & Kutner, M. (1990). *Applied linear statistical models.* Homewood, IL: Irwin.

Winer, B. J. (1991). *Statistical principles in experimental design.* New York: McGraw-Hill.

7

Nonparametric Analysis Procedures

W hen "Plan A" doesn't work out, it's always good to have a "Plan B." The good news is that when the normality assumption for a standard parametric procedure such as the *t*-test, correlation, ANOVA, or others cannot be verified, you have another option. A nonparametric procedure can often be used in place of a parametric procedure.

The basic technique used by nonparametric procedures to get around the normality assumption is that they do not use the raw data. Instead, in a nonparametric procedure, the ordered or ranked values are used in the analysis. That is, the smallest value receives a rank of 1, the next smallest a rank of 2, and so on. There will be some instances in which the data are ranked with respect to the entire data set and others in which the ranking will be done within groups. For more discussion on the use of ranks (e.g., how they are used in the case of ties, etc.), you should check a text with a good discussion of nonparametric analysis. Several good ones are Conover (1998), Gibbons (1993), Lehmann and D'Abrera (1998), and Siegel and Castellan (1988). Nonparametric procedures are also useful if you don't have exact data values but you do know how the data are ordered. This chapter presents descriptions of several commonly used and reported nonparametric statistical procedures. They include the following:

- *Spearman's rank correlation (measure association between two variables)*: a nonparametric alternative to Pearson's correlation

- *Mann-Whitney* U *(compare two independent groups):* a nonparametric alternative to a two-sample *t*-test
- *Kruskal-Wallis (compare two or more independent groups):* a nonparametric alternative to a one-way analysis of variance
- *Sign test or Wilcoxon test (compare two repeated measures):* nonparametric alternatives to the paired *t*-test
- *Friedman's test (compare two or more repeated measures):* a nonparametric alternative to a repeated-measures analysis of variance

The chi-square tests (e.g., for association and for goodness of fit) can also be considered to be nonparametric tests. These are covered in Chapter 5: Analysis of Categorical Data.

In this chapter, you will learn when, why, and how to perform a nonparametric test and how to present your results. The descriptions of the statistical tests in this chapter are sometimes abbreviated compared to other chapters because these procedures often mimic many of the design considerations of their parametric cousins.

Spearman's Rho

Spearman's rho (sometimes called Spearman's rank correlation) is a substitute for Pearson's correlation coefficient discussed in Chapter 4: Correlation and Regression when the normality assumptions for that measure cannot be assumed. Spearman's rho measures the strength of an increasing or decreasing relationship between two variables. Instead of using the raw observed data, Spearman's rho is based on the ranked data. Like Pearson's correlation, Spearman's rho takes on values from –1 to 1 and is interpreted in much the same way as Pearson's correlation. In fact, Spearman's rho is computationally equal to Pearson's correlation calculated on the ranks instead of the original data.

Appropriate Applications for Spearman's Rho

- *Is Your Car a Status Symbol?* Examine the association between people from five categories of socioeconomic level and model year of car driven. Note that socioeconomic level is an ordinal variable that may not satisfy the requirements of a quantitative variable. For discussion of variable types, see Chapter 2: Describing and Examining Data.
- *Tennis Rankings.* Tennis rankings of American tennis players and amount of income earned playing tennis (again, the tennis ranking variable is ordinal).

- *Is Crime Rate Related to Education?* A criminologist collects data on the crime rates and median educational level for a sample of U.S. cities to examine the relationship. There is concern that the variables may not be normal and that outliers may have too strong an effect on Pearson's correlation.

Design Considerations for Spearman's Rho

Situations in which Spearman's rho would be chosen over Pearson's correlation are as follows:

- *Data Benefits From Ranking.* When data values contain a few unusual values or outliers, we showed in Chapter 4: Correlation and Regression that the Pearson correlation can be unduly influenced by these values. Using Spearman's rho (which is based on ranks) in these situations can give a clearer measure of the actual strength of the association by minimizing the influence of the extreme values.
- *Data Observed as Ordinal Variables.* When data are observed in ordered values such as tiny, small, medium, large, very large, or < 10, 11–20, 21–30, 31–40, and so on, then Pearson's correlation is not appropriate, whereas Spearman's rho can still be correctly used.
- *Sample Size Too Small.* A measure of association between two variables is needed in a situation in which sample size is small and the normality of at least one of the variables is questionable.

Hypotheses for Spearman's Rho

The hypotheses being tested are the following:

H_0:   There is no monotonic relationship between the two variables.

H_a: There is a monotonic relationship between the two variables.

Tips and Caveats for Spearman's Rho

- *Verify Results With a Graph.* As illustrated in Chapter 4, you should always visually examine the relationship for your correlation using a scatterplot.
- *Correlation Does Not Imply Cause and Effect.* The finding of a significant correlation (either Pearson's or Spearman's) does not justify the conclusion of a cause-and-effect relationship. A properly designed prospective study is required before such a conclusion can be drawn.
- *Could Data Be Transformed?* If you are using Spearman's rho instead of a Pearson's correlation because your data distribution is nonnormal, another strategy might be to transform to data that are more nearly normal using a transformation such as the square root, logarithm, and so on.

EXAMPLE 7.1: Spearman's Rho

Describing the Problem

An educator wants to know how attendance (recorded as the percentage of classes attended) is related to the final letter grade received by freshmen students in an American history class at a community college. Because the grades are given as A, B, C, D, and F (recorded as 1, 2, 3, 4, and 5), Spearman's rho is used to measure the association. A scatterplot of the data is shown in Figure 7.1. The Spearman's rho calculation yields a correlation of -0.852 with $p < 0.001$. Spearman's rho is appropriate in this case because the letter grades (although coded with numbers) might not be considered to be of equal distance apart (depending on the grading criteria).

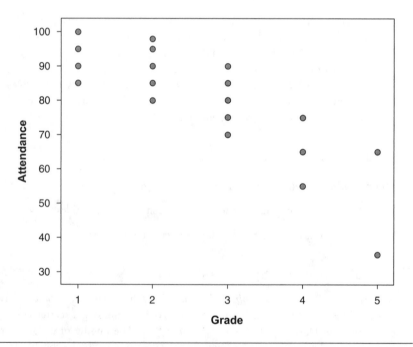

Figure 7.1   Scatterplot of Grade Versus Attendance Data

Reporting Results for Spearman's Rho

The following example illustrates how you might report this test result in a publication format.

Narrative for the Methods Section

"Spearman's correlation was used to examine the association between final letter grades and course attendance."

Narrative for the Results Section

"Spearman's rho for grade and course attendance was rho = –0.85, $p < 0.001$. This indicates that students with worse attendance had lower final grades in the course."

SPSS Step-by-Step. EXAMPLE 7.1: Spearman's Rho

To perform the analysis and generate the plot in SPSS, follow these steps:

1. Open the data set ATTENDANCE.SAV and select **Analyze/Correlate/Bivariate.**

2. Select *Grade* and *Attendance* as the variables to analyze.

3. Check the Spearman's checkbox and click OK to display the preliminary output shown for Spearman's rho.

4. To create the scatterplot, select **Graph/Scatter/Dot/Simple Scatter . . .** and Define.

5. Select *Attendance* for the *y*-axis and *Grade* for the *x*-axis and click OK.

Mann-Whitney (Two Independent Groups Test)

The Mann-Whitney test (sometimes referred to as the Mann-Whitney U) is similar to the two-sample *t*-test without the normality or equal variance assumption. However, the data must meet the requirement that the two samples are independent. Like other nonparametric procedures, the Mann-Whitney procedure uses ranks instead of the raw data values. Specifically, the data values are assigned ranks relative to both samples combined, and Mann-Whitney's test is designed to test whether observations in one population tend to have higher values (and therefore higher ranks) than those from the other population.

Typical settings appropriate for use of the Mann-Whitney test are those in which

- The sample sizes are small and normality is questionable.
- The data contain outliers or extreme values that, because of their magnitude, distort the mean values and affect the outcome of the comparison.
- The data are ordinal

Side-by-side boxplots are also useful in this setting. For more information on a two-sample *t*-test, see the discussion in Chapter 3: Comparing One or Two Means Using the *t*-Test.

Hypotheses for a Mann-Whitney Test

The hypotheses being tested by the Mann-Whitney test are the following:

H_0:   The two groups have the same distribution.

H_a: The two groups do not have the same distribution.

Note that Mann-Whitney tests equality of the distributions rather than means, as was the case in the two-sample *t*-test. Medians are usually reported for this type of data, but the Mann-Whitney test is not simply a test comparing medians unless the only difference in the two distributions is a shift in location.

EXAMPLE 7.2: Mann-Whitney Test

Describing the Problem

A researcher wants to know if one fertilizer (Brand 1) causes plants to grow faster than another brand of fertilizer (Brand 2). Starting with seeds, he grows plants in identical conditions and randomly assigns fertilizer "Brand 1" to seven plants and fertilizer "Brand 2" to six plants. Note: This is the same data set used in EXAMPLE 3.2. In the setting here, we assume that because of the small sample sizes, normality cannot be assumed. Output is shown in Table 7.1.

The "Ranks" table gives mean ranks for each group. As with other non-parametric procedures, the Mann-Whitney test is performed on the ranked data rather than on the actual values. Thus, the mean ranks are compared rather than the actual means of the data. The "Test Statistics" table shows a Mann-Whitney U statistic value of $U = 12.5$ and an exact *p*-value of $p = 0.234$. The asymptotic *p*-value is an approximation for large sample sizes. In this case, with sample sizes of 7 and 6, you should use the "exact"

Table 7.1   Mann-Whitney Analysis

Ranks

	TYPE	N	Mean Rank	Sum of Ranks
HEIGHT	1	7	5.79	40.50
	2	6	8.42	50.50
	Total	13		

Test Statistics[b]

	HEIGHT
Mann-Whitney U	12.500
Wilcoxon W	40.500
Z	-1.219
Asymp. Sig. (2-tailed)	.223
Exact Sig. [2*(1-tailed Sig.)]	.234[a]

a. Not corrected for ties.
b. Grouping Variable: TYPE

p-value. The Mann-Whitney test and the Wilcoxon rank sum test are different test statistics formed using the ranked data that yield equivalent p-values. It is most common to refer to this as the Mann-Whitney test. It is interesting to note that these results (i.e., not finding a significant difference between fertilizers) are consistent with those found in EXAMPLE 3.2 using the two-sample t-test.

Reporting Results for a Mann-Whitney Test

The following sample write-ups illustrate how you might report this Mann-Whitney test in publication format.

Narrative for the Methods Section

"A Mann-Whitney test was used to test the hypothesis that the distribution of heights of the plants for the two types of fertilizer was equal."

Narrative for the Results Section

"The distribution of plant heights given fertilizer Brand 1 was not significantly different from that given fertilizer Brand 2, Mann-Whitney $U = 12.5, p = 0.23$."

SPSS Step-by-Step. EXAMPLE 7.2: Mann-Whitney Test

To create the output for the Mann-Whitney test, follow these steps:

1. Open the data set FERTILIZER.SAV and select **Analyze/Nonparametric Tests/2 Independent Samples. . . .**

2. Select *Height* as the test variable and *Type* as the group variable. To specify the range of values for the grouping variable, click Define Range. Enter 1 for Group 1 and 2 for Group 2 (corresponding to the codes used for two groups) and click Continue.

3. Make sure the Mann-Whitney checkbox is selected. Click OK to display Table 7.1.

Kruskal-Wallis Test

The Kruskal-Wallis test is the nonparametric counterpart to the one-way analysis of variance. With the Kruskal-Wallis test, there are no normality or equal variance assumptions. Otherwise, the design considerations and data collection issues are the same as those for the one-way ANOVA discussed in Chapter 6: Analysis of Variance and Covariance. For more information on the appropriate applications for this type of analysis, refer to the description of the one-way ANOVA in Chapter 6. Graphical presentations discussed in Chapter 6, such as side-by-side boxplots, are also useful here.

Hypotheses for a Kruskal-Wallis Test

The hypotheses being tested are as follows:

H_0:   There are no differences in the distributions of the groups.

H_a: There are differences in the distributions of the groups.

EXAMPLE 7.3: Kruskal-Wallis Test

Describing the Problem

An agricultural researcher wants to know which of four possible feeds is best in producing weight gain for sheep. Twenty-eight sheep are randomly divided into four "feed" groups. Because the groups are small, the normality of the data cannot be adequately tested. Therefore, a Kruskal-Wallis test is used to compare the four groups. The data for this analysis (in the SPSS data editor) are shown in Figure 7.2. Notice how these data have been entered in the same way as the *t*-test or analysis of variance data in that there is one observation per line and there is a grouping variable (*Feed* in this case) that specifies a group identity for each observation.

	FEED	WEIGHT	var	v
1	1	50.80		
2	1	57.00		
3	1	44.60		
4	1	51.70		
5	1	48.20		
6	1	51.30		
7	1	49.00		
8	2	68.70		
9	2	67.70		
10	2	66.30		
11	2	69.80		
12	2	66.90		
13	2	65.20		
14	2	62.00		
15	3	82.60		
16	3	74.10		
17	3	80.30		
18	3	80.50		
19	3	81.50		
20	3	78.60		
21	3	76.10		
22	4	76.90		
23	4	72.20		
24	4	73.70		
25	4	74.20		
26	4	70.60		
27	4	75.30		
28	4	69.80		

Figure 7.2   Data for Kruskal-Wallis Example

The output for this analysis is shown in Table 7.2. The "Ranks" table shows the mean rank for each group, and the "Test Statistics" table reports the chi-square test statistic and associated *p*-value.

It should be noted that the ranking for the Kruskal-Wallis procedure is done on the basis of all 28 observations. Thus, the smallest value in the list, that is, 44.6 in Feed Group 1 (the third value from the top) in Figure 7.2, is assigned Rank 1, 48.2 (also in Group 1) is assigned Rank 2, and so on, and the largest value in the list, 82.6 (in Group 3), is assigned the largest rank of 28. It is interesting to note that the weights in Feed Group 1 have a mean rank of 4. Because 4 is the mean of the ranks $1, 2, \ldots, 7$, this implies that the seven smallest weights were in Feed Group 1, a fact that can be verified by examining the data in Figure 7.2. This information seems to suggest that weights

Table 7.2   Output for Kruskal-Wallis Analysis

Ranks

	FEED	N	Mean Rank
WEIGHT	1	7	4.00
	2	7	11.07
	3	7	24.43
	4	7	18.50
	Total	28	

Test Statistics[a,b]

	WEIGHT
Chi-Square	24.481
df	3
Asymp. Sig.	.000

a. Kruskal Wallis Test
b. Grouping Variable: FEED

in Feed Group 1 are smaller than those in other groups, and this leads us to us believe that the null hypothesis is not true. In fact, from the table, we see that $p < 0.001$, verifying our observations. There is sufficient evidence to reject the null hypothesis that the groups are the same and conclude that there is a statistically significant difference in the weight gains by feed.

SPSS does not offer a multiple comparison test for the Kruskal-Wallis test. Because the results are significant, you can safely conclude that the weight gains for Feed 3 (MEDIAN = 80.3) are significantly higher than the weight gains for Feed 1 (MEDIAN = 50.8). A description of how to do Tukey-style multiple comparisons for a Kruskal-Wallis test may be found in Zar (1999). In general, after obtaining a significant Kruskal-Wallis test, you could use multiple Mann-Whitney tests to examine pairwise differences. There would be six such comparisons. A conservative approach (Bonferroni) would be to perform these comparisons at the $0.05/6 = 0.0083$ level. We will not go into this analysis here.

Reporting Results for a Kruskal-Wallis Test

The following example illustrates how you might report this Kruskal-Wallis test in a publication format.

Narrative for the Methods Section

"A Kruskal-Wallis test was used to test for differences among feeds because normality was questionable and sample sizes within each group are small."

Narrative for the Results Section

"The Kruskal-Wallis test for comparison of feeds indicates that there is a statistically significant difference in the distribution of weight gain between the groups, $\chi^2(3) = 24.5$ and $p < 0.001$."

SPSS Step-by-Step. EXAMPLE 7.3: Kruskal-Wallis Test

To create the output for the Kruskal-Wallis test, use the following steps in SPSS:

1. Open the data set FEED.SAV and select **Analyze/Nonparametric tests/K independent samples.**

2. Select *Weight* as the test variable and *Feed* as the grouping variable. To specify the range of values for the grouping variable, click Define Range. Enter 1 as the minimum and 4 as the maximum (corresponding to the codes used for the four feeds) and click Continue.

3. Click OK to display the output for the Kruskal-Wallis test.

4. To calculate the medians by group, select **Analyze/Descriptive Statistics/ Explore.** . . . Select *Weight* for the dependent list and *Feed* for the factor list. Click OK. The resulting tables include the median values for each "feed" group.

Sign Test and Wilcoxon Signed-Rank Test for Matched Pairs

The sign test and the Wilcoxon signed-rank test can be used to compare paired data as nonparametric alternatives to the paired *t*-test. These tests are used when you cannot justify a normality assumption for the differences. Otherwise, the design considerations for these tests are the same as for the paired *t*-test described in Chapter 3. Applications of paired-data analysis are given in Chapter 3 and are applicable here.

The sign test is very simple in that it counts the number of differences that are positive and those that are negative and makes a decision based on these counts. The sign test can be used when the differences are ordinal or quantitative. The Wilcoxon signed-rank test goes one step further in that it uses information about the magnitude of the differences. Specifically, the absolute values of the differences are ranked from smallest to largest, and then the sum of the ranks associated with positive differences is compared with the sum of the ranks for the negative differences. It should be pointed out that the Wilcoxon signed-rank test assumes that the differenced data are quantitative and the distribution of the differences is symmetric.

Hypotheses for a Sign Test or Wilcoxon Signed-Rank Test

The hypotheses being tested by the sign test and Wilcoxon signed-rank test are as follows:

H_0: The probability of a positive difference is equal to the probability of a negative difference.

H_a: The probability of a positive difference is not equal to the probability of a negative difference.

EXAMPLE 7.4: Wilcoxon Signed-Rank Test and Sign Test

Using the Wilcoxon signed-rank test on the diet data in EXAMPLE 3.4 (analyzed in Chapter 3 as a paired t-test) produces the output shown in Table 7.3.

Table 7.3   Output for Wilcoxon Signed-Rank Test

Ranks

		N	Mean Rank	Sum of Ranks
after - before	Negative Ranks	10(a)	9.70	97.00
	Positive Ranks	5(b)	4.60	23.00
	Ties	0(c)		
	Total	15		

a. after < before
b. after > before
c. after = before

Test Statistics(b)

	after - before
Z	-2.108(a)
Asymp. Sig. (2-tailed)	.035

a. Based on positive ranks.
b. Wilcoxon Signed Ranks Test

The differences are calculated as "after weight minus before weight," and the "Ranks" table indicates that there were 10 negative differences, 5 positive differences, and no ties. The statistic calculated for the test is $Z = -2.108$

and $p = 0.035$. Similar output for the sign test (not shown) produces a p-value of 0.302. In this case, the Wilcoxon signed-rank test produced a significant result at the 0.05 level, and the less powerful sign test was not significant ($p = 0.302$). The Wicoxon test is in general more powerful, and in this example, it detected a difference when the sign test did not. Given these somewhat contradictory results, you would use the Wilcoxon signed-rank test if you can reasonably make the assumption that the distribution of the differences is symmetric. You might choose the more conservative sign test if you are uncomfortable with this assumption. It should be noted that in EXAMPLE 3.4 (where the data were analyzed using a paired t-test), the results were significant ($p = 0.02$).

Reporting the Results for a Wilcoxon Signed-Rank Test or Sign Test

The following illustrates how you might report the results of the Wilcoxon signed-rank test or sign test in a publication format.

Narrative for the Methods Section

"The Wilcoxon signed-rank test (or sign test) was used to ascertain whether the diet was effective."

Narrative for the Results Section

"The Wilcoxon test showed the diet to be effective, with 10 of 15 subjects losing weight ($p = 0.035$)."

or

"The sign test showed that the results were not significant, with 10 of 15 subjects losing weight ($p = 0.302$)."

SPSS Step-by-Step. EXAMPLE 7.4: Wilcoxon Signed-Rank Test and Sign Test

To create the output for the Wilcoxon signed-rank test and sign test example, follow these steps in SPSS:

1. Open the data set DIET.SAV and select **Analyze/Nonparametric Tests/ 2-Related Samples.**

2. Click on *Before* and *After* to highlight them and click the right arrow to place them in the "Test Pairs List."

3. Make sure the Wilcoxon and Sign checkboxes are selected and click OK. The output shown in Table 7.3 is displayed. Note that by default, SPSS calculates the difference as "after – before," regardless of the order you enter the variables in Step 2 above.

Friedman's Test

Friedman's test is a nonparametric alternative to a repeated-measures analysis of variance used to compare observations repeated on the same subjects. Unlike the parametric repeated-measures ANOVA, this test makes no assumptions about the distribution of the data (e.g., normality). Friedman's test, like many nonparametric tests, uses the ranks of the data rather than their raw values to calculate the statistic. If there are only two readings per subject, Friedman's test is equivalent to the sign test.

The design considerations for this Friedman's test are similar to those for the repeated-measures ANOVA discussed in Chapter 6, except for the normality assumption. We recommend that you review that discussion to understand how and when Friedman's test should be used.

Hypotheses for Friedman's Test

The hypotheses being tested in Friedman's test are as follows:

H_0: The distributions are the same across repeated measures.

H_a: The distributions across repeated measures are different.

EXAMPLE 7.5: Friedman's Test

We use Friedman's test to analyze the snoring data in EXAMPLE 6.3, where it was analyzed as a repeated-measures ANOVA. The data (shown in Figure 6.5) compare the effects of four drugs on snoring for eight patients. The output for Friedman's test is shown in Table 7.4.

The data are ranked within patients across drugs. For example, using the data in Figure 6.5, the snoring index for *Patient1* for *Drug1* through *Drug4* was 89, 78, 79, and 98, respectively. The resulting ranks are, then, 3, 1, 2, and 4, respectively. This ranking is done separately for each patient. If a certain drug tended to be assigned a preponderance of low ranks, then this would suggest it is better at reducing snoring. The output in Table 7.4 shows the ranks by drug along with a chi-square and associated *p*-value. In that

Table 7.4   Output for Friedman's Test

Ranks

	Mean Rank
DRUG1	3.06
DRUG2	1.25
DRUG3	1.75
DRUG4	3.94

Test Statistics[a]

N	8
Chi-Square	22.481
df	3
Asymp. Sig.	.000

a. Friedman Test

table, we see that *Drug2* had a mean rank of 1.25, while *Drug4* had a mean rank of 3.94. These mean ranks are consistent with the findings for *Patient1* and suggest that there is a general tendency for *Drug2* to perform best and *Drug4* to perform worst.

Table 7.4 shows that chi-square = 22.481 with $p = 0.000$ (usually reported as $p < 0.001$). SPSS does not offer any automated multiple comparison procedure as is available in the one-way repeated-measures analysis. A procedure for performing multiple comparisons following Friedman's test is discussed in Zar (1999, p. 267). A statement could be made that the results for *Drug4* were higher than for *Drug2* because those are the two extremes. Based on the fact that there is a significant difference among drugs, an ad hoc multiple comparison procedure could be used in which the sign test is used to compare all possible pairs of drugs (six total comparisons). These comparisons are shown in Table 7.5. If you wanted to take the conservative Bonferroni approach, then each of the *p*-values in Table 7.5 should be compared to $0.05/6 = 0.0083$.

Table 7.5   Multiple Comparisons for Friedman's Test

Test Statistics[b]

	DRUG2 - DRUG1	DRUG3 - DRUG1	DRUG4 - DRUG1	DRUG3 - DRUG2	DRUG4 - DRUG2	DRUG4 - DRUG3
Exact Sig. (2-tailed)	.008[a]	.008[a]	.016[a]	.219[a]	.008[a]	.008[a]

a. Binomial distribution used.
b. Sign Test

The resulting Bonferroni analysis shows that there is a significant difference between *Drug1* and *Drug2*, *Drug1* and *Drug3*, *Drug2* and *Drug4*, and *Drug3* and *Drug4*. A simple graphical presentation of these results is given in Table 7.6.

Table 7.6   Graphical Representation of Friedman's Multiple Comparisons

```
                    Drug  Drug  Drug  Drug
                     2     3     1     4
                                _____

           _____
```

In this graphical representation, any two means underscored by the same line are not significantly different at the 0.0083 significance level (i.e., at an overall 0.05 level of significance). Note that it may be possible, particularly because this is an ad hoc method, that the overall test could be significant while all of these individual comparisons are nonsignificant. However, the overall test at least specifies that the largest and smallest group medians are different. It should be noted that the results for these data are consistent with the findings for the repeated-measures ANOVA in EXAMPLE 6.4.

Reporting Results for Friedman's Test

The following illustrates how you might report this Friedman's test in a publication format.

Narrative for the Methods Section

"The difference between drugs was tested using Friedman's test because the assumption of normality could not be verified and the sample size for each group was small. In the presence of a significant overall test, follow-up pairwise comparisons were performed using the sign test, with the *p*-values adjusted using the Bonferroni correction to maintain an overall 0.05 comparison rate."

Narrative for the Results Section

"Friedman's test for comparison of feeds resulted in $\chi^2(3) = 22.5$ and $p < 0.001$. The drug producing the lowest snoring score was *Drug2*. Multiple comparisons indicate that *Drug2* and *Drug3* were more effective at reducing snoring than *Drug1* and *Drug4*, but there was no significant difference between *Drug2* and *Drug3* or between *Drug1* and *Drug4*."

SPSS Step-by-Step. EXAMPLE 7.5: Friedman's Test

To create the output for the Friedman's test example, follow these steps in SPSS:

1. Open the data set SNORING.SAV and select **Analyze/Nonparametric Tests/K-Related Samples.**

2. Select *Drug1* to *Drug4* as the test variables. Make sure the Friedman Test checkbox is selected. Click OK to display the test results for the Friedman test, as shown in Table 7.4.

3. To perform the multiple comparisons, select **Analyze/Nonparametric Tests/2-Related Samples.**

4. To specify the "Test Pairs" list, click on (and highlight) *Drug1* and *Drug2* and click the right arrow. Do the same for all pairwise comparisons (there should be a total of six pairwise comparisons). Make sure the Sign Test checkbox is selected. Click OK to display the results of the pairwise comparisons, as shown in Table 7.5.

Summary

Nonparametric tests are used when the assumptions for a standard parametric test cannot be reasonably assumed. Nonparametric tests are often less powerful than their parametric cousins and should be used only when the parametric test is not appropriate.

References

Conover, W. J. (1998). *Practical nonparametric statistics* (3rd ed.). New York: John Wiley.

Gibbons, G. D. (1993). *Nonparametric statistics: An introduction.* Newbury Park, CA: Sage.

Lehmann, E. L., & D'Abrera, H. J. M. (1998). *Nonparametrics: Statistical methods based on ranks.* Upper Saddle River, NJ: Prentice Hall.

Siegel, S., & Castellan, N. J. (1988). *Nonparametric statistics for the behavioral sciences* (2nd ed.). New York: McGraw-Hill.

Zar, J. H. (1999). *Biostatistics analysis* (4th ed.). Upper Saddle River, NJ: Prentice Hall.

8

Logistic Regression

Introduction to Logistic Regression

You've either got it or you don't. That's the point of logistic regression. Binary logistic regression is defined by a response variable that can take on only one of two values, typically 1 and 0 (often interpreted as yes or no, diseased or not diseased, alive or dead, etc.). Typical reasons a researcher would choose logistic regression for an analysis include the following:

- To predict the probability of an event occurring based on a list of one or more predictor variables
- To rank the relative importance of predictor variables in explaining the response variable
- To calculate an odds ratio that measures the importance of a predictor variable on the response

This chapter begins by describing simple logistic models and then discusses the more complicated process of selecting a model from a list of possible predictors and evaluating that model. Thus, the topics that are covered in this chapter include the following:

- *Simple logistic regression*: analyzing and interpreting a logistic regression model with one predictor variable
- *Multiple logistic regression*: development of a logistic regression model based on more than one predictor variable, including the following:

- *Model selection:* selection of the "best" variables to include in a model
- *Model interpretation:* interpretation of model coefficients and assessment of the model fit
- *Prediction:* using a logistic model for prediction

Although this chapter specifically covers binary logistic regression, there are also other types of logistic regression not discussed in this chapter, including multinomial logistic regression (where the dependent variable can have more than two outcomes) and ordinal logistic regression (where the dependent variable has two or more ordered categories). For the remainder of this chapter, the term *logistic regression* will refer to only binary logistic regression. To keep this discussion at the level of the rest of this book, we will discuss models that do not include interaction terms. However, although we've kept formulas to a minimum for most of the book, we felt it necessary to include a few more here than in previous chapters for explanatory purposes. If you need to delve deeper into this subject, we recommend that you refer to Cohen, Cohen, West, and Aiken (2002); Daniel (2004); Hosmer and Lemeshow (2000); Kleinbaum (1994); Neter, Wasserman, Nachtsheim, and Kutner (1996); and Tabachnick and Fidell (2001).

Appropriate Applications for Logistic Regression

- *What Variables Affect Voting Preference?* Investigators want to predict how a person will vote (two options) based on demographic characteristics of the individual.
- *Is This Customer a Good Candidate for a Loan?* A bank wants to predict whether a customer will default on a loan based on known demographic and financial information.
- *Will This Patient Develop Coronary Heart Disease?* In a longitudinal study of 450 patients, the independent variables age, gender, smoking behavior, and blood pressure are used to predict whether patients will develop coronary heart disease during the study.

As you can see from these examples, the characteristic that distinguishes logistic regression from linear regression (discussed in Chapter 4: Correlation and Regression) is the binary response (dependent) variable. Otherwise, as in linear regression, the predictor (independent) variables can be quantitative or binary.

Simple Logistic Regression

Simple logistic regression is a logistic model based on a single independent (predictor) variable that can be either dichotomous or quantitative. In logistic regression, the independent variable is sometimes referred to as a covariate. This section will examine the case in which the independent variable is quantitative. Understanding how to interpret the simple logistic model will help you understand the more complicated logistic regression equations later in this chapter. This simple logistic equation takes on the following form:

$$p = \frac{e^{\beta_0 + \beta_1 * Predictor}}{1 + e^{\beta_0 + \beta_1 * Predictor}} \qquad [8.1]$$

where p is the probability that the dependent variable is equal to 1, β_0 is the equation intercept (or constant), and β_1 is the coefficient for the predictor variable. Think of these coefficients in a similar way as those in a simple linear regression. As in simple linear regression, the parameters β_0 and β_1 are estimated from the data, and a statistical test is used to determine whether the coefficient β_1 can be considered to be nonzero.

Hypotheses for Simple Logistic Regression

The typical null hypotheses tested in a simple logistic regression are the following:

H_0: $\beta_1 = 0$ (the predictor variable is not related to the probability of occurrence).

H_a: $\beta_1 \neq 0$ (the predictor variable is related to the probability of occurrence).

The role of β_1 is specified in Equation 8.1. If β_1 is zero, then the logistic equation shows that there is no logistic relationship between the predictor variable and the probability of occurrence. If β_1 is found to be nonzero, then the independent variable plays a role in predicting p.

Tips and Caveats for Simple Logistic Regression

Cause and Effect

As in linear regression, the creation of a prediction equation does not necessarily imply a cause-and-effect relationship between the predictor and the response. Such a relationship can be implied only when the experimental design is prospective.

EXAMPLE 8.1: Simple Logistic Regression

Describing the Problem

A major automaker is experimenting with rebates on a new line of SUVs. At a local car show, 100 rebate coupons are handed out to attendees who are classified as strong prospects to purchase the SUV. Each coupon is randomly valued at anywhere between $250 and $5,150. During the following month, dealers keep track of which coupons were redeemed as a part of the purchase of an SUV. The automaker is interested in knowing how the value of the rebate coupon is related to the probability that a customer will purchase the SUV.

Because the rebate values are large (up to $5,150), it will help us obtain a more understandable prediction equation if we create a new variable called *Rebate100*, which has the value *Rebate* ÷ 100. (This will be illustrated in the upcoming example.) Otherwise, the coefficient for *Rebate* will be small and could lead to rounding errors for predictions.

By performing a logistic regression analysis with *Purchase* as the dependent variable and *Rebate100* as the independent variable, we create the output as shown in Table 8.1.

Table 8.1   Simple Logistic Regression Output

Variables in the Equation

		B	S.E.	Wald	df	Sig.	Exp(B)	95.0% C.I.for EXP(B)	
								Lower	Upper
Step 1[a]	Rebate100	.214	.043	24.597	1	.000	1.239	1.138	1.349
	Constant	-5.900	1.254	22.137	1	.000	.003		

a. Variable(s) entered on step 1: Rebate100.

One way to make use of the information in Table 8.1 is to use the results to predict the probability that a customer will redeem a coupon. To calculate this value, use the prediction equation shown in Equation 8.1.

The second column in Table 8.1 (labeled "B") refers to the estimates of the β coefficients (β_0 and β_1) mentioned above in the logistic equation and hypotheses. We will use the notation b_0 and b_1 to denote estimates of β_0 and β_1, respectively. The *Rebate100* coefficient is $b_1 = 0.214$ with $p < 0.001$. This indicates that *Rebate100* is a statistically significant predictor of the probability of a purchase. Because β_1 is deemed nonzero, it is appropriate to use the information in the table to construct a predictive logistic equation. This simple logistic equation takes on the following form:

$$\hat{p} = \frac{e^{b_0 + b_1 * Rebate100}}{1 + e^{b_0 + b_1 * Rebate100}}$$

where $\hat{p}$ denotes the predictor of the probability of purchase, p. In this case, $b_0 = -5.9$ and $b_1 = 0.214$. For a \$3,000 coupon (i.e., 3,000/100 = 30 is the value used in the equation), the predicted probability of purchase would be 0.627, as given by the following equation:

$$\hat{p} = \frac{e^{-5.9 + 0.214 * 30}}{1 + e^{-5.9 + 0.214 * 30}} = 0.627$$

A graphical technique for approximating the probabilities associated with this logistic regression without using Equation 8.1 is to produce the plot shown in Figure 8.1, a plot of the rebate values and the predicted probabilities of purchase based on the model. Notice the vertical line we've drawn at $Rebate100 = 30$. This line crosses the probability curve at about 0.63. This tells you that there is approximately a 63% chance that a customer with a \$3,000 coupon will redeem this coupon, which is consistent with the results of the computation above (which yielded the probability 62.7%). (For more information on decision cut-off values, see the discussion at the end of the section "Multiple Logistic Regression.")

Table 8.1 also contains information about the odds ratio (OR). The OR for $Rebate100$ is given in the column headed Exp(B) and is equal to 1.239. (If we had used $Rebate$ instead of $Rebate100$, the OR would have been 1.002, which would have been more difficult to interpret.) The corresponding 95% confidence interval for the OR is 1.138 to 1.349, which does not cover the value 1.0 and thus tells us that the OR is statistically significant (at the $\alpha = 0.05$ level). In this case, the OR is interpreted as the change in odds for each *unit change* in the predictor. That is, the odds of a customer purchasing an SUV are 1.239 times greater for each \$100 increase in the rebate coupon.

These preliminary concepts for interpreting logistic regression are an important foundation for the next section, which will discuss the development of a model that contains more than one predictor variable.

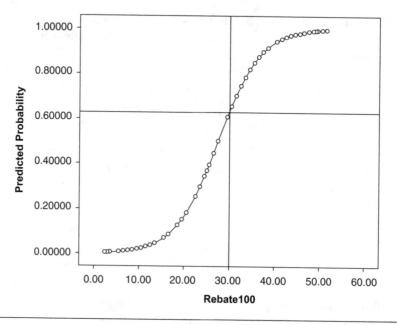

Figure 8.1   Graph of Logistic Regression for Car Rebate Data

Reporting the Results of a Logistic Regression

The following illustrates how you might report the odds ratio for the logistic regression in a publication format.

Narrative for the Methods Section

"To examine the effect of coupon value on sales, we used a logistic regression."

Narrative for the Results Section

"The odds ratio of a customer purchasing an SUV is 1.239. This implies that every $100 unit increase in the size of the coupon yields a 23.9% increase in the odds that a customer will use the coupon for a purchase."

SPSS Step-by-Step. EXAMPLE *8.1: Simple Logistic Regression*

To produce the output for EXAMPLE 8.1, follow these steps:

1. Open the data set REBATE.SAV and choose **Analyze/Regression/Binary Logistic.**

2. Select *Purchase* as the dependent variable and *Rebate100* as the covariate variable.

3. To produce the confidence intervals, click on Options and check CI for Exp(B). Click Continue.

4. To produce the data used for the graph, click on the Save button and check the Probabilities checkbox. Click Continue.

5. Click OK to produce Table 8.1.

To produce the plot in Figure 8.1, follow these steps.

1. Select **Graphs/Scatter/Dot/Simple Scatter** and click Define.

2. Select *Predicted Probability* as the y-axis and *Rebate100* as the x-axis. Click OK to produce the preliminary graph.

3. Double-click on the graph to enter the SPSS Chart Editor.

4. From the Options menu, select an x-reference line. Specify a value of 30 for the x-axis and click Close. Similarly from the Options menu, select a y-reference line with value 0.627. Click Close. (The y-reference line is drawn to assist the reader in visualizing the predicted probability.)

5. From the Elements menu, select the Interpolation line. Click Close.

6. Close the Chart Editor to display the graph shown in Figure 8.1.

Multiple Logistic Regression

A multiple logistic regression model has more than one independent variable (also referred to as predictor variables or covariates). As such, it is analogous to the multiple regression model in the case in which the dependent (response) variable is binary. A common setting is the situation in which there are several predictors to select from, and the task of the researcher is to select the best set of possible predictors. The purpose of the analysis includes the following:

- Determining which predictors are important and how they affect the response
- Creating a parsimonious and effective prediction equation

Tips and Caveats for Multiple Logistic Regression

Qualitative Predictor Variables

The predictor variables for a multiple logistic regression may be either binary or quantitative. If a potential categorical predictor variable has more than two categories such as race, brand of pickup truck, or socioeconomic status, the variable must be recoded into two or more binary indicator variables as in the multiple regression setting. For example, suppose an observed variable is hair color, categorized as 1 = black, 2 = blonde, 3 = brown, and 4 = red. To recode this, you must create $c - 1$ (i.e., the number of categories minus 1) new binary variables. Let's call these variables *Black, Blonde,* and *Brown.* Thus, a person with black hair would have the following values: *Black* = 1, *Blonde* = 0, and *Brown* = 0. A person with brown hair would have the values *Black* = 0, *Blonde* = 0, and *Brown* = 1. A person with red hair would have the values *Black* = 0, *Blonde* = 0, and *Brown* = 0, and so forth. (Some people refer to this process as "dummy coding" and the variables as dummy variables.)

Variable Selection

The process used to select the best variables for the model is similar to the process used in multiple linear regression.

Large Number Problem

If a continuous predictor variable contains values that are large, it may cause the estimate of the corresponding β coefficient as well as the corresponding OR to be small. This small number can lead to round-off errors in predictions and make interpretation difficult. It is advisable to divide large numbers by a constant to create smaller values for a predictor variable. This was illustrated for the *Rebate* variable in EXAMPLE 8.1 and for the *Price* variable in the upcoming example. Another strategy is to standardize predictor variables (i.e., subtract the mean and divide by the standard deviation). See EXAMPLE 8.2 for more discussion of these topics.

Use Binary Coding

If you have a variable that can take on only one of two values, it is common practice to code that variable using 0 and 1 values. If you use some other values, it will change the prediction equation and may make interpretation more challenging.

EXAMPLE 8.2: Multiple Logistic Regression

Describing the Problem

The sales director for a chain of appliance stores wants to find out what circumstances encourage customers to purchase extended warranties after a major appliance purchase. The response variable is an indicator of whether or not a warranty is purchased. The predictor variables they want to consider are the following:

- Customer gender
- Age of the customer
- Whether a gift is offered with the warranty
- Price of the appliance
- Race of customer

There are several strategies you can take to develop the "best" model for the data. It is recommended that you examine several models before determining which one is best for your analysis. One approach is to use a hierarchical technique in which you select the order of entry of predictor variables based on your knowledge of the problem. Another approach is to allow the computer to select variables in the model using strictly statistical criteria. We recommend a blend of these approaches in most situations. In this example, we allow the computer to help specify important variables, but it is inadvisable to accept a computer-designated model without examining alternatives. For this example, we begin by examining the significance of each variable in a fully populated model. Table 8.2 shows the output resulting from including all of the candidate predictor variables in the equation.

Table 8.2   Including All Predictor Variables in the Logistic Regression Equation

Variables in the Equation

		B	S.E.	Wald	df	Sig.	Exp(B)
Step 1[a]	Gender	-3.772	2.568	2.158	1	.142	.023
	Gift	2.715	1.567	3.003	1	.083	15.112
	Age	.091	.056	2.638	1	.104	1.096
	Price	.001	.000	3.363	1	.067	1.001
	Race			2.827	3	.419	
	Race(1)	3.773	13.863	.074	1	.785	43.518
	Race(2)	1.163	13.739	.007	1	.933	3.199
	Race(3)	6.347	14.070	.203	1	.652	570.898
	Constant	-12.018	14.921	.649	1	.421	.000

a. Variable(s) entered on step 1: Gender, Gift, Age, Price, Race.

Notice that the *Race* variable, which was originally coded as 1 = White, 2 = African American, 3 = Hispanic, and 4 = Other, has been changed (by the SPSS logistic procedure) into three (4 − 1) indicator variables called *Race(1)*, *Race(2)*, and *Race(3)*. These three variables each enter the equation with their own coefficient and *p*-value, and there is an overall *p*-value given for *Race*.

The significance of each variable is measured using a Wald statistic. (Note that SPSS reports a Wald chi-square and not the Wald *z* that is more commonly used. You can convert the Wald chi-square to a Wald *z* by taking the square root of the chi-square value and assigning the sign of the corresponding coefficient estimate, that is, b_i. Using $p = 0.10$ as a cutoff criterion for not including variables in the equation, it can be seen that *Gender* ($p = 0.142$) and *Race* ($p = 0.419$) do not seem to be important predictor variables. *Age* is marginal ($p = 0.104$), but we'll leave it in for the time being. The analysis is rerun without these "unimportant" variables, yielding the output in Table 8.3.

Table 8.3   Results of Reduced Model

Variables in the Equation

		B	S.E.	Wald	df	Sig.	Exp(B)
Step 1[a]	Gift	2.339	1.131	4.273	1	.039	10.368
	Age	.064	.032	4.132	1	.042	1.066
	Price	.000	.000	6.165	1	.013	1.000
	Constant	-6.096	2.142	8.096	1	.004	.002

a. Variable(s) entered on step 1: Gift, Age, Price.

This reduced model indicates that there is a significant predictive power for the variables *Gift* ($p = 0.039$), *Age* ($p = 0.042$), and *Price* ($p = 0.013$). Although the *p*-value for *Price* is small, notice that the OR = 1 and the coefficient for *Price* is zero to three decimal places. These seemingly contradictory bits of information (i.e., small *p*-value but OR = 1.0, etc.) are suggestive that the values for *Price* are hiding the actual OR relationship. If the same model is run with the variable *Price100*, which is *Price* divided by 100, the odds ratio becomes 1.041, and the estimated coefficient for *Price100* is 0.040, as shown in Table 8.4. All of the other values in the table remain the same. All we have done is to recode *Price* into a more usable number (similar to our creation of the *Rebate100* variable in EXAMPLE 8.1). Another tactic often used is to standardize values such as *Price* by subtracting the mean and dividing by the standard deviation (see the section "Transforming, Recoding, and Categorizing Your Data" in Appendix A for information on how to do this). Using standardized scores eliminates the problem observed with the *Price* variable and also simplifies the comparison of odds ratios for different variables.

Table 8.4   Revised Model Using *Price100*

Variables in the Equation

		B	S.E.	Wald	df	Sig.	Exp(B)
Step 1[a]	Gift	2.339	1.131	4.273	1	.039	10.368
	Age	.064	.032	4.132	1	.042	1.066
	Price100	.040	.016	6.165	1	.013	1.041
	Constant	-6.096	2.142	8.096	1	.004	.002

a. Variable(s) entered on step 1: Gift, Age, Price100.

The result is that we can now see that the odds that a customer who is offered a gift will purchase a warranty is 10 times greater than the corresponding odds for a customer having the same other characteristics but who is not offered a gift. We also observe that for each additional $100 in *Price,* the odds that a customer will purchase a warranty increases by about 4%. This tells us that people tend to be more likely to purchase warranties for more expensive appliances. Finally, the OR for age, 1.066, tells us that older buyers are more likely to purchase a warranty.

One way to assess the model is to use the information in the Model Summary table shown in Table 8.5. In general, when comparing models, the lower the –2*(log likelihood) (–2LL) value, the better the fit. To determine whether the inclusion of an additional variable in a model gives a *significantly* better fit, you can use the difference in the –2LL values for the two models to determine a chi-square test statistic. For example, for the model shown in Table 8.5, –2LL = 22.278. By removing the *Age* variable from the equation and rerunning the analysis, we get –2LL = 27.44. The difference (larger model –2LL minus smaller model –2LL) has a chi-squared distribution with 1 degree of freedom, and if this value is larger than 3.84, the log-likelihood criterion suggests that the new variable should be included in the model. For this example,

$$\chi^2 = \text{Larger model } (-2LL) - \text{Smaller model } (-2LL)$$
$$= 27.44 - 22.278 = 5.162$$

and we conclude that the model including *Age* is a better model. Other criteria (shown in Table 8.5) that can be used to assess the model are the Cox and Snell *R*-square and the Nagelkerke *R*-square, which are designed to provide information similar to the *R*-square in multiple regression.

Another model evaluation technique is the Hosmer-Lemeshow goodness-of-fit test. This test divides the data into several groups based on $\hat{p}$ values, then computes a chi-square from observed and expected frequencies of subjects falling in the two categories of the binary response variable within these groups. Large chi-square values (and correspondingly small p-values) indicate a lack of fit for the model. In Table 8.5, we see that the Hosmer-Lemeshow chi-square test for the final warranty model yields a p-value of 0.987, thus suggesting a model that fits the data. Note that the Hosmer-Lemeshow chi-square test is not a test of importance of specific model parameters (which may also appear in your computer printout). It is a separate post hoc test performed to evaluate a specific model.

Table 8.5   Model Diagnostics

Hosmer and Lemeshow Test

Step	Chi-square	df	Sig.
1	1.792	8	.987

Model Summary

Step	-2 Log likelihood	Cox & Snell R Square	Nagelkerke R Square
1	22.278[a]	.523	.753

a. Estimation terminated at iteration number 8 because parameter estimates changed by less than .001.

Interpretation of the Multiple Logistic Regression Model

Once we are satisfied with the model, it can be used for prediction just as in the simple logistic example above. For this model, the prediction would be

$$\hat{p} = \frac{e^{-6.096 + 2.339*Gift + .064*Age + .04*Price100}}{1 + e^{-6.096 + 2.339*Gift + .064*Age + .04*Price100}}$$

Using this prediction equation, we could predict the outcome for a customer having the following characteristics:

Age = 55

Price (of appliance) = $3,850

Gift = 1 (yes)

Placing these values in the equation yields the following:

$$\hat{p} = \frac{e^{-6.096 + 2.339*1 + .064*55 + .04*38.5}}{1 + e^{-6.096 + 2.339*1 + .064*55 + .04*38.5}} = 0.786$$

Thus, there is 78.6% chance a customer with these characteristics will purchase a warranty if a gift is offered. If a gift is not offered while the other characteristics stay the same, the equation becomes

$$\hat{p} = \frac{e^{-6.096 + 2.339*0 + .064*55 + .04*38.5}}{1 + e^{-6.096 + 2.339*0 + .064*55 + .04*38.5}} = 0.262$$

This information can be helpful in understanding the importance of the gift in selling a warranty for a particular age bracket or price. Using this information, it would be reasonable to predict that a person with the characteristics in the first example (i.e., *Age* = 55, *Price* = $3,850, and *Gift* = 1) would purchase a warranty because $\hat{p} = 0.786$, and the person in the second example (i.e., no gift offered) would not be predicted to purchase a warranty because $\hat{p} = 0.262$. The typical cutoff for the decision would be 0.5 (or 50%). Thus, using this cutoff, anyone whose score was higher than 0.5 would be predicted to buy the warranty, and anyone with a lower score would be predicted to not buy the warranty. However, there may be times when you want to adjust this cutoff value. Neter et al. (1996) suggest three ways to select a cutoff value:

- Use the standard 0.5 cutoff value.
- Determine a cutoff value that will give you the best predictive fit for your sample data. This is usually determined through trial and error.
- Select a cutoff value that will separate your sample data into a specific proportion of your two states based on a prior known proportion split in your population.

For example, to use the second option for deciding on a cutoff value, examine the model classification table that is part of the SPSS logistic output, as shown in Table 8.6.

Table 8.6   Model Classification

Classification Table[a]

Observed			Predicted		
			Bought		Percentage Correct
			No	Yes	
Step 1	Bought	No	12	2	85.7
		Yes	1	35	97.2
	Overall Percentage				94.0

a. The cut value is .500.

This table indicates that the final model correctly classifies 94% of the cases correctly. The model used the default 0.5 cutoff value to classify each subject's outcome. (Notice the footnote to the table: "The cut value is .500.") You can rerun the analysis with a series of cutoff values such as 0.4, 0.45, 0.55, and 0.65 to see if the cutoff value could be adjusted for a better fit. For this particular model, these alternate cutoff values do not lead to better predictions. In this case, the default 0.5 cutoff value is deemed sufficient. (For more information about classification, see Cohen et al., 2002, p. 516.)

SPSS Step-by-Step. EXAMPLE 8.2: Multiple Logistic Regression

To create the output for EXAMPLE 8.2 using SPSS, follow these instructions:

1. Open the data set WARANTY.SAV and choose **Analyze/Regression/Binary Logistic.**

2. Select *Bought* as the dependent variable and *Gender, Gift, Age, Price,* and *Race* as the covariates (i.e., the independent or predictor) variables.

3. Click on the Categorical checkbox and specify *Race* as a categorical variable. Click Continue and then OK. This produces Table 8.2.

4. To produce Table 8.3, again choose **Analyze/Regression/Binary Logistic;** select *Bought* as the dependent variable and *Gift, Age,* and *Price* as the covariates; and click OK.

5. To produce Table 8.4, repeat the steps in (4) with *Price100* substituted for *Price.*

6. To produce Table 8.5, click on the Options checkbox and select the Hosmer-Lemeshow goodness of fit. Click Continue and OK.

7. To choose a cutoff value other than the default 0.5, select the Options (see Step 6) dialog box and enter the desired cutoff value in the box titled "Classification Cutoff."

Summary

This presentation provides an example of a simple logistic regression. It also describes how to perform a multiple logistic analysis if your response variable is bivariate and your predictor variables are either categorical (converted to indicator variables) or quantitative variables. The purpose of this analysis is to discover which variables are significantly associated with the outcome and how predictions are performed once a suitable logistic model is obtained.

References

Cohen, J., Cohen, P., West, S. G., & Aiken, L. S. (2002). *Applied multiple regression/correlation analysis for the behavioral sciences* (3rd ed.). Mahwah, NJ: Lawrence Erlbaum.

Daniel, W. (2004). *Biostatistics* (8th ed.). New York: John Wiley.

Hosmer, D. W., & Lemeshow, S. (2000). *Applied logistic regression* (2nd ed.). New York: John Wiley.

Kleinbaum, D. G. (1994). *Logistic regression: A self-learning text.* New York: Springer-Verlag.

Neter, J., Wasserman, W., Nachtsheim, C. J., & Kutner, M. H. (1996). *Applied linear regression models* (3rd ed.). Chicago: Irwin.

Tabachnick, B. G., & Fidell, L. S. (2001). *Using multivariate statistics* (4th ed.). Boston: Allyn & Bacon.

Appendix A

A Brief Tutorial for Using SPSS for Windows

The SPSS program has been around for more than 35 years. Its origins are in social science (thus the original name Statistical Package for the Social Sciences), but it is now used in many other areas of research from medicine to business. Although this book (and, in particular, this appendix) is not meant to teach all the ins and outs of SPSS, this brief introduction provides enough information for you to use the examples in this *Quick Reference Guidebook*. (There is also a built-in tutorial in SPSS that can be accessed by selecting **Help/Tutorial** from the main SPSS menu.)

The examples throughout this book are based on SPSS Version 14, although most of the examples work in the same way for earlier (and probably later) versions of the program. In fact, SPSS is not one program but many.

The core SPSS program is called SPSS Base, which is the heart of the SPSS system. This SPSS Base program contains standard statistical procedures discussed in this *Quick Reference Guidebook*, including the following:

- *Descriptive statistics:* including frequencies and crosstabulations
- *Comparing means:* including *t*-tests and analysis of variance
- *Regression:* including correlation, simple linear regression, and multiple linear regression
- *Nonparametric tests:* including one-sample, two-sample, and related samples

We also discuss several analyses found in the SPSS Advanced Models and Regression Models Add-On products, including the following:

- *General linear models:* including repeated measures and analysis of covariance
- *Logistic regression*

These procedures are all contained in the SPSS Graduate Pack, which is available to students at many university bookstores. We recommend that you check with SPSS (spss.com) for information about the current status of the commercial and educational versions of the program.

Although the examples are analyzed using SPSS for Windows, all of the examples could be similarly analyzed using other versions of SPSS, including SPSS for Apple Macintosh.

This *Quick Reference Guidebook* assumes you have access to these modules in SPSS. Although SPSS offers many more analyses, these core features make up the analysis toolkit needed for the vast majority of data analysis projects.

When you first start up SPSS, the screen in Figure A1 is displayed. If a preliminary dialog box appears asking "What would you like to do?" click Cancel. The main SPSS screen looks a lot like a spreadsheet, but there are differences. Notice the two tabs at the lower left of the screen labeled "Data View" and "Variable View." These two views will be used in the upcoming examples to illustrate how to enter data into the program.

The SPSS menus at the top of this window will be referenced throughout this book to describe how to select an SPSS option or analysis. Briefly, these main menu items are as follows:

File: Create a new data file, open an existing data set, import and export data

Edit: Edit data in the SPSS spreadsheet, including copy, paste, and undo

View: Select options about how to view the SPSS data grid

Data: Manipulate data in the SPSS grid

Transform: Create new variables

Analyze: Perform a statistical analysis using the data in the SPSS data grid

Graphs: Create a graph from data in the SPSS data grid

Utilities: Select SPSS utility options

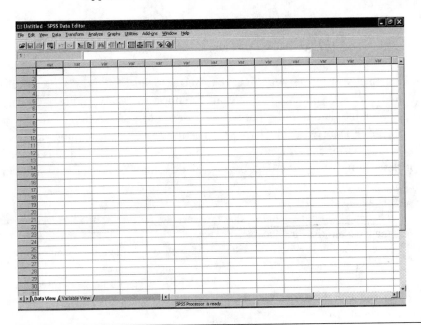

Figure A1   The SPSS Data Editor Grid

Add-Ons: Provides a listing of add-on packages to which you do not currently have access

Window: Manipulate windows

Help: Access the SPSS help system, including tutorials

In this *Quick Reference Guidebook,* we often refer to a series of menu choices using a command list such as **Analyze/Descriptive Statistics/ Frequencies . . . ,** which means to select the **Analyze** menu from the main SPSS menu followed by selecting the **Descriptive Statistics** submenu and then the **Frequencies** sub-submenu.

Working With Data in SPSS

Before performing any type of analysis, you must enter data into SPSS. There are three typical ways to make data available for use by SPSS. They are the following:

1. Open an existing SPSS data file (such as the example data files that are associated with the examples in this book).

2. Enter data into the SPSS spreadsheet using the keyboard.

3. Import data from another program such as Excel.

Whether you create your own data set or open or import a previously created data set, you should pay some attention to each variable name and type. Variable names and types were introduced in the section "Guidelines for Creating Data Sets" in Chapter 1. The information for naming variables in that discussion is sufficient for SPSS, but additional information is needed for describing the specific data types available in SPSS. For each variable in SPSS, you must select among the following list of data types.

- *Numeric.* Variables whose values are meaningful numbers. Subcategories of numeric variables in SPSS include the following:
  - *Comma:* numeric variables that are displayed with commas delimiting every three places and with the period as a decimal delimiter
  - *Dot:* numeric variables displayed with periods delimiting every three places and with the comma as a decimal delimiter (a numeric format used in some countries)
  - *Scientific notation:* numeric variables displayed with an imbedded E (single precision) or D (double precision) and a signed power-of-ten exponent such as 1.22D3 (meaning 1220) or 1.22E-2 (meaning 0.0122)
  - *Custom currency:* numeric variables displayed in accordance with a definition in the Currency tab of the Options dialog box
- *Date.* A variable that represents a calendar date or clock time.
- *String.* Categorical/text variables whose contents are not numeric. This can include text descriptions such as "Has the Flu," categorical designations such as "Male" and "Female" or "M" and "F," or noncalculated numbers such as a patient ID number. However, before you create a categorical variable that uses text instead of numbers, be aware that some procedures in SPSS (such as regression) do not allow text variables to be used in the analysis. If you choose to code categorical data using numbers (e.g., 1 and 0) instead of text (e.g., Y and N), you will be able to specify the meaning of your numeric code in the SPSS data editor using value labels.

The following sections provide examples describing how to enter data into SPSS using these techniques.

Before using the examples in this *Quick Reference Guidebook,* you should follow the procedures in Chapter 1: Introduction for downloading the example data files and placing them on your computer so you can use the hands-on exercises in this book.

SPSS Step-by-Step. EXAMPLE A1: Entering Data Into the SPSS Data Sheet

This example shows how to create a new data file in SPSS and how to enter data into the SPSS data sheet. To create an SPSS data file corresponding to the data specified by the data dictionary in Chapter 1, Table 1.2, follow these instructions:

1. On the main SPSS page, click in the "Variable View" tab at the bottom of the screen. Figure A2 shows the displayed grid.

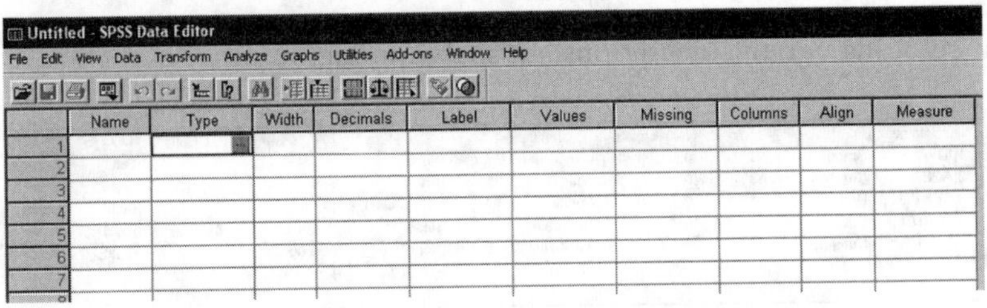

Figure A2   The SPSS Variable View Grid

Enter variable names and information into the Variable View grid, beginning with the variable ID:

2. In the "Name" column, enter ID.

3. In the "Type" column, click on the ellipsis (. . .), select "String," and click OK to designate that the ID variable is of string type.

4. In the "Width" column, change the value to 4. There are no decimals in a string variable.

5. In the "Label" column, enter "Identification Number." Ignore the other columns.

6. Enter the descriptions for the other variables by using the information in the data dictionary in Table 1.2. Using these criteria:
   a. Define the variable *Age* as 3 digits with no decimal places and a missing value of –99. To set the missing values code, click on the ellipse (. . .) in the Missing column, select "Discrete Missing Values," enter –99 as a missing value, and click OK.
   b. Define the variable *Sex* as 1 digit wide, no decimal places. (Hint: Set the decimals to 0 first, then the width to 1.) To enter the values for the *Sex* code:

(1) Click in the Values cell, then on the ellipse (. . .).

(2) Type in 1 as the value and Female as the value label and click Add.

(3) Type in 2 as the value and Male as the value label and click Add.

(4) Click OK.

c. Define the variable *Tdate* using mm/dd/yyyy, which automatically sets the width at 10 characters.

d. Define the variable *Score* as 6 digits wide, 2 decimal places (accommodates the maximum possible score of 100.00). (This designation would actually accommodate numbers up to 999.99.)

The resulting variable definitions are shown in Figure A3.

	Name	Type	Width	Decimals	Label	Values	Missing	Columns	Align	Measure
1	ID	String	4	0	Identification Number	None	None	8	Left	Nominal
2	AGE	Numeric	3	0	Age	None	-99	8	Right	Scale
3	SEX	Numeric	1	0	Gender	{1, Female}...	9	8	Right	Scale
4	TDATE	Date	10	0	Test Date	None	None	8	Right	Scale
5	SCORE	Numeric	6	2	Initial Test Score	None	-99.00	8	Right	Scale
6										

Figure A3   The SPSS Variable Grid Showing Entered Definitions

Once your variables are defined, click on the "Data View" tab at the bottom of the SPSS screen and enter the data in Table A1.

Table A1   Sample Data

ID	AGE	SEX	TDATE	SCORE
1001	23	1	10/22/2005	98.00
1002	43	2	10/23/2005	78.00
1003	24	2	11/03/2005	90.00
1004	36	1	11/06/2005	89.00
1005	29	2	11/10/2005	82.00
1006	26	2	11/15/2005	75.00
1007	19	1	11/20/2005	94.00
1008	32	1	11/23/2005	89.00
1009	35	1	11/30/2005	99.00

After you've entered the data, save the data file by selecting **File/Save As.** Save the data using the filename MYDATA1.SAV. These data are now ready to analyze.

SPSS Step-by-Step. EXAMPLE A2: Importing a Data File From Microsoft Excel

Data are sometimes entered and stored in a program other than SPSS. When you are ready to perform an analysis, you will want to import that data into SPSS. It is often useful to import a Microsoft Excel file into SPSS. This example shows how you would import an Excel file into SPSS. (The procedure is similar for other file types such as dBase files (.dbf) and Lotus (*.w*).)

Before importing Excel data into SPSS, review the guidelines in Chapter 1: Introduction in the section "Preparing Excel Data for Import." The following example uses the spreadsheet named EXAMPLE.XLS, located in the SPSS examples folder for this *Quick Reference Guidebook*. This file is already in the proper format for importing into SPSS, discussed in Chapter 1, and is shown in Figure A4.

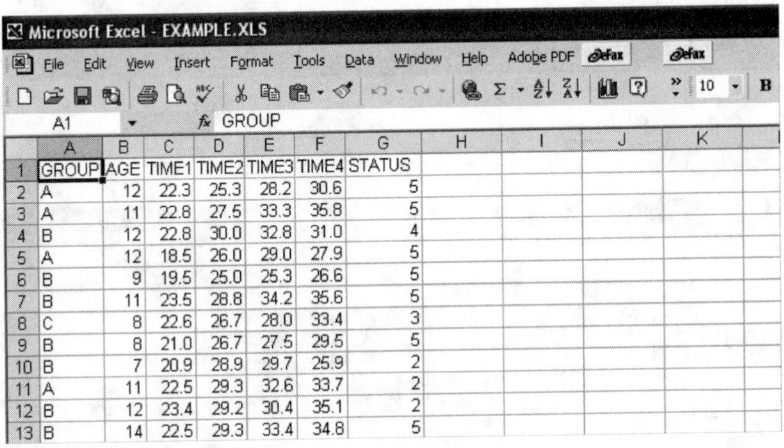

GROUP	AGE	TIME1	TIME2	TIME3	TIME4	STATUS
A	12	22.3	25.3	28.2	30.6	5
A	11	22.8	27.5	33.3	35.8	5
B	12	22.8	30.0	32.8	31.0	4
A	12	18.5	26.0	29.0	27.9	5
B	9	19.5	25.0	25.3	26.6	5
B	11	23.5	28.8	34.2	35.6	5
C	8	22.6	26.7	28.0	33.4	3
B	8	21.0	26.7	27.5	29.5	5
B	7	20.9	28.9	29.7	25.9	2
A	11	22.5	29.3	32.6	33.7	2
B	12	23.4	29.2	30.4	35.1	2
B	14	22.5	29.3	33.4	34.8	5

Figure A4 Data in Excel for Import Into SPSS

You do not need to open the Excel file to be able to import it into SPSS. To import this Excel file, use the following steps (in SPSS):

1. Select **File/Open/Data. . . .**
2. In the "Files of Type" option in the Open dialog box, select files of ".xls" type.

3. Select the file named EXAMPLE.XLS located in your C:\SPSSDATA directory (or wherever you stored the *Quick Reference Guidebook* examples files). The dialog box, as shown in Figure A5, appears.

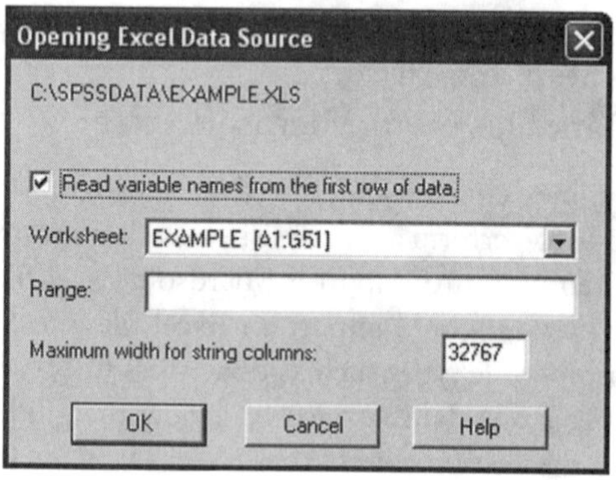

Figure A5 Dialog Box for Excel Import

4. Since the data in this file are formatted for import, you may accept all the defaults in this dialog box to import the data. (If there is information in columns and rows that you do not want to import, you will need to enter a specific range of cells to import.)

5. Click OK to import the data into SPSS. The SPSS file will automatically be opened in the SPSS Data View mode, as shown in Figure A6.

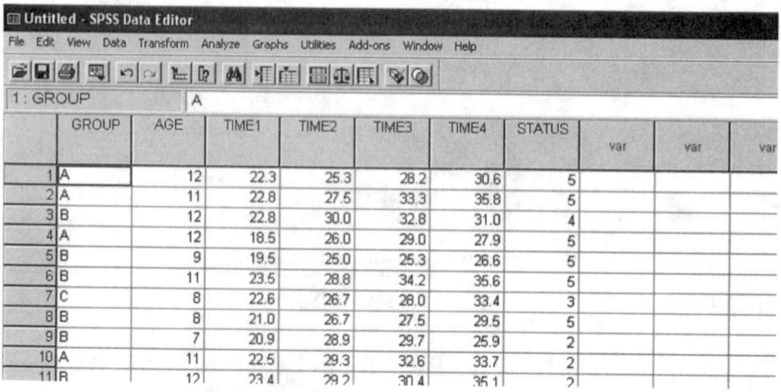

	GROUP	AGE	TIME1	TIME2	TIME3	TIME4	STATUS	var	var	var
1	A	12	22.3	25.3	28.2	30.6	5			
2	A	11	22.8	27.5	33.3	35.8	5			
3	B	12	22.8	30.0	32.8	31.0	4			
4	A	12	18.5	26.0	29.0	27.9	5			
5	B	9	19.5	25.0	25.3	26.6	5			
6	B	11	23.5	28.8	34.2	35.6	5			
7	C	8	22.6	26.7	28.0	33.4	3			
8	B	8	21.0	26.7	27.5	29.5	5			
9	B	7	20.9	28.9	29.7	25.9	2			
10	A	11	22.5	29.3	32.6	33.7	2			
11	B	12	23.4	29.2	30.4	35.1	2			

Figure A6 Data Imported From Excel

6. Click on "Variable View" and change any data definitions (labels, values, missing value codes) that were not properly imported.

7. Once your data file has been imported and you have added any "Variable View" changes, you should save the data as an SPSS data file. For this example, click on **File/Save As . . .** and save the file as IMPORTED.SAV.

8. The data are ready to analyze.

SPSS Step-by-Step. EXAMPLE A3: Performing an Analysis

Once you have entered data into SPSS by opening an existing file, typing in your data, or importing data from Excel, you can perform an analysis. For example, using the SPSS data file named TESTSCORES.SAV, you can calculate the means of AGE and SCORE for this data file following these steps:

1. Open the TESTSCORES.SAV data file by choosing **File/Open/Data. . . .**

2. From the main SPSS menu, select **Analyze/Descriptive Statistics/Descriptives.** . . . The dialog box shown in Figure A7 appears.

Figure A7   Dialog Box for Descriptives Analysis

3. Click on *Age* and the right arrow, then *Initial Test Score* and the right arrow. This selects these two variables for the analysis.

4. Click on OK, and the output shown in Table A2 appears in the SPSS output window showing descriptive statistics for these two variables.

Table A2   Output From Descriptives Procedure

Descriptive Statistics

	N	Minimum	Maximum	Mean	Std. Deviation
Age on Jan 1, 2005	9	19	43	29.67	7.550
Initial Test Score	9	76.00	99.00	88.3333	8.23104
Valid N (listwise)	9				

With these examples under your belt, you are ready to perform the analyses discussed in this book.

Transforming, Recoding, and Categorizing Your Data

Even when information is carefully entered into the computer, researchers often find it necessary to manipulate the data set to prepare it for analysis. This could include the following:

Creating a New Variable Using Computation. Suppose a data set includes height in inches, but the standard for an analysis is to work with centimeters. Using a conversion formula, you can use the SPSS Compute procedure to transform the inches measurement into centimeters. This technique may also be used to transform data that are not normally distributed, using a function such as a square root or logarithm to create a new variable that is more nearly normal in appearance.

• *Removing Selected Data From Analysis Using Filtering.* If a data set includes information for people outside the ZIP codes needed for a project, use the SPSS "Select Cases" option to filter out the unneeded records.

• *Combining Groups.* If a survey contains 14 different categories for race, but most categories include only a small number of entries, you can use the SPSS Recode procedure to combine the sparsely represented groups into an "other" category and thus reduce the number of categories for analysis.

Although not all data manipulation techniques can be covered in this brief discussion, the following examples illustrate some commonly used techniques for manipulating your data in SPSS.

SPSS Step-by-Step. EXAMPLE A4: Creating a New Variable Using Computation

SPSS allows you to calculate new variables as a function of current variables. This section illustrates how to perform this calculation and place the result into your data set. For example, suppose you want to compute an age-adjusted *Time1* variable from the EXAMPLE.SAV database in your analysis by creating a new variable, named *Time1adj,* defined by dividing *Time1* by the square root of *Age.* This can be accomplished using these steps:

1. Open the EXAMPLE.SAV data file and click on **Transform/Compute.**

2. In the Target text box, enter the new name *Time1adj.*

3. In the Numeric Expression text box, enter the following mathematical expression to perform the desired calculation:

$$TIME1/SQRT(AGE)$$

4. Click OK, and a new variable (column) appears in the SPSS data file, named *Time1adj.* For example, the value of *Time1adj* for Record 1 is 6.44, which is $22.3/\sqrt{12}$.

Be Aware: Unlike a Microsoft Excel Spreadsheet (which updates your calculations when you change a value involved in the calculation), a calculation in SPSS is a one-time event. If you go back to your data set and change a value of *Time1,* for example, the corresponding value for *Time1adj* will not change unless you perform the **Transform/Compute** procedure again.

SPSS Step-by-Step. EXAMPLE A5: Transforming Data to Make Data More Normally Distributed

Your data may be correctly entered but may still be in a form that is not ideal for analysis. In this case, you can transform the data using one of these techniques:

- Transforming quantitative data into standardized *z*-scores or other standardized values
- Transforming data to induce normality by creating new variables that are functions of current variables (using the Compute technique shown in the previous section)

For example, suppose you want to express the *Satisfaction* variable in the SURVEY.SAV data set as a standardized variable (*z*-score) by subtracting the mean and dividing by the standard deviation. The following procedure allows you to automatically create a standardized *z*-score variable in SPSS.

1. Open the data set SURVEY.SAV and select **Analyze/Descriptive Statistics/ Descriptives. . . .**

2. Select *Satisfaction* as the variable and check the box labeled "Save standardized values as variables."

3. Click OK. When the analysis is finished, notice that a new variable has been added to your data set, *ZSatisfaction,* which is the *z*-score for *Satisfaction.*

If you want the data to be standardized with mean 100 and standard deviation of 15, you can create a new variable from calculation (as described above) using the following expression:

$$ZSatisfaction100 = (ZSatisfaction * 15) + 100$$

You may also want to transform your data to make their distribution more nearly normal before applying an analysis procedure that assumes normal data. For example, taking the logarithm or the square root of the values in a right-skewed data set can sometimes produce data that are more nearly symmetric. The following example shows how a logarithmic transformation can improve normality. The variable *Skewed* in the TRANSFORM.SAV data set is highly skewed, as shown in Figure A8.

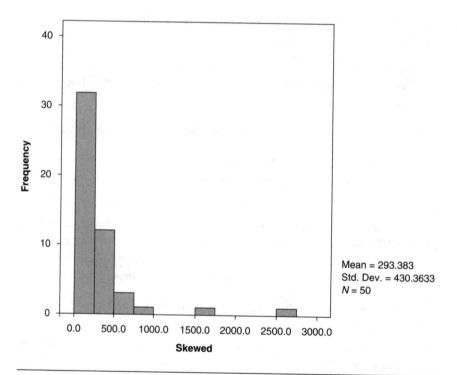

Mean = 293.383
Std. Dev. = 430.3633
N = 50

Figure A8   Skewed Data

We transform the data by taking the natural logarithm (the LN function in SPSS) of this variable. You can perform this calculation using the **Transform/ Compute . . .** procedure in SPSS and entering the following expression:

$$Trdata = LN(Skewed)$$

A histogram of the transformed data (*Trdata*) is shown in Figure A9, which appears to be much more "normal-like" in appearance than the histogram of the original data in Figure A8.

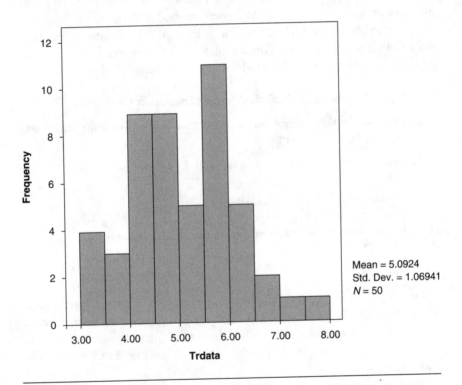

Mean = 5.0924
Std. Dev. = 1.06941
N = 50

Figure A9   Transformed Data

After transforming a variable for purposes of performing an analysis using the transformed data, the results reported should usually consist of statistics that have been transformed back into the original units.

SPSS Step-by-Step. EXAMPLE A6: Removing Selected Data From Analysis Using Filtering

Sometimes a data set contains records that you choose to exclude from your analysis. To exclude these records, you can filter them out (i.e., exclude) using the Data/Select Cases procedure in SPSS, as illustrated in the following example.

Filtering data in SPSS temporarily removes records from analysis. In the CARS2005.SAV data set, for example, suppose the analysis calls for cars with strictly combustion engines. Using Select Cases, you can define a filter that will exclude cars with hybrid electric engines from an analysis. To create such a filter, you must come up with some method of defining exclusion criteria. For example, the *Hybrid* variable in the CARS2005 data set indicates if the vehicle is a gas/electric hybrid vehicle. This variable can be used to filter these cars from the list. The following steps accomplish this:

1. Open the data set CARS2005.SAV select **Data/Select Cases.**

2. Click on the radio button option titled "If condition is satisfied . . . ," and click on the "If . . ." button.

3. In the "Select Cases: If" dialog box, enter the following expression:

$$Hybrid = 0$$

(That is, we want to use only vehicles that are NOT hybrids.)

4. Click on Continue and click OK.

Once you define this filter, the records for the hybrid models have a slash across the row label. This indicates that they will not be used in analyses as long as this filter is in effect. The filter should have detected and filtered out 12 cars in the data file, including the Toyota Prius, Honda Civic Hybrids, and several others.

Suppose you also want to eliminate any vehicles with more than eight cylinders from the analysis. You would use the same steps described above, but you would use the expression

$$Cylinders < 9$$

as your filter, which selects only those records with eight or fewer cylinders. If you want to use both of the criteria (not hybrid and eight or fewer cylinders), you would string the two expressions together with a "&" (AND) sign between them. For example,

$$Hybrid = 0 \ \& \ Cylinders < 9$$

This tells SPSS to include only those records that meet *both* criteria. To specify an OR condition instead of AND, you would use the vertical bar symbol "|" in the expression instead of the "&" sign.

To verify that the combination filter has worked correctly, you can perform the following check using the filtered CARS2005.SAV data.

1. Select **Analyze/Descriptive Statistics/Descriptives.** . . .

2. Select *CityMPG* as the variable to analyze and click OK.

3. The analysis should use only 1,058 of the 1,081 records in the calculations.

Note: To revert back to the nonsubsetted (nonfiltered) data file,

1. Choose **Data/Select Cases.** . . .

2. Click on the "All Cases" radio button.

3. Click OK.

All of the slash marks in the row designations are removed, signifying that all the data in the data file will now be used for future analyses.

SPSS Step-by-Step. EXAMPLE A7: Combining Groups and Creating Categories From Quantitative Data

At times, the categories of a categorical variable may be ill defined or too numerous to use in an analysis. In this case, you might want to recode the data into a more usable set of categories. Examples include the following:

- *Race.* Suppose you observe a number of Caucasians, African Americans, and Hispanics but very few Asians, American Indians, Eskimos, Pacific Islanders, and so on. As a result, you may consider recoding the sparse categories into an "other" category.

- *Income Bracket.* Suppose more than half of your sample falls in a particular income bracket (High), and the rest are scattered among other lower brackets. It might be appropriate to combine the other brackets and create a binary variable indicating subjects in HIGHINCOME or not.

- *Type of Trauma.* Suppose your original categories include penetrating wounds, blunt wounds, and burns, but there are very few burns in your data set. If, for your purposes, burn wounds are similar to penetrating wounds, you may want to combine burn and penetrating wounds into one category and analyze your data looking at blunt wounds versus all other types.

You must be careful when combining categories, and the combination should make sense in terms of your needs. It is good practice to describe any recoding you perform in your report or article.

Suppose you want to recode the variable *SBP* (systolic blood pressure) in the BP.SAV data set into two categories: hypertensive (coded 1) and not hypertensive (code 0), where *SBP* ≥ 160 means hypertensive. Follow these steps:

1. Open the data set BP.SAV and select **Transform/Recode/Into Different Variables. . . .**

2. Select *SBP* as your input variable.

3. Name your output variable *Hypertension*. Click Change.

4. Click the button labeled "Old and New Values."

5. On the Recode dialog box, click on the "Range, Lowest through" radio button and enter the value 159. For "New Value," enter 0, and click on the Add button. This defines *SPB* ≤ 159 as nonhypertensive.

6. To define hypertensive, click on the "All Other Values" radio button. For "New Value," enter 1, and click on the Add button. This defines *SPB* >159 as hypertensive.

7. To take care of missing values, click on the "System or User-Missing Values," enter –9 (or whatever missing value code you select) for the value, and click Add.

8. Click Continue. Click OK. Observe that the new *Hypertension* variable is included in the data set and contains the values 0 and 1.

9. Click on the "Variable View" tab on the datasheet and define the missing value code and your category values (0 = nonhypertensive, 1 = hypertensive) for your new *Hypertension* variable.

You can now use the new variable in an analysis. The trick with recoding continuous data into categories is to find the cut-point (i.e., the point that defines the categories into which the observations will be placed). A cut-point could be an obvious break in the data, a point that makes logical sense, or one that you can otherwise justify.

SPSS Step-by-Step. EXAMPLE A8: Transposing Data

Data for analysis are usually set up with one subject (or entity) per row and variables as columns. This was discussed in the Chapter 1 section titled "Planning a Successful Analysis." However, it is not uncommon for data to find their way into SPSS in just the opposite fashion (i.e., in which rows are variables and columns are subjects). In this case, you must transpose your data set before you can analyze it. The following example shows how this can be accomplished. For example, suppose your data set in SPSS looks like the data in Figure A10.

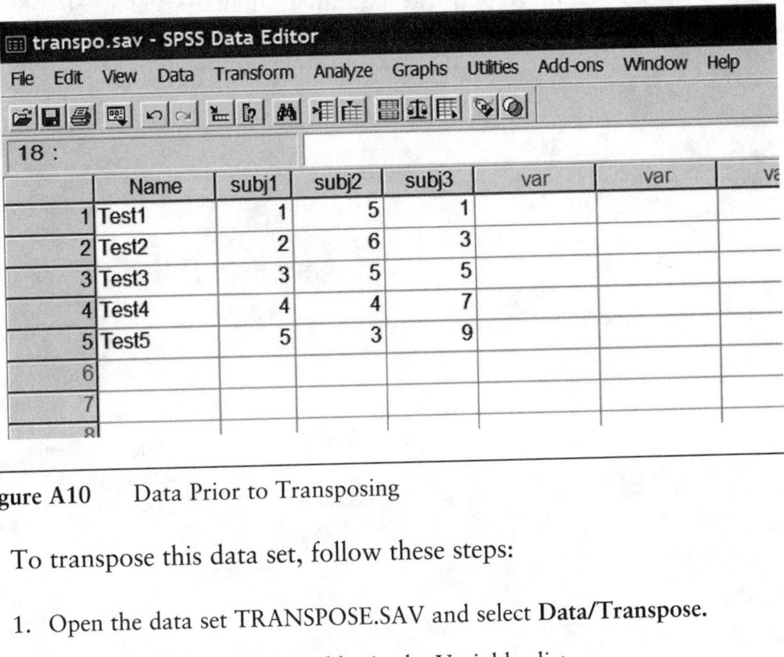

	Name	subj1	subj2	subj3	var	var	va
1	Test1	1	5	1			
2	Test2	2	6	3			
3	Test3	3	5	5			
4	Test4	4	4	7			
5	Test5	5	3	9			
6							
7							
8							

Figure A10   Data Prior to Transposing

To transpose this data set, follow these steps:

1. Open the data set TRANSPOSE.SAV and select **Data/Transpose**.

2. Place all three subject variables in the Variables list.

3. Place the *Name* variable in the Name list and click OK.

The resulting data set is shown in Figure A11. Notice that each row is now a "subject," and columns are variables. After transposing, you might need to use the Variable View to adjust the variable definitions for the reconstituted data.

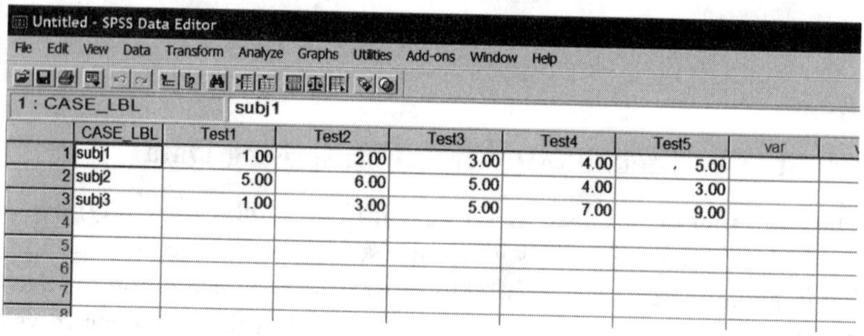

Figure A11   Data After Transposing

After going through the tutorials in this appendix, you will have the skills to use the SPSS program to perform the statistical analysis examples in this *Quick Reference Guidebook*.

Appendix B

Choosing the Right Procedure to Use

The ideal time to choose the type of analysis you will perform on your data is during the planning process. Knowing the analysis that will be performed is crucial in designing your data collection strategy and determining a sample size. However, many times, it is true that data are collected first, and only then is consideration given to the analysis that should be performed. In either case, this appendix will help you determine which analyses fit your needs. Remember, however, the earlier you address these statistical issues, the better.

To select a proper analysis, your experimental question must be well defined. If you do not know what hypotheses to test, then you cannot know the proper statistical analysis to apply. The following guide leads you through a series of questions that will assist you in deciding which statistical procedure or procedures will address your research questions. Begin by deciding which of the following scenarios addresses your analysis type:

1. Are you performing a *descriptive* analysis, a *comparative* (*inferential*) analysis, or a *correlation/association* analysis? These analyses are described in the section in Chapter 1 titled "Planning a Successful Analysis."

2. What types of variables are you analyzing? Are you using quantitative (numeric) or qualitative (categorical) data? Are your response (dependent) variables normally distributed? These are the types of questions that you will need to be able to answer to decide on the appropriate analysis. For more details, see Chapter 2: Describing and Examining Data.

Once you can answer these questions, the following decision tables help you decide which analyses are appropriate. This is not an all-inclusive decision-making tool and cannot substitute for the thoroughness that a professional statistician would apply to your experimental question. If your data and hypotheses do not conform to these simple rules, then your analysis may be more complex than those covered here, or you may not have properly defined your research questions.

How to Use the Tables

To use the following tables, first consider the type of analysis you want to perform. This topic was described in more detail in the section in Chapter 1 titled "Planning a Successful Analysis."

1. **A Descriptive Analysis.** *Is the purpose of your analysis to summarize your data into a few numbers?*

   For example, this would be the case if you want to characterize quantitative data using descriptive statistics (such as a mean and standard deviation) or you want to summarize information in a categorical variable using a frequency table or graph.

   If yes, go to Table B1, "Descriptive Statistics."

2. **A Comparative Analysis.** *Is the purpose of your analysis to compare one or more groups to each other or to a standard?*

   If yes, go to Table B2, "Comparison Tests."

3. **Association and Correlation.** *Is the purpose of your analysis to determine if there is a relationship between variables, or do you want to predict one variable using one or more other variables?* Examples of this would be a correlation or regression analysis as well as crosstabulation of categorical variables.

   If yes, go to Table B3: "Relational Analyses (Correlation and Regression)."

For example, suppose you have collected information from two independent groups of subjects and you have measured some characteristic for each subject. Suppose further that you want to know if the means of the measured characteristic are different for the two groups. This scenario fits the description of the second option. Therefore, you would go to Table B2 and, in the left-hand column, select the item labeled "You are comparing data from two INDEPENDENT groups." If you have determined that a normality assumption is plausible, then in the second column, you should select "Normal" as your data type. In the third column, you see that an appropriate analysis is a two-sample *t*-test. You can go to Chapter 3 and look over the hypotheses, assumptions, caveats, and description of a two-sample *t*-test to verify that this type of analysis is appropriate. If so, proceed with the analysis as described in Chapter 3.

If none of these options relates to what you want to accomplish, you should reexamine your research questions or consult a statistician to see what type of analysis best fits your goals. We emphasize that these tables contain only commonly used procedures and are not intended to provide an exhaustive listing of statistical techniques.

Table B1   Descriptive Statistics

Make a decision by reading from left to right.

	What Is the Data Type?	*Analysis Procedure to Use (Chapter)*
You want to describe a single variable.	Normal	Mean, SD, and so on, using the Descriptive or Explore procedure (Chapter 2)
	Quantitative	Median, histogram, and stem-and-leaf plot using the Explore procedure (Chapter 2)
	Categorical	Frequency table (Chapter 2)
You want to describe two related or paired variables.	Both are normal	Pearson's correlation (Chapter 4)
	Both are at least ordinal	Spearman's correlation (Chapter 7)
	Both categorical	Crosstabulations (Chapter 2)

Table B2   Comparison Tests

Make decision by reading from left to right.

You are comparing a SINGLE SAMPLE to a norm (gold standard).	*What Is the Data Type?*	*Procedure to Use*
	Normal	Single-sample *t*-test (Chapter 3)
	At least ordinal	Sign test (Chapter 7)
	Categorical	Goodness of fit (Chapter 5)
You are comparing data from two INDEPENDENT groups.	Normal	Two-sample *t*-test (Chapter 3)
	At least ordinal	Mann-Whitney (Chapter 7)
	Categorical	$2 \times c$ test for homogeneity/ chi-square (Chapter 5)
You are comparing PAIRED, REPEATED, or MATCHED data.	Normal	Paired *t*-test (Chapter 3)
	At least ordinal	Sign test (Chapter 7)
	Symmetric quantitative	Wilcoxon signed-rank test (Chapter 7)
	Binary (dichotomous)	McNemar (Chapter 5)
More than two groups: INDEPENDENT	Normal	One-way ANOVA (Chapter 6)
	At least ordinal	Kruskal-Wallis (Chapter 7)
	Categorical	$r \times c$ test for homogeneity/ chi-square (Chapter 5)
More than two groups: REPEATED MEASURES	Normal	Repeated-measures ANOVA (Chapter 6)
	At least ordinal	Friedman's test (Chapter 7)
	Categorical	Cochran Q (not covered)
You are comparing means where the model includes a covariate adjustment.	Normal	Analysis of covariance (Chapter 6)

NOTE: In this table, the term *Normal* indicates that the procedure is theoretically based on a normality assumption. In practice, normal-based procedures can be used if you have data for which a normality assumption is plausible or your sample size is sufficiently large that the normal-based procedures can be appropriately used. The term *At least ordinal* indicates that your data have an order. This includes ordinal categorical data and any quantitative data.

Table B3   Relational Analyses (Correlation and Regression)

Make decision by reading from left to right.

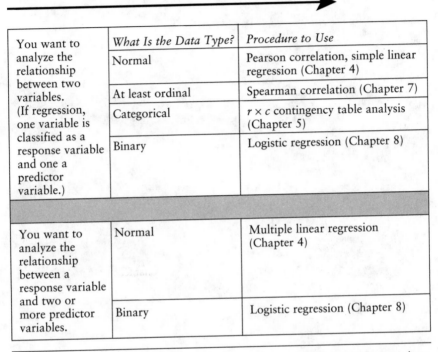

You want to analyze the relationship between two variables. (If regression, one variable is classified as a response variable and one a predictor variable.)	*What Is the Data Type?*	*Procedure to Use*
	Normal	Pearson correlation, simple linear regression (Chapter 4)
	At least ordinal	Spearman correlation (Chapter 7)
	Categorical	$r \times c$ contingency table analysis (Chapter 5)
	Binary	Logistic regression (Chapter 8)
You want to analyze the relationship between a response variable and two or more predictor variables.	Normal	Multiple linear regression (Chapter 4)
	Binary	Logistic regression (Chapter 8)

NOTE: In this table, the "data type" applies to the dependent variable for regression procedures. For assessment of association (e.g., correlation, crosstabulation, etc.), the variable type applies to both variables. See the footnote to Table B2 for a discussion of the normality assumption.

Index

Aiken, L. S., 210
Alternative hypotheses, 60, 65
Altman, D. G., 108
Analysis
  arranging *t*-test data for, 60–64
  choosing the right procedure
    to use in, 243–247
  how to use tables in, 244–247
  performance using SPSS, 233–234
  planning a successful statistical,
    10–12
  relational, *247*
Analysis of covariance (ANCOVA)
  appropriate applications
    for, 182
  defined, 182
  design considerations, 182–183
  examples, 184–189
  hypotheses for, 183–184
  results reporting, 188–189
  SPSS application, 189
Analysis of variance (ANOVA)
  one-way, 152–166
  repeated-measures, 175–181
  two-way, 166–175
APA (American Psychological
  Association) guidelines, 18
Applications. *See also* SPSS
  applications
  analysis of covariance, 182
  contingency table analysis, 114

correlation analysis, 79
goodness-of-fit test, 143
interrater reliability, 140
logistic regression, 210
Mantel-Haenszel analysis, 136
McNemar's test, 132
multiple linear regression, 96
one-sample *t*-test, 48
one-way ANOVA, 152
paired *t*-test, 69
prospective analysis, 128
repeated-measures, 175–176
retrospective analysis, 128
simple linear regression (SLR),
  87–88
Spearman's rho, 192–193
two-sample *t*-test, 54–55
two-way ANOVA, 167

Bickel, P. J., 139
Binary coding, 216
Bland, J. M., 108
Bland-Altman analysis
  defined, 107–108
  design considerations, 108
  examples, 108–111
  results reporting, 110
  SPSS application, 110–111
Bonferroni comparisons, 179, *180,
  181,* 186–187, 206
Boxplots, 28, *51*

Categorical data
  combining, 115
  considerations for examining, 39
  crosstabulation of variables
      in, 43–45
  defined, 39
  examples, 40–45
  frequency table for, 40–43
  nominal measures of, 148
  ordinal measures of, 148–149
  from quantitative data, 239–241
  SPSS applications, 42–43
  tips and caveats for, 40
  treated as quantitative data, 40
Cause and effect conclusions,
      81, 211–212
Central limit theorem (CLT), 26
Chi-square test, 120–121, 124, 134
  goodness-of-fit, 146
Cochran's test, 138
Cohen, J., 210
Cohen, P., 210
Comparative statistics, 5
Comparison tests, 246
Computer programs, reporting results
      using, 18
Confidence intervals
  one-sample t-test, 52
  paired t-test, 69
Conover, W. J., 191
Contingency coefficient, 148
Contingency table analysis
  appropriate applications of, 114
  criminal behavior versus drinking
      preference, 117–123
  defined, 114
  design considerations, 115
  examples, 117–126
  exposure to reagent versus reaction,
      123–126
  hypotheses, 116
  results reporting, 120–121, 125
  SPSS application, 121–123,
      125–126
Continuity correction statistic, 123

Contrasts, specified, 159, 160–161
Correlational statistics, 5–6
  data collection for, 11
Correlation analysis
  appropriate applications for, 79
  assumptions about linear
      relationships found using,
      82–83
  cause and effect
      conclusions using, 81
  defined, 78–79
  design considerations, 79–80
  examples, 83–87
  hypotheses for, 80
  one-sided tests, 80
  providing incomplete pictures
      of relationships, 81
  results reporting, 86
  scatterplots and, 81–87
  SPSS application, 86–87
  tips and caveats for, 80–83
  using scatterplots with, 81–83
  variables, 80–81
Cramer's V, 148
Crosstabulation of categorical
      variables, 43–45

Daniel, W., 210
Data
  arrangement, 60–64
  categorical, 39–45
  collection appropriate to testing
      hypotheses, 10–11
  dictionaries, 12–13
  entering SPSS, 229–231
  filtering, 238–239
  imported from Microsoft Excel,
      231–233
  outcome variable, 10–11
  predictor variable, 11
  quantitative, 24–38
  scales of measurement of, 11
  sets
      designed with one subject
          per line, 13

examples, 20
guidelines, 12–16
illustrated using graphs, 19
variables documented in, 12–13
SPSS, 227–234
transforming, recoding, and
    categorizing, 234–242
transposing, 241–242
Descriptive statistics, 4, 27, 171, 245
Design considerations
analysis of covariance, 182–183
Bland-Altman analysis, 108
contingency table analysis, 115
correlation analysis, 79–80
data set, 13
goodness-of-fit test, 144
Mantel-Haenszel analysis, 136
multiple linear regression, 96–97
one-sample t-test, 48–49
one-way ANOVA, 152–153
paired t-test, 70
repeated-measures ANOVA, 176–177
simple linear regression, 88–89
Spearman's rho, 193
two-sample t-test, 55–56
two-way ANOVA, 167–168
Dictionaries, data, 12–13
Distribution, quantitative data, 25
Documentation of variables, 12–13
Dunnett's test, 159–160

Elliott, A. C., 157
Extrapolation
multiple linear regression, 101
simple linear regression (SLR),
    89–90

Fidell, L. S., 210
Filtering using SPSS, 238–239
Formulation of testable research
    questions, 10
Frequency table for categorical data,
    40–43
Friedman's test
defined, 204

examples, 204–207
hypotheses for, 204
results reporting, 206
SPSS application, 207

Gamma statistic, 148
Gibbons, G. D., 191
Goodness-of-fit test
appropriate applications of, 143
defined, 143
design considerations, 144
examples, 145–147
Hosmer-Lemeshow, 220
hypotheses, 144
on Mendel's data, 145–147
results reporting, 146
SPSS application, 146–147
tips and caveats for, 144
Gossett, William, 47
Graphs
associated with two-sample
    t-test, 58
guidelines for creating and using, 19
one-way ANOVA, 155–156
scatterplot, 81–87
two-way interaction, 171, 172
Groups, quantitative data by, 34–36

Histograms, 28, 29, 30, 32
Homogeneity
of regressions, 183
test for, 115, 116
Hosmer, D. W., 210
Hosmer-Lemeshow goodness-of-fit
    test, 220
Hypotheses
alternative, 60, 65
analysis of covariance, 183–184
contingency table analysis, 116
correlation analysis, 80
data collection appropriate to
    testing, 10–11
deciding on type of analysis
    appropriate to test, 11
formulating testable, 10

Friedman's test, 204
goodness-of-fit test, 144
Kruskal-Wallis test, 198
Mann-Whitney test, 196
Mantel-Haenszel analysis, 136
McNemar's test, 132–133
multiple linear regression, 97–98
null, 6–8, 9–10, 51, 60
one-sample t-test, 49–50
one-way ANOVA, 154
paired t-test, 70–71
repeated-measures ANOVA, 177
sign test or Wilcoxon test, 202
simple linear regression (SLR), 89
simple logistic regression, 211
Spearman's rho, 193
testing, power and sample size, 6–9
two-sample t-test, 56–57, 65
two-way ANOVA, 168–170

Identity, plot of, 107, *108*
Independent samples, 55, 96, 115,
       116, 152, 167, 182
Indicator variables, 101
Interaction hypothesis, 169
Interpretation of results, 12
Interrater reliability
   appropriate applications of, 140
   defined, 140
   examples, 140–143
   results reporting, 141–142
   SPSS application, 142–143
Interval estimates, 91

Kendall's tau-b, 149
Kendall's tau-c, 149
Keppel, G., 170
Kleinbaum, D. G., 90, 210
Kolmogorov-Smirnov test, 25, 29
Kruskal-Wallis test
   defined, 198
   examples, 198–201
   hypotheses for, 198
   results reporting, 200–201
   SPSS application, 201

Kupper, L. L., 90
Kutner, M. H., 210

Lambda measure, 148
Least squares principle, 88–89, 97
Lehmann, E. L., 191
Lemeshow, S., 210
Levene's test, 155
Logistic regression
   appropriate applications for, 210
   introduction to, 209–210
   multiple, 215–222
   simple, 211–215
   tips and caveats for, 211–212, 216

Main effects test, 169–170
Mann-Whitney test
   defined, 195–196
   hypotheses for, 196
   results reporting, 197
   SPSS application, 198
Mantel-Haenszel analysis
   appropriate applications of, 136
   of Berkeley graduate
       admissions data, 136–140
   defined, 135
   design considerations, 136
   examples, 136–140
   hypotheses, 136
   results reporting, 138
   SPSS application, 138–139
   tips and caveats for, 139–140
McNemar's test
   for advertising effectiveness,
       133–135
   appropriate applications of, 132
   defined, 131
   examples, 133–135
   hypotheses for, 132–133
   results reporting, 135
   SPSS application, 135
Means
   and nonnormal distribution
       of data, 26–27
   two-sample t-test comparing, 55

Mendel, Gregor, 145
Model
    interpretation and evaluation for
        multiple linear regression,
        101–102
    interpretation of multiple logistic
        regression, 220–222
    selection for multiple linear
        regression, 99–100
Muller, K. E., 90
Multiple linear regression
    appropriate applications of, 96
    defined, 95
    design considerations for, 96–97
    examples, 102–107
    hypotheses for, 97–98
    model interpretation and
        evaluation for, 101–102
    model selection for, 99–100
    residual analysis in, 105–106
    R-square statistic in, 98
    scatterplots and, 102, 103
    SPSS application, 106–107
    tips and caveats for, 100–101
Multiple logistic regression
    defined, 215
    examples, 217–222
    model interpretation, 220–222
    SPSS application, 222
    tips and caveats for, 216

Nachtsheim, C. J., 210
Neter, J., 170, 210
Nizam, A., 90
Nominal measures of categorical
    data, 148
Nonparametric analysis
    procedures, 191–192
Normality
    analysis of covariance and, 182
    how to use information about, 26–27
    one-sample t-test and, 55
    one-way ANOVA and, 153
    paired t-test and, 70
    plots used to assess, 28–34

repeated-measures ANOVA
    and, 176–177
    testing, 25–26
    two-way ANOVA and, 167
Null hypotheses, 6–8
    p-value and, 9–10
    t-tests and, 51, 60, 65

Observed regression equations, 88–89
O'Connell, J. W., 139
One-sample t-tests
    appropriate applications for, 48
    confidence intervals, 52
    defined, 48
    design considerations, 48–49
    example, 50–54
    hypotheses for, 49–50
    results reporting, 53
    SPSS application, 53–54
One-tailed t-tests, 49–50, 56–57
    preplanning, 57
One-way ANOVA
    appropriate applications for, 152
    defined, 152
    design considerations, 152–153
    Dunnett's test and, 159–160
    equal variances in, 153
    examples, 154–166, 162–166
    hypotheses for, 154
    results reporting, 159
    specified contrasts and, 159,
        160–161
    SPSS application, 161–162,
        164–166
    tips and caveats for, 154
    with trend analysis, 162–166
Ordinal measures of categorical
    data, 148–149
Outcome variables, 10–11
Outliers, scatterplot, 81–83

Paired t-test
    appropriate applications for, 69
    associated confidence interval, 69
    defined, 68–69

design considerations, 70
examples, 71–75
hypotheses for, 70–71
results reporting, 73
SPSS application, 73–75
Pearson, Karl, 77, 78, 117
Phi coefficient, 148
Plot of identity, 107, 108
Power and sample size, 8–9
Predictor variables, 11
multiple linear regression, 101
multiple logistic regression, 216,
217–219
Procedures, choosing the right, 11
Prospective analysis, 128
example, 129–130
P-value, 9–10, 63–64, 67, 93, 124–125

Q-Q plots, 29
Quantitative data
with an unusual value, 28–34
combining groups and creating
categories from, 239–241
definition of, 24–25
description examples, 27–38
distribution, 25
by groups, 34–36
nonnormal distribution of, 26–27
normality testing, 25–26
reporting the mean of, 26–27
SPSS application, 33–34, 36, 37–38
tips and caveats for, 26–27
with unusual values, 36–38
when categorical variables can
be treated as, 40

Random selection, 153
Random split, 153
Regression. See Logistic regression;
Multiple linear regression;
Simple linear regression (SLR)
Relational analyses, 247
Repeated-measures ANOVA
appropriate applications for,
175–176
defined, 175

design considerations, 176–177
examples, 177–181
results reporting, 180–181
SPSS application, 181
Residual analysis in multiple
linear regression, 105–106
Residual plots, 90, 94
Results reporting
analysis of covariance, 188–189
Bland-Altman analysis, 110
contingency table analysis,
120–121, 125
correlation analysis, 86
crosstabulation, 44–45
frequency data, 41–42
Friedman's test, 206
goodness-of-fit test, 146
guidelines, 18–19
interrater reliability, 141–142
Kruskal-Wallis test, 200–201
logistic regression, 214–215
Mann-Whitney test, 197
Mantel-Haenszel analysis, 138
McNemar's test, 135
one-sample t-test, 53
one-way ANOVA, 159
paired t-test, 73
proper interpretation and, 12
quantitative data by groups, 35
quantitative data with an
unusual value, 33
repeated-measures ANOVA,
180–181
risk analysis, 130
Spearman's rho, 194–195
two-sample t-test, 64, 67–68
two-way ANOVA, 174
Wilcoxon or sign test, 203
Retrospective analysis
appropriate applications for, 128
example, 129
format for, 126–128
Risk ratio analysis
examples, 128–131
for exposure/reaction data,
128–131

prospective, 128
results reporting, 130
retrospective, 127–128
SPSS application, 130–131
R-square statistic, 98
P-value, 9–10

Samples
  independent, 55, 115, 116,
      152, 167, 182
  random selection, 153
  random split, 153
  size, 115, 170
  small size, 57–58
  strategies for, 115
Scales of measurement, 11
Scatterplots
  correlation analysis and, 81–83
  multiple linear regression
      and, 102, 103
Shapiro-Wilk test, 25, 29
Sign test
  defined, 201–202
  examples, 202–204
  hypotheses for, 202
  results reporting, 203
  SPSS application, 203–204
Simple linear regression (SLR)
  appropriate applications for, 87–88
  defined, 87
  design considerations, 88–89
  examples, 91–95
  extrapolation and, 89–90
  hypotheses for, 89
  interval estimates in, 91
  least square principle and, 88–89
  observed regression equation
      in, 88–89
  residual plots in, 90, 94
  SPSS application, 94–95
  theoretical regression line in, 88
  tips and caveats for, 89–91
  transformations and, 90–91
Simple logistic regression
  defined, 211
  examples, 212–215

  hypotheses for, 211
  results reporting, 214
  SPSS application, 214–215
  tips and caveats for, 211–212
Simpson's paradox, 140
Software programs, statistical, 8, 12.
    See also SPSS
Somer's d, 148
Spearman's rho
  appropriate applications for,
      192–193
  defined, 192
  design considerations, 193
  examples, 194–195
  hypotheses for, 193
  results reporting, 194–195
  tips and caveats for, 193
Specified contrasts, 159, 160–161
SPSS applications. See also
    Applications
  Advanced Models and Regression
      Models Add-On, 226
  analysis of covariance, 189
  Base, 225
  Bland-Altman analysis, 110–111
  combining groups and creating
      categories from quantitative
      data in, 239–241
  contingency table analysis,
      121–123, 125–126
  correlation analysis, 86–87
  creating new variables using
      computation in, 234–235
  crosstabulation of categorical
      variables, 45
  data files, sample, 20
  entering data into, 229–231
  frequency table for categorical
      data, 42–43
  Friedman's test, 207
  goodness-of-fit test, 146–147
  Graduate Pack, 226
  importing data from Microsoft
      Excel into, 231–233
  interrater reliability, 142–143
  Kruskal-Wallis test, 201

main menu, 226–227
Mann-Whitney test, 198
Mantel-Haenszel analysis, 138–139
McNemar's test, 135
multiple linear regression, 106–107
multiple logistic regression, 222
normality testing, 25
one-sample *t*-test, 53–54
one-way ANOVA, 161–162,
    164–166
paired *t*-test, 73–75
performing analyses in, 233–234
quantitative data by groups, 36
quantitative data with an unusual
    value, 33–34
quantitative data with unusual
    values, 37–38
removing selected data from analysis
    using filtering in, 238–239
repeated-measures ANOVA, 181
risk ratio analysis, 130–131
simple linear regression (SLR),
    94–95
simple logistic regression, 214–215
step-by-step instructions for,
    229–242
transforming, recoding, and
    categorizing data in, 234–242
transforming data to make data
    more normally distributed,
    235–237
transposing data in, 241–242
two-sample *t*-test, 60–63, 65, 68
two-way ANOVA, 175
Wilcoxon or sign test, 203–204
working with data in, 227–234
Standard deviation (SD),
    reporting, 27
Standard error of the mean (SEM), 27
*Statistical Analysis Quick Reference
    Guidebook*
appendices, 3
purpose of, 2
topics covered by, 1–2

Statistics
    comparative, 5
    correlational, 5–6, 11
    descriptive, 4, 27, 171, 245
Stem-and-leaf plots, 29

Tabachnick, B. G., 210
Tables, how to use, 244–247
Task Force on Statistical Inference, 11
Testing
    chi-square, 120–121, 124, 134
    comparison, 246
    deciding on type of analysis
        appropriate to hypothesis, 11
    homogeneity, 115, 116
    hypothesis, 6–9
    independence, 115, 116
    normality, 25–26
    one-sided, 144
    p-value and, 9–10, 63–64, 67,
        93, 124–125
Theoretical regression lines, 88
Tips and caveats
    categorical data, 50
    contingency table analysis, 116–117
    correlational analysis, 80–83
    goodness-of-fit test, 144
    Mantel-Haenszel analysis, 139–140
    multiple linear regression, 100–101
    multiple logistic regression, 216
    one-way ANOVA, 154
    simple linear regression (SLR),
        89–91
    simple logistic regression, 211–212
    Spearman's rho, 193
    two-sample *t*-test, 57–58
    two-way ANOVA, 170
Transformations, 90–91
Transposition of data, 241–242
Trend analysis, 162–166
T-tests
    appropriate applications for, 48,
        54–55
    confidence intervals, 52

design considerations, 48–49, 55–56
determining which statistic
    to use from, 58–59
examples, 50–54, 60–68
hypotheses for, 49–50, 56–57, 65
misuse of, 57
multiple, 58
one-sample, 48–54
one-tailed, 49–50, 56–57
origins, 47
paired, 68–75
results reporting, 53
tips and caveats for, 57–58
two-sample, 54–68
two-tailed, 49, 56
types of, 47–48
Tufte, Edward, 19
Tukey test, 157–158, 173, *174*, 200
Two-sample *t*-tests
    appropriate applications for, 54–55
    defined, 54
    design considerations, 55–56
    with equal variances, 60–65
    examples, 60–68
    graphs, 58
    hypotheses for, 56–57
    misuse of, 57
    performing multiple, 58
    preplanning, 57
    results reporting, 64, 67–68
    small sample sizes in, 57–58
    SPSS application, 60–63, 65, 68
    tips and caveats for, 57–58
    with variance issues, 65–68
Two-tailed *t*-tests, 49, 56
Two-way ANOVA
    appropriate applications for, 167
    defined, 166
    design considerations, 167–168
    equal variances assumed by,
        167–168
    examples, 171–175

hypotheses for, 168–170
results reporting, 174
SPSS application, 175
tips and caveats for, 170

Uncertainty coefficient, 148

Variables
    abnormal distribution in
        correlation analysis, 83
    correlation analysis, 80–81
    crosstabulation of categorical,
        43–45
    deciding on and documenting,
        12–13, 99–100
    independent, 55, 96
    indicator, 101
    and model selection for multiple
        linear regression, 99–100
    outcome, 10–11
    predictor, 11, 101, 216, 217–219
    qualitative predictor, 216
Variances
    equal, 55–56, 60–65, 153,
        167–168, 176–177
    issues with, 65–68
*Visual Display of Quantitative
    Data, The,* 19

Wasserman, W., 210
West, S. G., 210
Wickens, T. D., 170
Wilcoxon test
    defined, 201–202
    examples, 202–204
    hypotheses for, 202
    results reporting, 203
    SPSS application, 203–204
Wilkinson, L., 11
Woodward, W. A., 157

Zar, J. H., 200, 205